MANHATTAN

ON FILM

Walking Tours of

Hollywood's Fabled Front Lot

MANHATTAN ON FILM

Walking Tours of Hollywood's Fabled Front Lot

Revised and Expanded Edition

Chuck Katz

Limelight Editions

First edition 1999

Published in 2005 by
Limelight Editions (an imprint of Amadeus Press, LLC)
512 Newark Pompton Turnpike
Pompton Plains, New Jersey 07444, USA

For sales, please contact
Limelight Editions
c/o Hal Leonard Corp.
7777 West Bluemound Road
Milwaukee, Wisconsin 53213, USA
Tel. 800-637-2852
Fax 414-774-3259

Website: www.limelighteditions.com

Interior design by Mulberry Tree Press, Inc.
(MulberryTreePress.com)

Printed in Canada

Library of Congress Cataloging-in-Publication Data

Katz, Chuck.
  Manhattan on film : walking tours of Hollywood's fabled front lot /
Charles D. Katz.-- Rev. and updated ed.
     p. cm.
  Includes index.
  ISBN 0-87910-319-1 (pbk.)
  1. Motion picture locations—New York (State)—New York—
Guidebooks. 2.
Manhattan (New York, N.Y.)—Guidebooks. I. Title.
PN1995.67.N7K384 2005
384'.8'097471--dc22
                    2005006053

To Mom
For every day it becomes increasingly clear
how you were the glue
that held together
our little corner of the world

ACKNOWLEDGMENTS

A number of years ago I stumbled across a wise sentiment from an anonymous author in a compilation of wise sentiments from anonymous authors. In his (or her) words, "A man with a large bank account has a lot of money. A man with good friends and loved ones has great wealth." Based on that yardstick, I am a rich man, indeed.

For helping to put together this volume of *Manhattan on Film*, I would like to thank John Cerullo, my publisher, for the excitement he has shown for this project and for embracing some of the less wacky ideas I have for getting this book into the hands of every man, woman, and child on the planet. In addition, I would like to thank Jenna Young (promotion), Gail Siragusa (editing), and Joe Gannon of Mulberry Tree Press (design). A special thanks to Nancy Menna, my assistant, who devoted many hours on her own time helping with all the thankless tasks that go into getting a book like this ready. A hearty thanks to Mel Zerman, my former publisher, for being the first to take a chance on an unknown with an idea about a book on movie locations and for helping to make it a reality. And finally, thanks to Professor Read Mercer Schuchardt, whose Metaphilm Web site will help bring New York movie locations and *Manhattan on Film* to everyone and vice versa.

There are a great many people who have helped make my life what it is, and I feel they all deserve mention. In all of our lives, people stay and people go. I am fortunate that, in my life, those who have stayed far outnumber those who have gone.

When it comes to friends, no one has been luckier than I, who can still count among my dear friends a vast array of people from all stages of my life. If my life could be viewed as a train ride, I have friends who have boarded at many stations along the way: Scott Bloom, who boarded when we were five years old and remains a very close friend (despite the fact that he fed me dog biscuits when we were ten and told me they were cookies his sister had baked; I'd still be angry at him, had they not tasted so good); Churn (Paul Tschernia to everyone else), who boarded in junior high school (even though he invited everyone to his bar mitzvah except me); Doug Spector, Michael Fishbin, Tom Sheahan, Mark Blumkin, and Geri Crane, who boarded during my days at Union College—think the college scenes from *The Way We Were*—and continue to be good, good friends; Alejandro Schwed, Ray Keane, Scott Koltun, and Bill Weisner, who hopped aboard during our days at Fordham Law School, when we wanted to take over the world—now, with eleven kids among us, we just want to get some sleep; Steven Lapidus, Mike Rotondi, Michela Daliana, Lisa Soeder, and Lieutenant Colonel David McCarthy, who jumped on during our early "adult" years living and working in Manhattan and have remained ever since; Paul Eisenberg, who managed to sneak on when the conductor was looking the other way, but we let him stay, because nobody can imagine the ride without him.

For those few who no longer ride the train (Larry from Tampa, Moltner from wherever Moltner is from, and particularly, Richard from Montreal), you made the ride richer and there will always be the good memories.

To the good folks at Duane Morris, with whom I hang my legal hat, many thanks for making me a part of your ever expanding family and your plans for the future; to my friends at De-Cotiis, FitzPatrick, Cole and Wisler, thanks for treating me as one of your own.

I miss my mom. Finally succumbing to a long illness only days after the first volume of *Manhattan on Film* hit the stores in early 2000, she never got to share the thrill of my getting published. She had a knack for making everyone feel as if they were the most important person in the world, and all those whose lives she touched feel her absence every day—nobody more than I. This volume is dedicated to her.

Many thanks and much love to my dad, who was our rock growing up, who has devoted his life to taking care of others and making our lives the best that they can be, and who continues to overcome all obstacles he encounters along the way. Many thanks to Phyllis, whose caring, love, and support for Dad have served as a reminder to us all that we should never give up, because even when things seem darkest, we never know what joy a new day will bring.

I grew up in a loving home with two wonderful parents and three great brothers. As with all families, we had our ups and downs. When David sold my childhood ring for a few pieces of candy, that was a down. When he and I journeyed through Alaska, finding the forest that must have inspired the illustrations of Dr. Seuss, it was a definite up. Jim refusing to acknowledge that I was his brother when we were both at West Hempstead High was a big down. Being with him when his short film won first prize at the Marco Island Film Festival was a great up. Having Jeff join us for a round of golf was always an up (even though watching him slice into the woods was certainly a down). But our golf-school weekend was an amazing time and a reminder of what a close family is meant to be. May our ups always exceed our downs as we forge ahead.

As the train pulls into the next station, I ask that Amy, Jacquie, and Lyndsay climb aboard, as the ride cannot be the same without them, and there are a few new passengers who are making the ride the most rewarding experience of my life.

To my wife, my Ashley, my love, for her support, her love, and her strength. An added thanks for coming along when she did, for taking my hand as we take this ride together, and for sharing with me two of God's miracles:

Jaden and Austin. Two stunning examples of how wonderful life can be. They demand everything, but give back even more. My two boys have redefined what it means to love. They have taught me what is important. They remind me on a daily basis of the reason I was put on this Earth, and even if one day a statue of me is erected in Times Square, Jaden and Austin will still be the greatest achievement of my life.

Contents

FOREWORD

In the summer of 2003 I offered an experimental film course at Marymount Manhattan College titled Manhattan Movie Experience. The first time I taught the class I was looking around for reading material that the students would find direct, accessible, and interesting. I was very excited by the fact that Marymount Manhattan College is on East 71st Street, since that is also the location of arguably three of popular culture's most enduring fictional characters: Holly Golightly from *Breakfast at Tiffany's* lived in an apartment just up the block; James Bond (in the person of Sean Connery) apparently had an apartment on the same street (though I don't know if any Bond scenes were ever actually filmed on the block); and no less a literary hero than the 20th century's most famous protagonist, Holden Caulfield from *Catcher in the Rye*, lived somewhere on East 71st Street, according to its author, J. D. Salinger, between Fifth Avenue (where his sister caught the downtown bus) and Lexington Avenue (where his mother did her shopping). I wanted to give my students a feel for that excitement of place and for the thrill of knowing they were studying film in a physical location that was within walking distance of these significant film locations. Never mind that *Catcher in the Rye* still hasn't been committed to celluloid: my students and I agreed it would be an instant classic the minute someone could get the rights to do what Salinger never wanted done. We were also just a few blocks away from Carrie Bradshaw's apartment in *Sex and the City*, a fact that impressed them more than

Holden Caulfield. So there I was, wishing there was something that could provide students with the feeling of immediacy and importance of just about every street corner in New York's filmed history. And then I found it in *Manhattan on Film*, Chuck Katz's guidebook to walking tours of famous New York City film locations. The students ended up taking the book with them to work, on the train, anywhere in the city where they might come across one of the locations. The class became an instant hit, and we've offered it at the college every subsequent summer.

I not only added the book to the required reading list for the course, but I also took advantage of the fact that Mr. Katz was only a local phone call away, and presuming that meant he was only a few subway stops away, invited him to come and give a talk to the class. He did, and they've loved him ever since.

As a result of his lecture, I invited Chuck Katz to write an essay for Metaphilm, the film interpretation site that I've published since its launch in the summer of 2001. And that's when the wheels started turning. It struck me that what Mr. Katz was offering in print deserved a wider audience, and it was one that I could provide via Metaphilm without competing with his publisher. So what you see before you is not only Chuck's wonderfully useful book of Manhattan film locations, it is also the first time he is being introduced as the official brain behind the Metaphilm Movie Mapper, an interactive online version of the movie locations in this book but with a few key differences. Online you can't actually find all of the information that's in the book in one fell swoop; but online you get more locations, pictures, and an interactive map-maker feature that shows you exactly where each scene took place. More locations mean you can find older, more obscure, and less commercially successful films. More pictures mean you can see a picture of the location as it appeared in the movie versus how it appears now. And on each page of the online mapper you'll have the opportunity to not only buy (another) copy of Chuck's book to give to family and friends, but also to "Ask Chuck" where your favorite New York film scene took place, in the rare chance that it's not already in the database. If you become a real film buff or Manhattan location expert, you'll even get to add a location and get the credit for it in future editions of the book.

So I hope you'll enjoy the book, enjoy the double pleasure of walking through Manhattan that the book provides, and when you're home or outside the city, take a minute to look up Chuck online at www.metaphilm.com/mapper. See you at the movies in Manhattan!

—Read Mercer Schuchardt
Publisher, Metaphilm

PREFACE

Over the past three-quarters of a century, and increasingly so in recent years, Manhattan has served as the location of choice for thousands of movies. And while most of the action in some movies takes place almost entirely within the city (*On the Town, My Man Godfrey, Sea of Love, Ghostbusters, One Fine Day*), and others even within one particular neighborhood (*Once Upon a Time in America, After Hours, You've Got Mail*), still others find a reason to stop in for a brief, but memorable, scene (*Moonstruck, Sleepless in Seattle, Midnight Run*).

Gone are the days when most films are shot entirely on a Hollywood back lot or soundstage. Not to say that a good deal of filming does not still take place in studios and on back lots, only that filmmakers use an increasingly large number of exterior shots, which enable the moviegoers to "place" a particular scene. It is one thing to show a scene in a hotel room, quite another to show the exterior of the Plaza Hotel, suggesting that the ensuing scene takes place within. A "real" location lends a touch of realism.

And I've discovered that both dyed-in-the-wool New Yorkers and visitors to this great metropolis love to see where their favorite actor stood while filming that memorable scene from their very favorite film. Hence, *Manhattan on Film*.

I have limited the book to locations that are still in existence. In a fast-paced, ever changing cultural, social, and economic society, where stores and restaurants close and reopen almost overnight, this has not been an easy task. Although I had always presumed that some locations (e.g., the Empire State Building) would be here forever, the destruction of the World Trade Center on September 11, 2001, proved how naïve such a view had been. Therefore these locations, like all the good things with which we have been blessed, must not be taken for granted and must be enjoyed while they are here. For we may never know when it will be too late, until it is.

The focus of the Walking Tours in this book is exteriors. When I point out a building and indicate that it is where somebody lived (e.g., Thomas Crown [Pierce Brosnan] in *The Thomas Crown Affair*), I do not mean to suggest, since I do not in fact know, that any of the movie's interior scenes were filmed inside this location. Furthermore, these Walking Tours do not require entrance to a building. However, where a building, store, and so on, is open to the public, feel free to enter. But please be on your best behavior. TourWalkers have a reputation to uphold.

I employed no magic in determining which locations were used in a film and made no inquiries of filmmakers or others in the movie industry. I found most locations by watching the film and doing a little research. For example, I found Location 2 of **Walking Tour 10: The Chelsea Circle** (the home of Kate [Jennifer Aniston] in *Picture Perfect*) by (1) drawing a picture of the building's front railing, (2) noting the store she passes when she leaves the building and turns the corner, (3) finding that store, and (4) finding the building that matched the picture of the railing I had drawn. I admit, my process was embarrassingly low-tech, but it worked. A few locations were easier for me to find because I know Manhattan and most of its neighborhoods particularly well, but almost all locations can be found by anyone willing to take the time and make the effort. Hopefully, this book now makes such effort unnecessary.

Each Walking Tour is obviously best enjoyed

on foot, and it is strongly recommended that all Walking Tours be followed during daylight hours, when it is easier to see and enjoy the locations in detail.

As I often refer to a location in terms of direction (e.g., the northeast corner of a particular intersection, or the west side of a particular avenue), it will be necessary for the TourWalker to understand these directional references. The city's "compass" is easier to grasp than you might imagine. For example, walking uptown and standing at the intersection of Second Avenue and 85th Street, you will find that 86th Street is ahead of you, to the north, while 84th is behind you, to the south, and First Avenue is to your right, east of Second Avenue, while Third Avenue is to your left, west. If you are unsure of the directions for a particular location, ask one of the friendly New Yorkers walking by. They will be only too happy to help.

For TourWalkers who, like me, also enjoy television, I have also included a few locations from some of the more popular television shows of recent years that have Manhattan backdrops.

Finally, I sincerely hope that TourWalkers enjoy taking these tours as much as I enjoyed putting them together.

—Chuck Katz
April 1, 2005

Walking Tour 1

IN THE SHADOW OF THE PLAZA

All of the locations in this first walking tour have one thing in common: they sit atop some of the most expensive real estate in the world. From luxurious hotels, to stores whose names are synonymous with elegance and class, to homes inhabited by some of the wealthiest people around, this neighborhood has no peer when it comes to offering the finest of just about everything that New York City has to offer.

Walking Tour 1: In the Shadow of the Plaza begins at the southeast corner of Central Park, at the intersection of 59th Street (Central Park South) and Fifth Avenue. If you are not already there, cross to the west side of Fifth Avenue and enjoy an unobstructed view of the Plaza Hotel, which stands grandly before the southeast entrance to Central Park.

1. The Plaza Hotel. 59th Street, west of Fifth Avenue. The Plaza. These two words are sufficient to let people know you are referring to the magnificent structure standing proudly at the southeast entrance to Central Park in New York City. A symbol of luxury and grandeur, the Plaza is not only surrounded by numerous wonderful movie locations but has itself appeared in more films than possibly any other location in Manhattan. Whatever the genre, whoever the stars, the Plaza has been the backdrop for many memorable films of the past half-century.

It has seen people fall in love, as Tony Hunter

(Fred Astaire) and Gabrielle Girard (Cyd Charisse) did in *The Band Wagon*. Tony's movie career was on the wane, so he decided to try his hand on the Broadway stage. At first, he was oil to the beautiful but tempestuous ballerina's water, and they couldn't have irritated each other more. And then one evening they left this hotel, where they were staying (separately), hopped on a horse-drawn carriage, and went for an enchanting ride around the city. After that, the success of their collaboration was all but assured, both onscreen and off.

And when love leads to marriage, there is often a honeymoon. And what better place to spend time with your newly betrothed than here? Young hotshot attorney Paul (Robert Redford) and his new bride Corie (Jane Fonda) spent their seemingly endless honeymoon in one of the hotel's suites in Neil Simon's *Barefoot in the Park*. Interestingly enough, when Paul did, in fact, go "barefoot in the park," it was not in Central Park, which would have been the logical choice, given its proximity to the Plaza. After the honeymoon ended, Corie found Paul barefoot (and drunk) in Washington Square Park (see **Walking Tour 11: Greenwich Village,** Location 14).

Neil Simon located a few of his scenes in *Barefoot in the Park* in the Plaza, but he actually incorporated the famed hotel in the title of his *Plaza Suite*, which involved three different stories played out inside this hotel, starring Walter Matthau, Maureen Stapleton, and Lee Grant, among others.

Making a business pitch? What better location than the Palm Court in the hotel's ornate lobby? Having already been told by producer Arnold Kreplich (Alan King) that movie star Alice Detroit (Dyan Cannon) had agreed to do his play, playwright Ivan Travalian (Al Pacino) was surprised to learn that there was still one small detail that he and Arnold had to take care of: Go ask

Alice. Less than pleased with Arnold's little white lie, Ivan accompanied him when they met the star at the Palm Court and got her to agree to sign on in *Author! Author!*

Already have the job? Janice Courtney (Debbie Reynolds) was being worked to the bone and running on all cylinders, but she kept on going, working so hard that she finally collapsed during a photo session inside her hotel room here in *My Six Loves*. That was enough for her doctor, who prescribed six weeks of uninterrupted rest and banished Janice to the country, where she learned there was more to life than work.

Business leans more toward the illegitimate? After his release from prison, Frank White (Christopher Walken) used the Plaza as his base of operations as he attempted to reclaim his crown as *King of New York*.

Business borders more on the less conventional? In *Love at First Bite*, Count Dracula (George Hamilton) also stayed at this hotel. But unlike most guests, who use their rooms primarily at night, the Count preferred to spend his evening hours out on the  town, catching up on his sleep during the day.

Out-of-towners gravitate to the Plaza. Kevin McAllister (Macaulay Culkin) boarded the wrong plane and found himself in New York alone at Christmas. He checked in under the suspicious eye of the hotel's concierge (Tim Curry) in *Home Alone 2: Lost in New York*. In *"Crocodile" Dundee*, another fish out of water, Mick Dundee (Paul Hogan), stayed here and charmed the hotel staff.

Kevin McAllister "grew up" during his stay

in New York, and Mick Dundee taught others to focus on what is important. But underage *Rolling Stone* reporter William Miller (Patrick Fugit) probably learned the biggest lesson of all. When the band he was covering, Stillwater, got to New York, William found Penny Lane (Kate Hudson) in a room in this hotel in *Almost Famous*. Penny had overdosed as a way of dealing with the pain of seeing her boyfriend, rock star Russell (Billy Crudup), go back to his wife. A painful lesson indeed.

Monty Brewster (Richard Pryor) resided here during the thirty-day period in which he had to spend $30 million in *Brewster's Millions*.

Hailing from a small town, just in from the airport, and mistaken for a pair of twins, one identical to each of them, Sadie (Bette Midler) and Rose (Lily Tomlin) Ratliff were dropped off here by a limousine and shown to their room. Well, actually, the other twins' room. A few minutes later, their other halves, Sadie (Bette Midler) and Rose (Lily Tomlin) Shelton, who were bigwigs in *Big Business*, showed up and were given a room adjacent to the one occupied by the Sisters Ratliff. With two sets of twins in the hotel, both played by Midler and Tomlin, havoc was sure to follow. And it did.

When I was in school, we gathered on suburban street corners, at the mall, or at the local diner for a burger and fries. Not so, the young adults in *Metropolitan*. They were young, but having grown up in New York, they acted like adults. Dressed in their best formal attire, it was not unusual for the friends to gather in a room here and while away the hours talking and being, or at least acting, mature.

In a fancy restaurant within the Plaza, smitten and besotted Arthur Bach (Dudley Moore) dined with a hooker he had picked up on the streets in *Arthur*. He expressed surprise (to the consternation of the other diners) when he learned that his "date" was a hooker. He had simply thought he was doing really well with her.

In front of the steps leading to the Plaza's elegant front door, you may see doormen and guests coming and going. It's the perfect place to get your point across to the passersby.

2. In Front of the Plaza Hotel. Ever the political activist, Katie (Barbra Streisand) handed out leaflets for the American Soviet Benefit in front of the hotel. Years later, with a lot of turbulent water under the bridge, Katie ran into her lifelong love, Hubbell Gardner (Robert Redford), on the same spot. They had parted ways long before and were no longer a couple, but their eyes couldn't hide the feelings they still harbored for one another in *The Way We Were*.

Take a look at the fountain in front of the Plaza.

3. Plaza Hotel Fountain. He was unhappily married to Mary (Joanne Woodward), a very cold woman, ironically his wife in real life. But he realized that he would rather be happy with someone else than miserable with his wife, so Alfred (Paul Newman) in *From the Terrace* arranged a late-night rendezvous by this fountain with Natalie (Ina Balin).

While Alfred learned after he got married that his wife was not the one for him, another man sensed on the eve of his wedding that he was destined to be with someone else. Not willing to leave things entirely to chance, Jonathan Trager (John Cusack) took the initiative and canceled his wedding on the very morning he was to walk down the aisle. Afterward, not certain if he had done the right thing, Jonathan walked near this fountain with best friend Dean Kansky (Jeremy Piven). Dean was supportive of his friend's actions, realizing after his own marriage had broken apart that sometimes it is necessary to act and other times it is okay to rely on *Serendipity*.

Just out front, near the fountain, FBI Agent Mike Downey (Matthew Modine) trailed mob widow Angela Demarco (Michelle Pfeiffer) as she searched for a job. While she was inside a building across the street, Agent Downey passed the time singing with a group of street minstrels in *Married to the Mob*.

Turn to the north, leaving the Plaza on your left. Cross 59th Street (Central Park South) until you reach the small plaza just north of 59th and west of Fifth Avenue. The small block is known as Grand Army Plaza. Continue north a few steps along Fifth. Note the statue on the left.

4. Fifth Avenue between 59th and 60th Streets. Statue. After his life took a tragic turn, once-hot radio talk show host Jack Lukas (Jeff Bridges) sat at the base of this statue, trying to drink away his sorrows. When that didn't work, he considered ending it all, until he met the mysterious and troubled Perry (Robin Williams). The rest is the stuff of fantasy in *The Fisher King*.

Years earlier, before the statue was even there, journalist Phil Green (Gregory Peck), a new arrival to New York, walked through this plaza with his son Tom (a young Dean Stockwell) and sat on a bench on this small block, talking about many things in *Gentleman's Agreement*.

Look across Fifth Avenue to the restaurant at the Sherry Netherland Hotel, Harry Cipriani.

5. Harry Cipriani, in the Sherry Netherland Hotel. After meeting at a fundraiser the night before, insurance investigator Catherine Banning (Rene Russo) and billionaire industrialist Thomas Crown (Pierce Brosnan) came here for dinner in

The Thomas Crown Affair. But Catherine's intentions were not pure. While Catherine kept Crown occupied, the police made copies of his house keys, which she had swiped from him, and searched his home for evidence linking him to a brazen art theft. But, as always, Crown was one step ahead of them all.

Look just north to the hotel itself.

6. Sherry Netherland Hotel. 781 Fifth Avenue.

Detective Danny Madigan (Richard Widmark) came to meet his wife, Julia (Inger Stevens), in Suite 1004 of this hotel before escorting her to the Captains' Association Dinner Dance in *Madigan*.

The Sherry Netherland was home to Miss Zoe Montez (Heather McComb), where she essentially lived alone with her butler, because her parents were always jetting around the world, in Francis Ford Coppola's "Life Without Zoe" segment of *New York Stories*.

Walk north on Fifth to 60th Street. Note the building on the southeast corner.

7. Fifth Avenue and 60th Street. Southeast Corner.

In a building on this corner, in *Tales of Manhattan*, actor Paul Allman (Charles Boyer) waited patiently for a tailcoat to be delivered to his apartment. With much fanfare, the coat was delivered and placed on a mannequin in Allman's home. He didn't seem concerned when he learned the tailcoat was supposedly cursed. But, as he would later learn, perhaps he should have been.

———·•·———

Continue north half a block until you are across from the Pierre Hotel.

8. The Pierre Hotel. Fifth Avenue (between 60th and 61st Streets). Weddings weren't supposed to be his thing, and he never imagined he would want to fall into such a trap himself, but when playboy Charlie Reader (Frank Sinatra) returned from Europe, he came here from the airport to attend a wedding. He arrived just in time to blow a kiss to the bride, catch the bouquet, and realize that falling into a tender trap wouldn't be so bad, if the trap was the one set by Julie Gillis (Debbie Reynolds) in *The Tender Trap*.

This hotel was named "the Bradbury" in the movie *For Love or Money*. It is where concierge Doug Ireland (Michael J. Fox) worked to get anything and everything for his well-tipping guests.

In another film where the hotel was called "the Bradbury," finance whiz Laurel (Whoopi Goldberg) met Mr. Fallon (Eli Wallach) to try to convince him to do business with her and her fictional partner, Robert S. Cutty, in *The Associate*.

———·•·———

Look up at the tower above the Pierre.

9. 2 East 61st Street. Pierre Hotel Tower. As his sixty-fifth birthday approached, wealthy communications mogul William Parrish (Anthony Hopkins) received an unwelcome visit from a mysterious stranger (Brad Pitt) during a family dinner in his New York City apartment. In *Meet Joe Black*, that luxurious apartment was high atop this building.

Walk north to the end of the block until across from the Café Pierre.

10. Fifth Avenue and 61ˢᵗ Street. Cafe Pierre. Soon after receiving unwanted custody of a baby, J. C. Wyatt (Diane Keaton) attended a lunch meeting here, where, with limited success, she tried to leave the baby with the coat check girl in *Baby Boom.*

Continue north to 64ᵗʰ Street.

11. Fifth Avenue and 64ᵗʰ Street. After finally agreeing to adopt a baby with his wife Amanda (Helena Bonham Carter), Lenny (Woody Allen)

became the model father in *Mighty Aphrodite*. In the first scene shown with the baby, Amanda and Lenny, with carriage in tow, walked north along Fifth in front of this entranceway.

Walk north until you are halfway between 65ᵗʰ and 66ᵗʰ Streets.

12. Fifth Avenue, between 65ᵗʰ and 66ᵗʰ Streets. West side of the street. She made a habit of coming to New York on Sundays, and on a particular *Sunday in New York,* that is exactly what she did. During her visit, Eileen (Jane Fonda), a wide-eyed innocent from upstate New York, tried to hail a cab from this spot, then boarded a bus that was headed south. She would soon find herself attached to Mike (Rod Taylor) when her flower got caught on his jacket pocket.

Near the almost identical spot where she boarded the bus as Eileen, Jane Fonda was back a few years later. As Brice Daniels, Fonda was no wide-eyed innocent, but rather a high-priced call girl, and she found herself embroiled in an investigation of the disappearance of one of her occasional clients. In *Klute*, after finally convincing private investigator John Klute (Donald Sutherland) that she had told him everything she could, they met here, and Klute gave her the surveillance tapes he had made of her during his investigation. Brice took the tapes and tossed them into a trashcan against the wall.

Continue north until you are between 67th and 68th Streets. Look across to number 860.

13. 860 Fifth Avenue (between 67th and 68th Streets). Flanders Kittredge (Donald Sutherland) and his wife, Ouise (Stockard Channing), lived in lavish style in this building until the tranquility and sterility of their lives was ultimately shattered by a mysterious visitor, Paul (Will Smith), in *Six Degrees of Separation*.

Turn and head south to 63rd Street. Cross Fifth and stand on the southeast corner.

14. 817 Fifth Avenue (at 63rd Street). What would a whirlwind New York City weekend be without a little rendezvous with a member of the fairer sex? If you are Lieutenant Colonel Frank Slade (Al Pacino) and you have very little to look forward to in your life, such a pick-me-up might be just the thing you need. In *Scent of a Woman*, while his "chaperone," Charlie (Chris O'Donnell), waited in a car at the curb, Frank visited a woman in this building.

———◆·◆———

Walk south one block to the south side of 62nd Street. Turn left and walk the short distance until you are in front of 8 East 62nd.

15. 8 East 62nd Street. Having just been promoted to detective, New York City policeman Michael Keegan (Tom Berenger) received his first assignment: protecting wealthy socialite Claire Gregory (Mimi Rogers), who had witnessed a murder, in *Someone to Watch Over Me*. Miss Gregory lived in this building, where Detective Keegan learned that more was at stake than just a murder conviction or the safety of the witness: his marriage.

———◆·◆———

Return to Fifth, turn left and walk two blocks to 60th Street. Turn left and walk until you reach number 1.

16. The Metropolitan Club. 1 East 60th Street. Having just moved to New York, Finn (Ethan Hawke) was thrilled to run into his long-term friend and childhood crush, Estella (Gwyneth Paltrow). And he was even more excited when she invited him to join her and her friends for a drink here, fueling his *Great Expectations*. But he left deflated, having learned that Estella was dating Walter (Hank Azaria) and seemed to view Finn as nothing more than an old friend. So distraught was he that he left with a jacket the club had given him to wear while inside. Outside these gates, a club employee caught up with Finn, and he had to return the jacket.

———◆·◆———

Again return to Fifth Avenue, turn left, and walk south until you reach 58th Street. The famed toy store FAO Schwarz should be on your left.

17. 767 Fifth Avenue and 58th Street. FAO Schwarz. A tourist attraction in its own right, this fabled and always crowded toy store is where Mr. MacMillan (Robert Loggia) went every Saturday to get the pulse of the people, and where he ran into Josh Baskin (Tom Hanks), in *Big*. It is where the two of them performed a memorable duet of "Heart and Soul" and "Chopsticks" on the "foot piano."

A few years after they became friends, Lenny (Woody Allen), with his adopted son Max (Jimmy McQuaid), ran into Linda (Mira Sorvino) with her daughter inside the store in *Mighty Aphrodite*. Neither Lenny nor Linda knew the full extent to which their lives were intertwined.

If you choose to enter the store, I cannot be responsible for how much money you end up spending while inside, but it is certainly a great temptation. You might end up like hardworking concierge Doug Ireland (Michael J. Fox), who entered the store empty-handed and emerged with a large stuffed giraffe, which he then drove around, neck out of the sunroof in his hotel's limousine, in *For Love or Money*.

On her first trip to the big city in *Big Business*, Sadie Ratliff (Bette Midler) went on a window-shopping spree that brought her to this world-famous toy emporium. There she was spotted by

Jason (Seth Green), who mistook her for his mother, Sadie Shelton (also Bette Midler), and tried out his toy boxing gloves on her. It took them a long time to finally figure out who was who, but not before they had all endured a great deal of confusion and mayhem.

A number of years before, while his colleague Arthur (Blaine Novak) kept her son occupied, undercover sleuth John (Ben Gazzara) initiated contact with the subject of his surveillance, Angela (Audrey Hepburn), while she was shopping in the store. The movie was *They All Laughed,* and at the time the store was located across 58th Street from this location.

Continue south one block until you are in front of Tiffany's, at 727 Fifth Avenue.

18. 727 Fifth Avenue. Tiffany's. The name alone should give it away. Mysterious, beautiful "socialite" Holly Golightly (Audrey Hepburn), eating her breakfast pastry and drinking her coffee, stood in front of the store and admired the window displays at the beginning of *Breakfast at*

Tiffany's. Later on, she got to wander inside with her suitor and neighbor, Paul (George Peppard).

Soon after arriving in New York and filled

with wonder and excitement, Joe Buck (Jon Voight) noticed a man lying on the pavement in front of this store in *Midnight Cowboy*. What seemed to trouble him most was the seeming callousness of the passersby, who barely looked at the figure on the ground. TourWalkers will learn that New Yorkers are not like that.

Walk south on Fifth half a block.

19. Fifth Avenue (between 56th and 57th Streets). In front of Trump Tower. Molly (Meryl Streep) and Isabelle (Dianne Wiest) worked in the city and often walked in front of Trump Tower. And when they walked, they talked. They discussed work, their respective relationships, and their lives. But one thing Molly didn't discuss with Isabelle was the fact that, though married, she was *Falling in Love* with Frank (Robert De Niro).

And, of course, somewhere inside the building is the famous boardroom where week after week in *The Apprentice* brilliant young hopefuls sit before "the Donald" and wait to see to whom the dreaded "you're fired" will be directed.

Resume your southward trek on Fifth and stop at the corner of Fifth and 55th Street. Note the grand Peninsula Hotel diagonally across the street.

20. 700 Fifth Avenue (at 55th Street). The Peninsula Hotel. Radical attorney Edward J. Dodd (James Woods) was invited to come here to meet with Manhattan District Attorney Robert Reynard (Kurtwood Smith) to discuss a case that both men were working on in *True Believer*.

One minute she was rooting on her favorite team, the New York Knicks, the next she was plucked from obscurity to coach the team. A dream come true for any avid fan, but at a dinner

here with the eccentric team owner, "Wild Bill" Burgess (Frank Langella), Eddie Franklin (Whoopi Goldberg) learned that "Wild Bill" intended to move New York's beloved basketball team to St. Louis. Willing to walk away from her dream, Eddie left the dinner and the hotel, and hailed a passing cab in *Eddie*.

Sometimes the stars of the movies never even make it inside. In the typical disaster movie, the audience is introduced to the cast of characters prior to the onset of the disaster. In *Daylight*, taxi driver Kit (Sylvester Stallone) picked up two nasty passengers in front of this hotel and had the harrowing task of driving them through the ill-fated Holland Tunnel. To find out whether they make it, you'll have to see the movie.

Ratso Rizzo (Dustin Hoffman) waited in the shadows outside the hotel (named "the Barclay" in the movie) while his friend and client, self-styled lothario Joe Buck (Jon Voight), went inside to offer his "services" to one of New York's supposedly lonely women in *Midnight Cowboy*. Apparently, the staff of the Barclay Hotel didn't share Joe's sense of the importance of his task, because they tossed Joe out on his rear end.

Turn to the left and walk east the short distance on 55th Street until you are across from another fine hotel, the St. Regis.

21. 2 East 55th Street. The St. Regis Hotel.
The St. Regis was the site of the first secret rendezvous between Elliot (Michael Caine) and his wife's sister Lee (Barbara Hershey) in Woody Allen's *Hannah and Her Sisters*.

Inside, at the famed King Cole bar, "spurned first wife" Elise Eliot (Goldie Hawn) tried to drown her sorrows with the help of a sympathetic bartender in *The First Wives Club*. Elise was bemoaning the fact that she had been offered the role of a mother in a play, confirming her fears that she was, indeed, getting older.

In front of this hotel, cab driver Travis Bickle (Robert De Niro) picked up the beautiful Betsy (Cybill Shepherd) at the end of *Taxi Driver*.

———

Return to Fifth Avenue, cross to the west side of the street, turn to the right at the corner, and walk north a half-block or so until you reach the Henri Bendel store.

22. Henri Bendel Store. 712 Fifth Avenue (between 55th and 56th Streets). After winning the lottery, Muriel (Rosie Perez) and husband, Charlie (Nicolas Cage), went on a shopping spree to spend some of their newfound wealth. In *It Could Happen to You*, it happened to them, and this fashionable emporium was one of the many stops on their spree.

———

Continue walking north to Harry Winston, just before the corner of 56th Street.

23. 718 Fifth Avenue. Harry Winston Jewelers. Holden (Edward Norton) wanted to buy his girlfriend, Skyler (Drew Barrymore), an engagement ring and brought along his girlfriend's sister D. J. (Natasha Lyonne) for help. As with everything else in the Woody Allen film *Everyone Says I Love You*, their shopping spree turned into a full-scale musical number, right here in this store.

Continue north to 57th Street. Note Bergdorf-Goodman on the northwest corner.

24. Bergdorf-Goodman. 754 Fifth Avenue (at 57th Street). After agreeing to accompany Phillip Shane (Cary Grant) to Bermuda, and thereafter on a trip around the world, the less-than-worldly Cathy Timberlake (Doris Day) first had to get some new clothes. With Mr. Shane picking up the tab, in this the cinematic predecessor to Julia Roberts' shopping spree in *Pretty Woman*, Cathy came here in *That Touch of Mink*, tried on a vast array of clothes, and left with a whole new wardrobe.

Although Mr. Hobson (Sir John Gielgud) remarked that one would ordinarily have to go to a bowling alley to meet someone of Linda's (Liza

Minnelli) stature, millionaire lush Arthur Bach (Dudley Moore) did just fine outside this store, where he watched, with admiration, Linda's sticky fingers and quick wit in *Arthur*.

Cross 57th, turn left, and walk the short distance until you are before 7 West 57th.

25. 7 West 57th Street. After unleashing her wild side while on vacation in Greece, Ann (Liv Ullman) returned to her normal existence, which included working in a real estate office located in this building. But when Peter (Edward Albert), her vacation "fling," surfaced in New York, Ann found that it might not be so easy to return to the life she had known before. For Ann's life in *40 Carats*, that turned out not to be such a bad thing.

Walk the few short yards to the building behind the big red "9".

26. 9 West 57th Street. After quitting their high-stress lives and dropping out of society in an effort to "find themselves," David (Albert Brooks) and Linda (Julie Hagerty) instead found that chucking it all was not as easy as they thought it would be. Finally realizing that withdrawing wasn't the answer, they left their most recent jobs in Arizona (he was a school crossing guard, and she sold hotdogs at a fast-food stand), drove their recreational vehicle all the way to New York City, and pulled up at the curb in front of this building. They may have gotten *Lost in America*, but they found themselves in New York. Many people do.

In *Superman*, a burglar improbably scaled the front of this building. As he made his way up, he had planned for everything except the possibility that he might find Superman (Christopher Reeve) standing in his path, throwing a wrench in his plans. Startled, the burglar fell, but, luckily, Superman was there to catch him before he hit the ground.

Fans of television's *Friends* may be interested to know that Chandler (Matthew Perry) worked in data processing in this building. And then again, they may not.

Head west on 57th and stop in front of Rizzoli Books, at 31 West 57th.

27. Rizzoli Books. 31 West 57th Street. They came in separately, doing their last-minute Christmas shopping. Each loaded down with packages from other stores, Frank (Robert De Niro) and Molly (Meryl Streep) wandered through the store, looking for the perfect gift for their significant

others, and then collided on the way out, never dreaming that this collision was just the first time their paths would cross. In *Falling in Love*, Frank and Molly were destined to meet again and again.

***

Continue west, cross Avenue of the Americas (Sixth Avenue), and continue until you are across from the Parker Meridien Hotel.

28. 118 West 57th Street. Meridien Hotel. As-

sistant District Attorney Tom Logan (Robert Redford) had been roped into giving the keynote address before the Manhattan Legal Society, which met here. The stress he felt about giving the speech would soon be eclipsed by what he would encounter in *Legal Eagles*.

Belinda (Shelley Long) developed feelings for Chuck (Henry Winkler), who, thanks to the cleverness of Billy (Michael Keaton), had become a pimp of sorts for Belinda and her cohorts in *Night Shift*. Sitting in a car with Billy in front of the back entrance to this hotel, with a customer waiting upstairs, Belinda had a decision to make, and, surprisingly, Billy came through with some solid advice. Confused? See the movie. Most reviewers predicted Michael Keaton's future stardom based upon his performance in this film. Love arcane movie trivia? Watch for a young Kevin Costner attending a party in a scene at the morgue.

———•◦•———

Head west a little bit more until you are across from the tall, monolithic structure that is the Metropolitan Tower, at 146 West 57th Street.

29. 146 West 57th Street. Metropolitan Tower. Jack Lukas (Jeff Bridges) was a successful radio personality. In *The Fisher King*, Jack lived here until a shooting spree, which he may have convinced a caller to his radio show to undertake, turned his life upside down.

———•◦•———

There are two ways to get to Carnegie Hall. One, as the old saying goes, is to practice. The other, and much quicker, way is to walk west a very short distance. One of the world's most famous music venues is just east of the corner of Seventh Avenue, across 57th Street from you.

30. 154 West 57th Street. Carnegie Hall. Some TourWalkers may remember a 1947 movie called *Carnegie Hall*. It featured such classical music artists as Artur Rubinstein, Leopold Stokowski, Jascha Heifetz, Ezio Pinza, and the New York Philharmonic, and you are looking at where much of it was filmed.

After developing a crush on world-renowned pianist Henry Orient (Peter Sellers), wide-eyed schoolgirls Valerie Boyd (Tippy Walker) and Marion Gilbert (Merrie Spaeth) came here to attend a concert at which Henry was performing in *The World of Henry Orient*. But Henry, who had previously noticed the two girls on a number of occasions, and never with good results, was clearly unnerved by their appearance.

Well-known symphony conductor Claude

Eastman (Dudley Moore) suspected that his much younger and very beautiful wife Daniella (Nastassja Kinski) was cheating on him. To make things worse, Claude thought the affair was with fellow musician Max Stein (Armand Assante), with whom Claude was currently working, here, in *Unfaithfully Yours*.

They were a long way from their school in East Harlem, but thanks to a tremendous amount of hard work and enthusiasm and some helping hands along the way, particularly from Roberta (Meryl Streep), who had taught them to play the violin, the students had their big-time debut here, in *Music of the Heart*. They played before a packed house, and shared the stage with such music world luminaries as Isaac Stern and Itzhak Perlman.

———————

Walk west to Seventh Avenue, turn right, and walk north one block to 58th Street. Note the building on the southeast corner.

31. Seventh Avenue and 58th Street. Caterers Holly (Dianne Wiest) and April (Carrie Fisher) met David (Sam Waterston, in an unbilled role), an attractive and interesting architect, at a party they were catering in *Hannah and Her Sisters*. After the party, David took the two women on a tour of what he considered to be some of Manhattan's more interesting architectural structures. This building was one of the attractions on that tour.

———————

Head north on Seventh Avenue, one block to Central Park South.

32. Central Park South and Seventh Avenue. On the park side of the street, the out-of-their-element cowboys Pepper (Woody Harrelson) and Sonny (Kiefer Sutherland) bade farewell to their friend Sam (Ernie Hudson), a cop who longed to be a cowboy, before heading back to New Mexico in *The Cowboy Way*.

Turn right and head east on Central Park South (same as 59th Street). Stop at the New York Athletic Club.

33. New York Athletic Club. 180 Central Park

South.   Abruptly  leaving this club, Phillip (Cary Grant) stood under the awning to stay out of the rain and asked a friend to arrange for a job for Cathy (Doris Day). Later on, in *That Touch of Mink*, Phillip came charging out of the club in nothing but a towel to hail a cab.

Walk a few feet to the east until you are halfway between Seventh and Sixth Avenues.

34. Central Park South (Between Seventh and Sixth Avenues). Chivalry wasn't dead. At least not where Leopold, Duke of Albany (Hugh Jackman) came from. Or more accurately, "when" Leopold came from. Having passed through a time tunnel of sorts, Leopold found himself defending the honor of the thoroughly modern Kate McKay (Meg Ryan) on more than one occasion. And in one particular instance, after a mugger snatched Kate's purse and climbed the low wall into the park along this stretch, Leopold commandeered a horse from one of the horse-drawn carriages and, with the damsel Kate riding

behind him, gave chase through the park in *Kate and Leopold*.

Walk east until you reach 160 Central Park South.

35. 160 Central Park South. Essex House. Upon arriving in New York for his ill-fated rendezvous with Terry (Annette Bening), in *Love Affair*, Mike Gambril (Warren Beatty) checked in here.

Continue walking east until you reach 112 Central Park South.

36. 112 Central Park South. The Westin. In the movie *Regarding Henry*, Henry Turner (Harrison Ford) had been a cutthroat attorney before he was shot in a holdup. Afterward Henry struggled to remember even the simplest things from his prior life. The first word he spoke after his ordeal was "Ritz." He was remembering the Ritz-Carlton, which was the previous name of this hotel. In the movie, Henry went to the hotel and sat in a room. An unexpected visit by co-worker Linda (Rebecca Miller) helped Henry remember that some parts of his prior life had not been so simple after all.

Walk east a bit further, crossing Sixth Avenue, and continue until you are across from the subway entrance, which is on the park side of 59th Street.

37. Central Park South Subway Entrance (between Fifth and Sixth Avenues). But a short distance from his appearance in *The Cowboy Way*, Woody Harrelson (playing Charlie) found himself here, in *Money Train*. After another "chewing out" by Donald Patterson, their boss (Robert Blake), Charlie and John (Wesley Snipes) emerged from this staircase and headed east on this street, just as you have been doing.

———————

Walk east just a bit further until you reach the Oak Room in the Plaza Hotel.

38. Oak Room in the Plaza Hotel. While having a drink in the Oak Room, advertising executive Roger Thornhill (Cary Grant) innocently went to send a wire and was mistaken for a man named George Kaplan. He was ushered (at gunpoint) into a car waiting out in the street and whisked away to an estate on Long Island, in *North By Northwest*. Thornhill eventually escaped his captors and made his way back here, hoping to uncover the mystery of George Kaplan.

Frank Slade (Al Pacino) and Charlie (Chris O'Donnell) came here for a meal in *Scent of a Woman*.

You have reached the end of **Walking Tour 1: In the Shadow of the Plaza**.

Walking Tour 2
CENTRAL PARK WEST

W. 86TH ST.

W. 72ND ST.

W. 59TH ST.

RIVERSIDE DR.

WEST END AVE.

AMSTERDAM AVE.

COLUMBUS AVE.

CENTRAL PARK WEST

BROADWAY

ELEVENTH AVE.

TENTH AVE.

NINTH AVE.

EIGHTH AVE.

UPTOWN

WEST SIDE

EAST SIDE

DOWNTOWN

Walking Tour 2
CENTRAL PARK WEST

The Arch in St. Louis, Missouri, is meant to symbolize that city as the Gateway to the West (and, presumably, to the East, if one happens to be traveling in the opposite direction) in the United States. By the same token, Columbus Circle has often been called the Gateway to Manhattan's Upper West Side. Once the turf of the Jets and the Sharks, whose battleground in *West Side Story* was razed by the construction of Lincoln Center for the Performing Arts in the 1960s, this area of Manhattan is now one of the most artistically and culturally rich in the world.

From Columbus Circle, walk east along Central Park South (59th Street) until you are in front of 240 Central Park South.

1. 240 Central Park South. Plucked from the obscurity of a small town, he grew to be a fixture on radio, then television. But he made some bad choices along the way and his fall was as rapid as his rise. In the end, "Lonesome" Rhodes (Andy Griffith) screamed from a balcony near the top of this building, while Marsha (Patricia

Neal) and Mel (Walter Matthau) stood on the street in front, realizing that Rhodes had reached the end of his meteoric ascent and would soon be, once again, nothing but *A Face in the Crowd*.

Walk to the front of San Domenico, the upscale restaurant connected to this building.

2. 240 Central Park South. San Domenico. A very popular and highly acclaimed eatery, this is where concierge Doug Ireland (Michael J. Fox) looked through the window to see the woman he liked, Andy (Gabrielle Anwar), having dinner with Christian (Anthony Higgins) in *For Love or Money*. Days later, Doug would again look in and, much to his chagrin, see Christian, who was married, in the restaurant with a different woman. In film, as in life, it seems that nice guys often do finish last. Then again, the movie didn't end here.

Turn back and enter Columbus Circle. Walk along the eastern road that fronts Central Park and stand before the large monument that stands guard over the park.

3. Columbus Circle. Memorial to Seamen of the Maine. A priest should not be having such thoughts, but young Brian Flynn (Edward Norton) couldn't help himself. Realizing that he was in love with his childhood friend Anna (Jenna Elfman), a forlorn and lovelorn Father Brian sat on the base of this statue and bemoaned his unenviable dilemma in *Keeping the Faith*.

In a short period of time, Travis Bickle (Robert De Niro) went from offering his services as a volunteer for the presidential campaign of Senator Charles Palantine (Leonard Harris) to considering an assassination of the man. Sporting a mohawk, Travis looked upon the rally being held on this spot and made his way through the crowd, hand suspiciously kept inside his jacket. Luckily, he was scared off by the senator's bodyguards, in *Taxi Driver.*

Continue in the same direction and stop at the concrete bench built into the wall.

4. Columbus Circle and Central Park West. Corner. Look to make sure that book editor Will Randall (Jack Nicholson) isn't on the prowl, as he was in *Wolf.*

Continue along to the newsstand at 60th Street.

5. Central Park West and 60th Street. Newsstand. Presumably as long-lived as the Empire

State Building, this newsstand appeared in the Gene Kelly/Frank Sinatra classic *On the Town*, one of the earlier films filmed on location in New York. Gabey (Gene Kelly) was on a mission to find "Miss Turnstiles," Ivy Smith (Vera Ellen). She boarded a subway, and Gabey, Chip (Frank Sinatra), and Ozzie (Jules Munshin) hopped a cab and got out here. They rushed down the staircase across from the newsstand to find her. But they didn't see Ivy Smith come up the same staircase a moment later and disappear down the street.

Head north on Central Park West and stop across from the Prasada, near 65th Street.

6. 50 Central Park West. The Prasada. This beautiful building, with its magnificently carved front pillars, has appeared in several movies in recent decades. In *Three Men and a Baby*, the building was home to the playboy triple-threat of Peter (Tom Selleck), Jack (Ted Danson), and Michael (Steve Guttenberg).

In a lesser-known film but, coincidentally, one also starring Steve Guttenberg, *It Takes Two*, the Prasada was home to Steve Guttenberg's wealthy but bitchy fiancée Clarisse (Jane Sibbett). In the movie, the incomparable Olsen twins played identical twins, one rich, one poor, who tried to bring together the father of one, Roger Calloway (Guttenberg), with Diane (Kirstie Alley), the camp counselor of the other. Mary-Kate played Amanda, and Ashley played Alyssa. Or was it the other way around? Does it really matter? Jane Sibbett went on to become well-known as Carol, the ex-wife of Ross in the television show *Friends*.

They had a very strange relationship, Gordon Hocheiser (George Segal) and his senile mother (Ruth Gordon), who was given to asking on a pretty regular basis, *Where's Poppa?* The two of them lived in this building, and even at the end of

34

the movie the bizarre dynamic between them was not quite clear.

The Prasada was also home to Broadway star Sally Ross (Lauren Bacall), who had many fans, but only one (Michael Biehn) who could consider himself *The Fan*. He had a terrible effect on Sally and those around her, and his stalking made all of their lives a living hell.

Walk north until just before 66th Street and look across to 55 Central Park West.

7. 55 Central Park West. Movie buffs will recognize this building as the home of Dana Barrett (Sigourney Weaver) and Louis Tully (Rick Moranis). The corner penthouse of "Spook Central" is where Dana lived, according to Ray Stantz (Dan Aykroyd). This building was also the crossover point for Zool, Gozer, the Keymaster, and the

Gatekeeper, as well as all of the other ghosts, ghouls, and goblins that invaded New York City. After the final showdown, the *Ghostbusters* emerged from the building and greeted their adoring and appreciative fans.

The address indicated in the movie was 550,

probably a gesture toward privacy for the building's residents, a privacy now shattered. My apologies.

Walk north to 67th Street, cross over to the west side of the street and continue west on 67th until you are in front of Café Des Artistes.

8. 1 West 67th Street. Café Des Artistes. After the funeral of their friend, former college chums Annie (Diane Keaton), Elise (Goldie Hawn), and Brenda (Bette Midler) came here to eat, drink, and reminisce in *The First Wives Club*.

Walk a few feet to your left.

9. 1 West 67th Street. The Templetons, Bill (John Beck), Janice (Marsha Mason), and their daughter, Ivy (Susan Swift), lived in splendor in a spacious multilevel apartment in this building. And then Mr. Hoover (a young Anthony Hopkins, looking like a cross between Rowan Atkinson and Major Healy from the television show *I Dream of Jeannie*) showed up, making the unfathomable claim that their little Ivy was the reincarnation of his daughter, *Audrey Rose*, who had died in a fiery car crash years before. They thought he was nuts. But they would soon learn that it wasn't always a good idea to jump to conclusions.

Turn back and walk east to Central Park West. Turn left and walk north one block to 68th Street. Look to the sewer plate in the street.

10. Central Park West and 68th Street. Sewer Plate. After the longest night of their lives, having been forced to sleep in Central Park because the hotel gave away their room, small-town denizens George (Jack Lemmon) and Gwen (Sandy Dennis) had had enough. They stood on this corner and argued about what to do next.

George then walked out into the street and onto a sewer plate, fortuitously stepping aside just before steam from below blew the plate into the sky. For these *Out-of-Towners*, where everything that could go wrong did, it was the final straw.

Head north until you reach 91 Central Park West, at 69th Street.

11. 91 Central Park West. Midge Carter (Ossie Davis) had a tough choice to make. He could spend his free time in this building, where he worked the outmoded boiler somewhere down below, or he could venture into Central Park and idle away his time listening to the ravings of fellow bench-sitter Nat (Walter Matthau). He chose the latter. Otherwise, *I'm Not Rappaport* would have been a much shorter (and, dare we say, less interesting) film.

Continue north on Central Park West until you reach 72nd Street. Cross to the far side of the street and turn left, walking the short distance until you are before the guard booth that sits in front of the entranceway to the famed Dakota.

12. 1 West 72nd Street. The Dakota. New York lore has it that this building was named the Dakota because at the time it was built, the wealthy people lived on Fifth Avenue, and any building as far west as this one might as well have been in the Dakotas (North or South wasn't specified). Most people know this New York City landmark, however, as the home of John Lennon, and the place where he was gunned down by Mark David Chapman on a cold December night in 1980.

Film buffs will know that demonic forces were at work on Rosemary Woodhouse (Mia Farrow) here in the classic *Rosemary's Baby*. Rosemary's husband Guy (John Cassavetes) made a pact with

the devil, along with his henchmen, who happened to be the Woodhouses' neighbors in the building, chief among them Minnie (Ruth Gordon) and Roman (Sidney Blackmer) Castevet. The film is a horror classic, and Charles Grodin had an early non-comedic role as Dr. Hill.

Return to Central Park West, turn left, and walk north to 73rd Street. Stop at number 135.

13. The Langham. 135 Central Park West. He may have made a good living, but Jonathan Balser

(Richard Benjamin) did very little to make his wife, Tina (Carrie Snodgrass), feel appreciated. So

much did he take her for granted that she found comfort in the arms of another man, George Prager (Frank Langella). The unhappy Balsers, and their two kids, lived in this building in *Diary of a Mad Housewife*.

Continue north to 75th Street and stop at number 151.

14. 151 Central Park West (at 75th Street). The Kenilworth. Stranded in New York, mistakenly suspected of murder, and with nowhere else to turn, the hapless foursome Billy (Michael Keaton), Jack (Peter Boyle), Henry (Christopher Lloyd), and Albert (Stephen Furst) showed up at the apartment of Billy's former girlfriend Riley (Lorraine Bracco), which was in this building, in *The Dream Team*.

Keep heading north and stop at the far side of 77th Street. The Museum of Natural History, the favorite destination of many school field trips, as well as millions of adults, will tower before you.

15. Museum of Natural History. Central Park West and 77th Street. On the eve of Thanksgiving, this street is blocked off as balloons for the legendary Macy's Thanksgiving Day Parade are inflated and kept overnight. The event has turned into one of New York's most festive of the year and is well worth a visit. In *Miracle on 34th Street*, the start of the parade was captured on film and began on this very street in front of the museum's entrance. It was here that Kris Kringle (Edmund Gwenn) discovered that the Santa Claus who was scheduled to ride on one of the floats was drunk and had to be replaced. Which he was.

In another film, Alonzo (Harvey Keitel) pulled up in front of the 77th Street entrance, half a block to the left from where you stand, and confronted Randy (Molly Ringwald) to collect on a debt in *The Pick-Up Artist*.

Still hoping to track down the witness who could corroborate his allegations of sanitation industry corruption and hopefully save his job, Jack Taylor (George Clooney) took time out to bring his daughter Maggie (Mae Whitman) and her schoolmate Sammy (Alex D. Linz) here to kill some time. Sammy was the son of Melanie Parker (Michelle Pfeiffer), Jack's antagonist and love interest, in *One Fine Day*. In the movies, it is possible to be both.

The museum is also where Walter Kornbluth (Eugene Levy) was first ridiculed when he revealed that he had seen a mermaid with his own eyes. Later on, when the mermaid, Madison (Daryl Hannah), was captured and brought in for testing, Dr. Kornbluth received the respect he so craved. All of this occurred against the wishes of Allan Bauer (Tom Hanks), who had a less scientific, more romantic interest in the mermaid. And all of this happened in *Splash*.

Continue north on Central Park West and stop at the subway entrance, just to the north of the museum's front steps.

16. Subway Entrance. South of Entrance to Museum of Natural History. Angie (Christina Vidal) lifted his wallet, prompting Mikey (Michael J. Fox) to chase her down these stairs to the subway. When she pulled a small knife on him and kicked him, Mikey knew he was in over his head and let her go. He knew better than to mess with such a tough cookie. But when he found her, having pulled the same stunt on someone else outside the museum, performing a wonderful display of histrionics, Mikey thought it might be worth taking a risk, and he did what any self-respecting talent agent would do: he signed her up in *Life With Mikey*.

Walk north to the near corner of 81st Street. Look west at the tree-lined block.

17. 81st Street, west of Central Park West. Getting to know one another, Judy (Mia Farrow) and Michael (Liam Neeson) strolled along this street in *Husbands and Wives*.

Note the Planetarium, the glass-enclosed sphere just to the west and south of you.

18. Hayden Planetarium's Rose Center for Earth and Space. Jamal (Rob Brown) was doing his best to fit in at his new school, and his new friend Claire (Anna Paquin) was doing her best to make his transition easier. Later on, Jamal would devote his energies to *Finding Forrester*, but right

now he just wanted to find a friend. One afternoon the two of them came here, discussed how
Claire ended up at the Mailor-Callow School,
and the possibility that their friendship might
move to another level.

Cross 81st Street and walk north to number
225, between 82nd and 83rd Streets.

19. 225 Central Park West. After dumping the
only girl he ever loved, Sebastian (Ryan
Phillippe) camped out across the street from this
building where Annette (Reese Witherspoon)
lived and waited for her to read his journal. He
hoped she would realize that he truly loved her,
and that his *Cruel Intentions* were not only a mis-
take, but also a thing of the past.

Continue north to number 257, just south of
86th Street.

20. 257 Central Park West. Orwell House.
Ruthless financier Lawrence Garfield (Danny
DeVito) finally met his match. Beautiful, sexy,
smart, and a lawyer, she was also the daughter of
the head of the company that Lawrence intended
to take over. Her name was Kate (Penelope Ann
Miller), and she lived here in *Other People's
Money*.

Look to the busy intersection of Central Park
West and 86th Street.

21. 86th Street and Central Park West. In a car
chase that is still one of the most memorable in
screen history, New York City cop Buddy
Manucci (Roy Scheider) pursued one of the bad
guys through just about every inch of Manhattan's streets. At one point, the two cars raced up
Central Park West and made screeching left turns
onto 86th Street and continued on their way,

heading west toward the Hudson River, in *The Seven-Ups*.

Cross 86th Street and walk north until you are in front of number 262 (between 86th and 87th Streets).

22. 262 Central Park West. Marjorie (Natalie Wood) was still in school and still lived here with her parents, but a summer with Noel Airman (Gene Kelly) was going to make her grow up fast. And although she wanted a life in the theater, she would eventually question whether Noel was going to figure in her plans, as life with him would make her grow up more quickly than she wished, in *Marjorie Morningstar*.

Look across Central Park West to the wall enclosing the park.

23. Along the Central Park Wall. They were both powerful people in the world of television news program-ming, and for a while they did more than just work for the same *Network*: they shared a ro-mance so torrid that it caused Max (William Holden) to leave his wife for Diane (Faye Dunaway). Try-ing to get away

from the rigors of their industry, they took a stroll and stopped here to share a few affectionate moments.

Turn back on Central Park West and head south to the south side of 83rd Street. Turn right on 83rd and walk west until you are in front of number 46.

24. 46 West 83rd Street. There were 8 million stories in *The Naked City*, and one of them took place here. Although the building's address was shown to be number 52 in the movie, this is where a woman's body was found, a crime the police did their best to solve before the final credits started to roll.

————•—•————

Continue heading west on 83rd Street until you reach Amsterdam Avenue. Turn right on Amsterdam and walk until you are just north of 86th Street. The church should be on your right. Stop in front of Barney Greengrass.

25. 541 Amsterdam Avenue. Barney Greengrass. Time for a NitPick. In the movie *Smoke*, Auggie (Harvey Keitel) managed a smoke shop somewhere in the heart of Brooklyn. He befriended Paul (William Hurt), a man who had suffered greatly. Near the end of the movie, they decided to leave the store and get something to eat, mainly because Auggie wanted to tell Paul a nice Christmas story. To get some food, they ended up here in Manhattan at Barney Greengrass, famous for such delicacies as smoked salmon, sturgeon, and whitefish.

Is the food good? Absolutely. But is it likely that these two guys would come here all the way from Brooklyn when the movie suggests that they were just going nearby to get a bite? If you agree that the answer is no, congratulations. You are now an official NitPicker.

Because it was in the neighborhood, it made more sense for Kathleen (Meg Ryan) and Birdie (Jean Stapleton) to share a meal here, which they did in *You've Got Mail*.

Head back south and stop at the southeast corner of Amsterdam and 83rd Street.

26. 477 Amsterdam Avenue (at 83rd Street). Hi-Life Bar & Grill. Poor Ray (Campbell Scott). Every bartender in town seemed to be in his debt, and before he could lend his sister money, he had to make the rounds and call in their IOUs. Ray was a bartender here, and before the night was over he was to come across some old faces and some new, including his ex-girlfriend Maggie (Daryl Hannah), his sister's worthless boyfriend Jimmy (Eric Stoltz), and a bookie named Fatty (Charles Durning), in *Hi-Life*, a movie named after the bar.

Cross Amsterdam and walk west on 83rd until you are across from Café Lalo.

27. 201 West 83rd Street. Cafe Lalo. Kathleen (Meg Ryan) was here, book and flower in hand, ready to meet her secret e-mail pal. And then Joe (Tom Hanks) had to show up and ruin things. But Joe knew something that Kathleen didn't, and moviegoers knew something that neither Kathleen nor Joe would discover until the end of *You've Got Mail*.

Return to Amsterdam and turn right. Walk south to the south side of 78th Street, then cross Amsterdam and continue east a short distance. Stop in front of 170 West 78th Street.

28. 170 West 78th Street. Within the confines of this building, thanks to the insensitivity of their mutual acquaintance, two struggling yet ambitious actors, Elliot (Richard Dreyfuss) and Paula (Marsha Mason), were thrown together as roommates. Although it sounds like Neil

Simon's *The Odd Couple*, it is really Neil Simon's *The Goodbye Girl*.

Continue east until just before Columbus Avenue.

29. 78ᵗʰ Street. Just West of Columbus Avenue. *The Goodbye Girl* again. Briefly considering heroics, Elliot chased a car down this street to retrieve groceries that men in a car had stolen from Paula. Just before reaching the corner, the men got out of the car brandishing a weapon. Sensing that his strength lay more in his acting ability than his fists, Elliot dropped his own groceries and beat a hasty retreat.

Continue east to Columbus. Look to the left. The eatery Ocean Grill should be in front of you, a few feet up Columbus.

30. 384 Columbus Avenue. Ocean Grill. Again in *You've Got Mail* (an Upper West Side staple). Kathleen (Meg Ryan) was trying to figure out the identity of her e-mail friend, and enemy-turned-friend Joe (Tom Hanks) was only too happy to help. While eating lunch here, they tried to decipher the meaning of the screen name "NY 152."

Turn south on Columbus and walk to the north side of 77ᵗʰ Street. Cross Columbus and head east until you are across from 20 West 77ᵗʰ Street.

31. 20 West 77ᵗʰ Street. In a car parked right at the curb where you are standing, writer of detective novels Phillip (Ben Masters) accompanied a real detective, Carabello (Danny Aiello), on an actual stakeout in *Key Exchange*. The building they were watching was 20 West 77ᵗʰ Street.

Return to Columbus, turn left, and walk to the near corner of 76th Street. Look east.

32. 76th Street, East of Columbus Avenue.

Lonely guy Larry Hubbard (Steve Martin) decided to make one last effort to avoid a life of utter loneliness and to try and win back his true love, Iris (Judith Ivey), who was about to marry Jack (Steve Lawrence) in *The Lonely Guy*. Beginning his mad dash to the church to stop the wedding, Larry rushed from his apartment and headed west, past where you are standing, to catch a cab on Columbus Avenue.

Cross to the south side of Columbus, turn left, and head east to the entrance to number 60.

33. 60 West 76th Street.

This building was the home of Bronte (Andie MacDowell) and, for the purposes of fooling immigration officers, her "husband" Georges (Gerard Depardieu) in *Green Card*. Filmgoers will remember the curved staircase leading up from the lobby, easily visible from the street.

Return to Columbus. Turn left and walk south until you reach the south side of 75th Street. Look at the restaurant across Columbus.

34. 316 Columbus Avenue (at 75th Street). Pappardella.

Observant fans of *Seinfeld* will recognize this recurring restaurant exterior (although it no longer wears the green and white colors it had in the show) as a site of an occasional meal and date for the Seinfeld four.

Look down at your feet, but watch for cruising Casanovas.

35. 60 West 75th Street.

Jack Jericho (Robert Downey, Jr.) had spotted Randy Jensen (Molly

Ringwald) and approached her, using his best lines and proving that he was, in fact, a pick-up artist of the highest order in *The Pick-Up Artist*. They turned the very corner where you are now standing, headed east on 75th Street, and stopped in front of the first building off Columbus. Having told her she had the "face of a Botticelli and the body of a Degas," Jack did surprisingly well with Randy. And many other women.

Walk south on Columbus Avenue. Turn right on 69th Street and walk west until you are in front of number 115.

36. 115 West 69th Street. Gladys Glover (Judy Holliday) came to town to make it big, and while

she was here, she lived in this building, along with fellow tenant Pete (Jack Lemmon), a documentary filmmaker, in *It Should Happen to You*.

Head back the other way on 69th and stop when you are across from Maya Schaper's Cheese and Antiques. But don't be fooled.

37. 106 West 69th Street. Maya Schaper Cheese & Antiques. A neighborhood institution for years, this picturesque shop was the actual location of the independent book shop owned by

Kathleen (Meg Ryan) and forced out of business by the opening of a large "chain" bookstore owned by Joe (Tom Hanks) in *You've Got Mail*. The interior scenes of Kathleen's book shop were also filmed within the store.

You have now reached the end of **Walking Tour 2: Central Park West.** If the store is open, please feel free to go inside and look around. New York wouldn't be New York without stores like this.

Walking Tour 3

UPTOWN BROADWAY

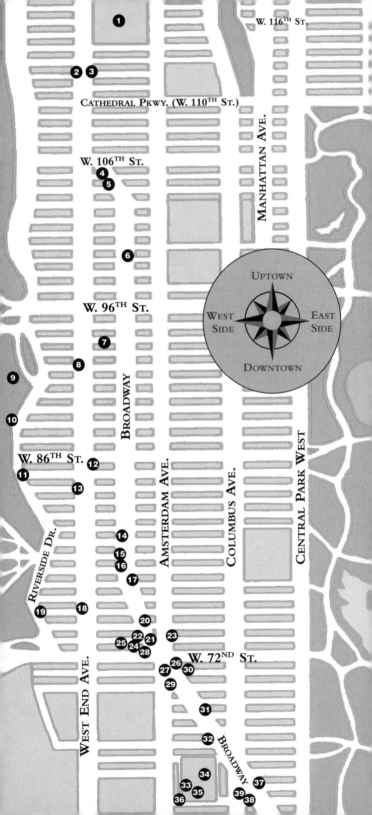

Walking Tour 3
UPTOWN BROADWAY

Put your walking shoes on because **Walking Tour 3: Uptown Broadway** covers a lot of ground, but the locations to be seen will make it well worth the trip. Some of the treasures contained in **Walking Tour 3: Uptown Broadway** are out in plain sight (like Columbia University, the Ivy League institution that begins our tour). Others, like a community garden and neighborhood monument, are known mostly to locals. Still others, like a private street off the beaten path, are rare gems unknown even to many who live only a few blocks away.

Grand old homes, small neighborhood haunts, and the world's premier cultural enclave, this Walking Tour will cover it all. **Walking Tour 3: Uptown Broadway** begins at 116th Street and Broadway, in front of the gates to Columbia University. Feel free to go through the gates and admire the campus from within.

1. Columbia University. 116th Street and Broadway. Paul (David Selby) was a history professor here, and one day, in *Up the Sandbox*, his wife Margaret (Barbra Streisand) stopped by after her doctor's appointment to tell him that she was pregnant. But Paul was in a meeting, and she didn't get the chance.

The academic life must have made an impression on Ms. Streisand, though, because years later she, too, would play a professor at this school in *The Mirror Has Two Faces*. Several scenes in the film took place on these memorable and picturesque grounds.

Before getting their funding revoked and getting thrown off campus, Peter (Bill Murray), Ray (Dan Aykroyd), and Egon (Harold Ramis) worked here at Columbia in *Ghostbusters*. After they were evicted from their office, they sat out on campus and pondered their next move.

⎯⎯◆◆⎯⎯

If you entered the campus, return to the west side of Broadway. Turn left and head south on Broadway until you reach the north side of 112th Street. Note the store on the northwest corner with the flowers out front.

2. Broadway and 112th Street. Northwest corner. After a reward had been offered for his capture, Nicky (Adam Sandler), Satan's childlike son, stopped here to smell the flowers. But people recognized him, and pretty soon a large crowd chased *Little Nicky* down Broadway.

⎯⎯◆◆⎯⎯

Look directly across Broadway. If it hasn't jumped out at you by now, then you probably are not a true *Seinfeld* devotee.

3. 2880 Broadway (at 112th Street). Tom's Restaurant. This is the well-known façade from the long-running television show. Now you may ask why, if Jerry and Kramer lived on 81st Street

(a fact often referred to on the show), did they frequent this coffee shop on 112th Street, a full mile-and-a-half away? Considering that many New Yorkers never travel such a distance to do anything, ever, it is a fair question. And a legitimate NitPick.

Continue south on Broadway. At 107th Street, Broadway veers left, and West End Avenue begins. Bear left and stay on the west side of Broadway, continuing south. When you get to 106th Street, continue to the middle of the next block, between 105th and 106th.

4. Smoke. 2751 Broadway. After a tough day on the job, three good cops named Artie (Michael Keaton), Stevie (Anthony LaPaglia), and Felix (Benjamin Bratt) thought about going for a drink at the bar that was located here, but when they saw their commanding officer, Lieutenant Danny Quinn (Kevin Conway), inside, they decided to pick a different place to spend their off-duty hours in *One Good Cop*.

Continue south the short distance to another well-known tavern, Tap-A-Keg.

5. 2731 Broadway. Tap-A-Keg. After Michael (Daniel Stern) got dumped by his wife, he and Phillip (Ben Masters) hoisted a few, then wheeled their bicycles out of this venerable tavern in *Key Exchange*.

Resume your southward trek until you reach 100th Street. Continue walking until you are halfway down the next block. Look across Broadway to The Metro.

6. The Metro. Broadway (between 99th and 100th Streets).

This longstanding movie house was the site of redemption for Mickey Sachs (Woody Allen) in *Hannah and Her Sisters*. Having fallen to the depths of despair, wondering if there was anything worth living for, questioning the meaning of life, and even having tried (unsuccessfully) to end it all, Mickey wandered the streets of Manhattan and ended up here. *Duck Soup*, the Marx Brothers classic, was on the screen, and watching it, Mickey came to realize that maybe life didn't have to have some deep-seated meaning, after all. It may be enough just to be alive. Renewed and reborn, Mickey left the theater and picked up the pieces of his life, finding happiness in the unlikeliest of places along the way.

Continue south on Broadway and turn right on 94th Street. Walk halfway down the block until you get to the stone and brick archway on the right.

7. 265 West 94th Street. Pomander Walk.

A breathtakingly serene respite from the hustle and bustle of Manhattan, this charming block of small houses was one of the locations on the architectural tour of the city given to Holly (Dianne Wiest) and April (Carrie Fisher) by David (Sam Waterston), the architect the two friends had met at a party and were about to fight over in *Hannah and Her Sisters*.

Unfortunately, the gate is locked because the short street is private, but you can get a glimpse of

the houses on either side of the walkway beyond
the wrought-iron fence.

―――――・・―――――

Continue west on 94th Street (in the same direction that got you to Pomander Walk) until you
reach West End Avenue. Turn left on West End
and head south until you reach 92nd Street. Look
across West End Avenue.

**8. West End Avenue and 92nd Street. North-
west Corner**. Troubled writer Harry (Woody
Allen) was being honored at his old school, and
wanted to bring his son along for the occasion.
But that would require taking the boy out of
school and getting the consent of his ex-wife,
Joan (Kirstie Alley), in *Deconstructing Harry*. Harry
confronted Joan and they ended up bickering on
this corner. Harry lost the argument.

An interesting note about this film. Visiting his
son's school, Harry talked with his son while a
mother sitting at the next table eavesdropped on
the conversation. She was played by Mariel Hemingway, who had appeared as Woody Allen's
young love interest in an earlier film, *Manhattan*
(see **Walking Tour 5: East of the Park,** Location 35).

―――――・・―――――

Cross West End Avenue and head west on 92nd
Street to Riverside Drive. Turn left on Riverside

and head south to 91st Street. If it is spring or summer and it is daylight, it may be worth venturing into Riverside Park here to see the community garden where Joe Fox (Tom Hanks) and Kathleen Kelly (Meg Ryan) shared a very special moment. If you choose, enter the park at 91st Street and follow the path down, bearing left as the path forks. The playground should be on your left. The path lets out, up a slight incline, at the garden.

9. Riverside Park at 91st Street. Community Garden. They started out disliking each other, then the ice melted and they developed a mutual attraction. But it was too late. Kathleen (Meg Ryan) was going to meet her e-mail pal here at

the community garden. In the late spring and summer, the garden is in full bloom, as it was at the end of *You've Got Mail*, when Joe (Tom Hanks) showed up and foiled Kathleen's rendezvous. Or did he? As their eyes met, Kathleen was moved to tears, Joe's loyal dog, Brinkley, scampered nearby, and someone began singing about something being somewhere over the rainbow. A classic Hollywood ending to be sure.

If you entered Riverside Park, return up the path to Riverside Drive. If not, you should still be at 91st Street. Continue south on Riverside Drive (the park should remain on your right) until you are halfway between 89th and 88th Streets. Note the monument on your right.

10. Riverside Drive (near 89th Street). Soldiers' and Sailors' Memorial Monument. They may have been the least likely of roommates. In fact, they were quite *The Odd Couple*,

but they were still the best of friends. One evening, Oscar Madison (Walter Matthau) and Felix Unger (Jack Lemmon) sat near this monument and talked.

———•+•———

Continue south to 131 Riverside Drive (at 85th Street).

11. 131 Riverside Drive. After sitting on the bench, *The Odd Couple* returned here, where they lived. This building is not to be confused, however, with the apartment in the television series of the same name (see **Walking Tour 5: East of the Park,** Location 37).

———•+•———

Turn back north on Riverside Drive. Then turn right on 86th Street. Walk east to West End Avenue and look at number 530, on the southeast corner of the intersection.

12. 530 West End Avenue (at 86th Street). Joan Wilder (Kathleen Turner) wrote novels about romance and adventure. Her heroines were beautiful; her heroes dashing and brave. And then on a trip to Colombia, her life imitated her art, and she had the adventure of a lifetime in *Romancing the Stone*. After she returned to New York, Joan handed in a novel that made her agent weep and resumed her normal, staid life. But not for long. Returning home with groceries, she was astounded to find her dashing real-life hero, Jack Colton (Michael Douglas), polishing his boat in front of this building. She discarded the groceries, admired Jack's boots—which resembled a certain reptile they had battled in Colombia—and climbed aboard to head off on another adventure.

———————

Turn right and walk south on West End Avenue until just before 84th Street. The next location is the building on your right, number 505.

13. 505 West End Avenue. This building is where Rose (Barbra Streisand) went to live with her mother, Hannah (Lauren Bacall), after leaving husband Greg (Jeff Bridges) in *The Mirror Has Two Faces*. A highly memorable scene at the end of the film had Rose and Greg waltzing outside the building here on West End Avenue. I was living ten blocks down from here at the time and can attest to the fact that, even though the finished product looks good on screen, it is no fun being woken up in the middle of the night by the sounds of a helicopter overhead, from which the waltzing scene was being filmed.

———————

Cross West End Avenue and walk east one block. Turn right on Broadway and walk south until you reach Zabar's, halfway between 81st and 80th Streets.

14. 2245 Broadway. Zabar's. This popular West Side institution is where Kathleen (Meg Ryan) found herself in the cash-only checkout line with too little cash when her nemesis, Joe (Tom Hanks), came to her rescue in *You've Got Mail*.

————•—•————

Head down Broadway to the south side of 79th Street. Locate the entrance to the subway.

15. Broadway and 79th Street. Subway Entrance. After discovering that his friend George (Ricky Jay) had been murdered and knowing that he would be blamed, Joe (Campbell Scott) climbed out the window of George's apartment and entered the subway down this staircase just as the cops were racing to George's building in *The Spanish Prisoner*.

————•—•————

Walk south a short distance until you are before the grand entranceway to the Apthorp, a block-long building on your right.

16. The Apthorp. 2211 Broadway (between 78th and 79th Streets). This enormous building, with its beautiful façade, was home to Alison (Faye Grant), a friend of the mayor's daughter Bernadette (Mary Elizabeth Mastrantonio), in *The January Man*. After Alison was found murdered, for reasons somehow made clear in the film, the only person deemed capable of solving the mystery was Nick Starkey (Kevin Kline).

The Apthorp is also where Vera Cicero (Diane Lane) lived and consorted with the likes of Dutch Schultz (James Remar) and Dixie Dwyer (Richard Gere) in *The Cotton Club*.

————•—•————

Continue south and stop halfway between 78th and 77th Streets. Look across Broadway.

17. Ruby Foo's. 2182 Broadway. His wife was using their newly earned wealth to blend into the world of caviar and champagne, but Ray (Woody Allen) preferred pizza and beer. While passing by here one afternoon in *Small Time Crooks*, Ray was greeted by his wife's cousin May (Elaine May), who was dining inside.

Walk south and turn right on 75th Street. Walk west one block to West End Avenue. Number 325 should be across West End from you.

18. 325 West End Avenue. They thought it would be a step in the right direction when they moved out of this building and headed for the suburbs. But Joanna and Walter Eberhart (Katherine Ross and Peter Masterson), along with their daughter, Kim (a seven-year-old Mary Stuart Masterson), didn't quite know what they were getting themselves into when they put down roots in the seemingly idyllic town of Stepford, Connecticut. But they would soon learn why the town was just a little bit too peaceful, in *The Stepford Wives*.

Cross West End Avenue and head west on 75th Street until you are in front of the building on the corner, number 33.

19. 33 Riverside Drive. Having just returned from a wonderful vacation at a resort island, Paul Kersey (Charles Bronson) and his wife Joanna (Hope Lange) tried to ease back into their New York City existence. However, their calm was short-lived when three men broke into their apartment, which was in this building, and attacked Joanna and their daughter, Carol (Kathleen Tolan), in *Death Wish*.

That Paul should want revenge for his wife's murder and his daughter's attack should come as no surprise. What may be surprising, though, is that one of the thugs who took part in the attack was played by Jeff Goldblum. Quite a different role from the intellectual good guys he played in such blockbusters as *Jurassic Park* and *Independence Day*.

Turn back and walk east on 75th to the east side of Broadway. Turn right and head south until you reach the Beacon Theater, between 75th and 74th Streets.

20. Beacon Theater. 2124 Broadway. After blowing up an underground garage, the so-called party crasher (Stephen Lang) ran in here, followed closely by Lieutenant John Moss (James Woods), for what should have been the final showdown. But nothing ever seemed to work easily for Moss, and ever since movie star Nick Lang (Michael J. Fox) started tagging along, everything seemed to be done *The Hard Way*.

Turn to the right and head south on Broadway until you reach Apple Bank for Savings, between 74th and 73rd Streets.

21. 2100 Broadway. Apple Bank for Savings. In *One Fine Day*, Melanie Parker (Michelle Pfeiffer) and Jack Taylor (George Clooney), after dropping off their respective children at the Ninth Street Dropoff Center, left the center and walked around the corner. The next shot showed Melanie and Jack walking south past this bank. A nice film, but one deserving of a NitPick. Why? Well, assuming the Ninth Street Dropoff Center is located on 9th Street (a reasonable assumption to make, I would argue), which would be some 65 streets south of this spot, how likely is it that the two of them would have been walking here a few seconds after leaving the dropoff center? And heading in the wrong direction, to boot? (From 9th Street to 74th, you would be walking north.)

In a city as large as New York, how likely is it that a seemingly random location such as Broadway and 74th Street would be used as a movie location for more than one film? If the answer to that question is "not very," then how likely would it be for the same seemingly random location to be used in two films starring the same star? Enough said. But that is exactly what happened here.

The movie *One Fine Day* was filmed in 1996. Now, while Michelle Pfeiffer was walking along this stretch of Broadway with co-star George Clooney, did it cross her mind that eight years before, in *Married to the Mob*, she had gotten off the M104 public bus on the corner and walked by this same Apple Bank? In that movie, Angela de Marco (Pfeiffer) exited the bus next to this building, not aware that FBI agent Mike Downey (Matthew Modine) was on the bus, tailing her. When Angela got off the bus, Mike, who couldn't blow his cover, had to kick out a vent and climb out the top of the bus.

Look across Broadway to the Ansonia, another wonderful home on the Upper West Side.

22. The Ansonia. 2109 Broadway. There was a time when Willie Clark (Walter Matthau) had been one half of the legendary vaudeville team of Lewis and Clark. Al Lewis (George Burns) had been the other half. The duo, once best of friends, now arch enemies, went by the name *The Sunshine Boys*. But many years had passed since then,

and Willie spent his days living a curmudgeonly existence in a cluttered apartment in this building, where his primary contact with the outside world was the weekly visit from his nephew Ben (Richard Benjamin).

This imposing structure served as the home of Allie (Bridget Fonda) and her fiancé, Sam (Steven Weber), and for a while the disruptive Hedra (Jennifer Jason Leigh), in one of those "it really could happen to anyone" thrillers, *Single White Female*.

This building was also home to esteemed psychiatrist Dr. Nathan Conrad (Michael Douglas), his wife, Aggie (Famke Janssen), and their daughter, Jessie (Skye McCole Bartusiak), in *Don't Say a Word*. They went to sleep the night before Thanksgiving hoping to see the Bart Simpson balloon in the parade the next day, but when Dr. Conrad woke to find that young Jessie had been kidnapped, the day's itinerary understandably changed.

Continue south to 73rd Street and turn toward the left. P & G Bar/Café is on Amsterdam and 73rd, a stone's throw away.

23. P & G Bar/Cafe. 279 Amsterdam Avenue. A favorite hangout of the local underworld figures who populated the gang that FBI undercover agent Joe Pistone, aka *Donnie Brasco* (Johnny Depp), infiltrated.

Although his girlfriend Linda (Andie MacDowell) wanted him to follow a more secure and more legitimate career path, Gary (Andy Garcia) thought he had *Just the Ticket* to a great life, and his habits were hard to break. After long days of scalping tickets to various sporting and cultural events around town, Gary and his friends came here to eat, drink, and unwind.

Cross Broadway at 73rd Street and walk west,

keeping the Ansonia on your right. When you reach the end of the building, you will come to an alleyway running north.

24. Alleyway Next to Ansonia. 73rd Street, West of Broadway. Although the alleyway now leads to an underground parking garage, it was a passage strewn with garbage cans back when Joe Turner (Robert Redford), on his way to meet his CIA colleagues, was shot at in *Three Days of the Condor*.

———•◆•———

Look across 73rd Street, to number 240.

25. 240 West 73rd Street. Proving that an exterior is often nothing more than that, this building was made out to be a hotel in *Broadway Danny Rose*. After their long sojourn in the swamps of New Jersey, Danny (Woody Allen) and Tina (Mia Farrow) returned to New York. Fearing that

Danny was in danger should he return to his apartment, Tina convinced Danny to try to find a hotel room for the night. They entered this building together. Tina stopped to use the pay phone in the entranceway (not there in real life), and Danny continued on to the reception desk in the lobby. A peek into the building will reveal a wall of mailboxes where the hotel's desk was purported to be. Told that there were no rooms available, Danny exited the hotel, passing the phone that Tina had used. Moments later outside the hotel, a Cadillac pulled up to the curb, and two men took Danny and put him in the trunk.

Return to Broadway and turn right. Walk to the northwest corner of Broadway and 72nd. Look diagonally across the intersection to Gray's Papaya.

26. Gray's Papaya. 72nd Street and Broadway. Southeast Corner. In addition to its obvious popularity, judging by the big crowds that surround the place at all hours of the day and night, you might remember that Gray's Papaya was a favorite of Alex (Matthew Perry) in *Fools Rush In*. In fact, Gray's Papaya was one of the things that Alex feared he would miss most about New York when he was contemplating forsaking his hometown and moving to Nevada to be with Isabel (Salma Hayek) and their baby. Camping out under the stars by the Grand Canyon or eating hot dogs and drinking papaya juice from Gray's Papaya? For regulars of this place, it would be a difficult decision, indeed.

Doug Ireland (Michael J. Fox) was asked by one of his hotel's guests to look after Andy (Gabrielle Anwar), so he did. In *For Love or Money*, this is one of the places he took her.

More recently, Joe (Tom Hanks) and Kathleen (Meg Ryan) stopped in here for hot dogs in *You've Got Mail*.

He finally got Sontee (Regina King) to go on a date with him, and he took her here. But Lance Barton (Chris Rock) had great difficulty realizing that Sontee and everyone else didn't see him as the *Down to Earth* person he used to be, but as Charles Wellington, the middle-aged white man whose body Lance had been given to use on a temporary basis. And when, trying to impress

Sontee, Lance started singing rap, he got his lights punched out by some bystanders.

———•◆•———

Without moving, let your eyes drift to the right.

27. 72nd Street Subway Station Entrance.
This entrance has appeared in several movies over the years. With one glance at the exterior, you can see why.

Across the street from the subway station entrance, Larry (Steve Martin), who couldn't help being *The Lonely Guy*, ran into Jack (Steve Lawrence), who obviously was not cut from the same cloth. While Larry couldn't get a date, Jack had a girl on each arm, Verna (Jolina Collins) and Frieda (Lena Pousette).

In a memorable scene from *Fools Rush In*, Alex (Matthew Perry), pining away for Isabel (Salma Hayek), was confronted in front of this small building by a strange man, a soothsayer perhaps, who hinted at Alex's dilemma and urged him to follow his love, predicting that he would see signs that would show him the way.

Those who prefer more action-oriented films might recall that John McClane (Bruce Willis) and partner-in-adversity Zeus (Samuel L. Jackson) raced to this station to answer both the pay phone to the left of the entrance and the riddle that had been posed to them, in order to beat the deadline imposed by the mad bomber Simon (Jeremy Irons), in *Die Hard With a Vengeance*. The pay phone does not exist, but the station itself, as you can see, is very real.

Not enough action in that movie for you? A rally in the Bronx had gotten out of hand, and after a shooting, utter chaos ensued. The street gang known as *The Warriors* knew they wouldn't be safe until they returned to their home turf in Coney Island, Brooklyn, and they had a long, grueling night ahead of them as they made their way through the city. When the subway didn't work out as planned, a few of them got off here and raced through the back door of the station entrance, only to find a rival gang, with painted faces, wearing baseball uniforms and waving baseball bats. The Warriors fled, and the bat wielders followed in hot pursuit.

———————

Now turn and gaze up at the Alexandria, behind you on the northwest corner of Broadway and 72nd Street.

28. The Alexandria. 201 West 72nd Street (at Broadway).

Her face graced the pages of fashion magazines, but her personal life was in complete disarray. Her best prospect seemed to be a self-absorbed actor named Bob (Maxwell Caulfield), who only called when he was feeling low. Her name was Sahara (Bridgette Wilson), she lived in this building, and she didn't reveal until the end of *The Real Blonde* that she wasn't, in fact, a real blonde.

———————

Cross 72nd Street and walk south until you reach 71st Street. The various corners abutting Broadway and 71st Street, including the benches on the median between the uptown and downtown lanes on Broadway, were once known as Needle Park.

29. Needle Park. Vicinity of Broadway and 71ˢᵗ Street. The neighborhood has changed significantly, and most of the stores and eateries from those days have evolved into what you see, but back in the early 1970s, Bobby (Al Pacino), Helen (Kitty Winn), and the rest of their so-called friends spent a good deal of time hanging around this area, scoring or using drugs. It was *The Panic in Needle Park*, and they would learn that good times were often followed by bad, and a friend was only a friend until somebody else came along and made a better offer.

Tour 3

Cross to the south side of 71ˢᵗ Street, then turn left and cross first Amsterdam, then Broadway and continue east until you are across from the entrance to 171 West 71ˢᵗ Street.

30. 171 West 71ˢᵗ Street. While television reporter Tony Sokolow (Sigourney Weaver) pursued her story, night janitor and possible *Eyewitness* to murder Daryll Deever (William Hurt) courted her. One evening, Daryll gave Tony a lift home on his motorcycle to this building.

Return to Broadway and turn left. Walk south and stop at number 2000, at 69ᵗʰ Street.

31. 2000 Broadway (at 69ᵗʰ Street). Before he was given a glimpse of what might have been, finance wiz Jack Campbell (Nicolas Cage) had no regrets about the path his life had taken.

A high-powered business mogul and free-living bachelor, Jack lived in the largest apartment in this building. But after waking in "his" bed in a suburban home with a wife, Kate (Tea Leoni), and children, Jack imagined he was having a bad dream. He drove into Manhattan and came here, but nobody knew who he was, and he realized that his suburban experience was not a dream. He had actually become *The Family Man*.

Continue south on Broadway and stop at 66th Street, across Broadway from Tower Records.

32. Tower Records. 1961 Broadway. Although the original layout was changed when the store was renovated in the mid-1990s, this is the same place where Mickey (Woody Allen) spotted former sister-in-law Holly (Dianne Wiest) in *Hannah and Her Sisters*. Years before, the two had shared a memorably horrific blind date and could not have been less compatible, but on reuniting, they discovered that they, indeed, had much in common.

Cross Broadway at 66th, then turn left and walk south to 65th Street. At 65th, Broadway veers left, and Columbus Avenue veers to the right. The world-renowned cultural complex Lincoln Center for the Performing Arts fronts Columbus Avenue to your right. Walk along the roadway that leads into Lincoln Center and stop when you reach the open plaza (at 64th Street).

Turn to your right and face the full majesty of the buildings on all three sides. Focus first on the Metropolitan Opera House, before you on the far side of the fountain.

33. Metropolitan Opera House. 30 Lincoln Center Plaza. To keep peace in the family, Alby Sherman (Elliott Gould) ended things with his non-Jewish girlfriend and agreed to date Cheryl (Carol Kane), of whom his family approved. On one of their dates, Cheryl and Alby came here to see an opera. Although Cheryl enjoyed the performance, Alby slept through most of it in *Over the Brooklyn Bridge*.

Apparently, not all men are bored by opera. To Ronny Cammareri (Nicholas Cage), a night at the opera was a rare treat. And to be there with Loretta (Cher) made it a very special night, indeed. And when Loretta, dressed to the nines, met up with Ronny on this plaza for his dream date, a performance of *La Boheme*, Ronny knew that fairy tales could come true. Of course, the fact that Loretta was engaged to Ronny's brother Johnny (Danny Aiello) provided a complicating factor, but Ronny was lovestruck, and in *Moonstruck*, that might just be enough.

Similarly, at the end of *The Secret of My Success*, new couples Bradley Foster (Michael J. Fox) and Christy Wills (Helen Slater), along with Fred Melrose (John Pankow) and Vera Prescott (Margaret Whitton), attended the opera while their limousine awaited their return in a very unlikely spot—right next to this fountain.

And speaking of the fountain.

34. The Fountain at Lincoln Center. Sitting around this fountain one evening, creative producer Max Bialystock (Zero Mostel) convinced timid accountant Leo Bloom (Gene Wilder) to become his partner and try to produce a Broadway flop. After agreeing to join forces, *The Producers* celebrated their new alliance in style.

Peter Venkman (Bill Murray) waited alongside the fountain for Dana Barrett (Sigourney Weaver)

to emerge from the building. When she did, she was accompanied by a fellow musician (Timothy Carhart), whom Dana described as "one of the finest musicians in the world." Peter didn't mind, though. To Peter, who was one of the *Ghostbusters*, the man was a "stiff" and no competition, because Peter was a ghostbuster, and Dana was being plagued by ghosts.

Turn to the left and note the New York State Theater.

35. New York State Theater. 20 Lincoln Center Plaza. In *Fame*, some wanted to dance, some wanted to sing, some wanted to act, and some wanted to play musical instruments. But in *Center Stage*, everybody wanted to dance. Much of the action in the film was set in this building and around the plaza itself.

Cross to the far side of the fountain and head left, keeping the Metropolitan Opera House on your right. You will soon be in Damrosch Park, a concrete oasis with a bandshell on one end.

36. Damrosch Park. Lincoln Center. During a frenetic day, the seemingly ordinary people who became disciples in *Godspell* sang and danced their way throughout New York City. In one scene, they related the story of Lazarus while here in this park, and even put on a show onstage, although nobody else was around to enjoy it.

Leave the park and walk to 62nd Street (the park should be on your right). At 62nd, turn left and walk east. Cross Columbus Avenue and continue until you reach Broadway. Turn left on Broadway and walk north to the north side of 63rd Street. Fiorello's will be across Broadway from where you stand.

37. Fiorello's. 1900 Broadway. While Broadway director Joe Gideon (Roy Scheider) was in the hospital recovering from a heart attack, the producers and backers of his show were more interested in the bottom line. Not certain when or if Gideon would return to work, they met here with another director, Lucas Sergeant (John Lithgow), in *All That Jazz*, and threw out to him the possibility of his stepping in and taking over the reins from Joe.

Turn around and walk the short distance to Columbus and 63rd. Look at the restaurant on the south side of 63rd.

38. 48 West 63rd Street. In the television series *Friends*, Monica Geller worked as a chef here when it was called Merlot.

In *Sea of Love*, Frank Keller (Al Pacino) and Sherman Touhey (John Goodman) played New York City cops who went undercover to capture a serial killer believed to be preying on people who responded to "personal ads." They set up a sting operation at this location, which at the time was the longstanding New York City tavern O'Neal's Balloon. At a table not far from the window onto 63rd Street, first Keller and then Touhey posed as "personal ad" placers and met, one after another, those who responded to the ads. One of

the women answering Keller's ad was the beautiful, sexy, sultry Helen (Ellen Barkin).

---

39. Columbus and 63rd Street. Before leaving this intersection, it may interest you to know that you are standing on the exact spot where Alvie Singer (Woody Allen) parted ways with Annie Hall (Diane Keaton) at the very end of *Annie Hall*.

Alas, it is now time to part ways with **Walking Tour 3: Uptown Broadway.**

Tour 3

Walking Tour 4
CENTRAL PARK

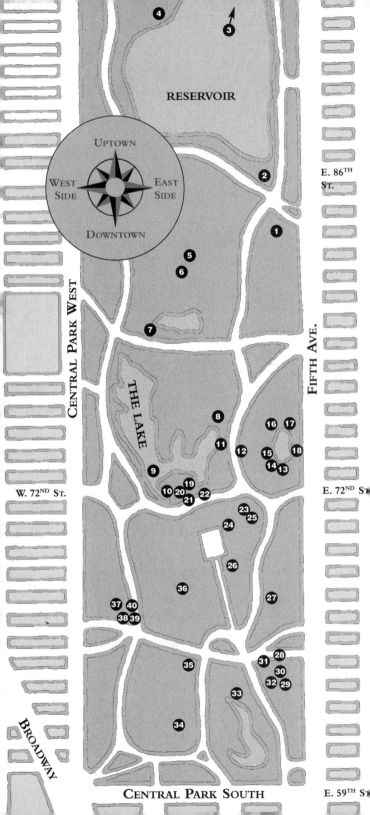

Walking Tour 4
CENTRAL PARK

A beautiful example of the marriage of nature and design, Central Park is for visitors one of the most unexpected treasures of New York. Most people from elsewhere only hear horror stories about this New York City gem and believe it to be one of the most dangerous places on Earth, but nothing could be further from the truth. Hopefully, a brief trip through Central Park should convince the TourWalker of its beauty and abundance of pleasures.

Walking Tour 4: **Central Park** begins at the southwest corner of Fifth Avenue and 84th Street. At the northern tip of the Metropolitan Museum of Art, there is a path running along the roadway that leads into the park. Walk west and then bear left on the path as it curves up into the park. You will see the enormous glass wall of the Egyptian Pavilion on your left.

1. Metropolitan Museum of Art. Egyptian Pavilion. *When Harry Met Sally…,* the two of them did not get along at all. But over the years, a friendship began and then blossomed. One sunny afternoon, they wandered through this pavilion, with Harry (Billy Crystal) giving Sally (Meg Ryan) amusing diction lessons ("pecan pie" featured prominently in the lesson), during which Harry asked Sally if she would like to see a movie that night. But Sally had a date. And, though he was not sure why, that fact upset Harry. From that point forward, they realized their interest in each other might be blossoming even more, and maybe Harry had been right all along when he said that men and women cannot be just friends.

Continue up the path until you reach Park Drive East. Being careful to avoid the cars, joggers, rollerbladers, and bikers, cross the roadway and turn to the right. You will find stairs leading up to the Gate House at the southeast tip of the Reservoir. Take the stairs and walk to the Gate House, again doing your best to avoid the joggers circling the fenced-in body of water.

2. Reservoir. South Gate House. Although he wasn't sure how, Babe (Dustin Hoffman) had found himself embroiled in matters of interna-

Tour 4

tional intrigue. In a final scene here, this young *Marathon Man* had led Szell (Sir Laurence Olivier) into this building, where the fate of a treasure trove of diamonds was to be determined.

While you are welcome to circle the Reservoir (it is roughly 1.6 miles around), it is not necessary to do so for purposes of **Walking Tour 4: Central Park**. A few movies have had scenes filmed here, but I will save you the need to circumnavigate the Reservoir.

3. Reservoir. Northeastern Side, East of North Building. Fearing that young upstart Kevin Lomax (Keanu Reeves) may be after his job as head of the law firm, Managing Partner Eddie Barzoom (Jeffrey Jones) went out for a run along the path, wrestling with many demons, in *The Devil's Advocate*. It would be his last run, as Eddie was pursued by demons who assumed the forms of New York's homeless before beating him to death just off the Reservoir path.

———•·•———

4. Reservoir. Northwestern tip. Running Track. Depressed about the meaning of life and pondering the thoughts of such great thinkers as Socrates, Nietzsche, and Freud, Mickey Sachs (Woody Allen) walked north along the west side of the Reservoir in *Hannah and Her Sisters*. In the movie, the Citicorp Building was clearly visible in the background.

Along the same stretch, Patrick (Mike McGlone), one of *The Brothers McMullen*, confronted Susan (Shari Albert) while she jogged here. Susan had jilted Patrick before he could break things off with her.

———•·•———

Retrace your steps away from the Reservoir, down the stairs, and turn right. Walk south along the path (the museum will be on your left, across Park Drive East). The great expanse known as the Great Lawn will be a few hundred feet to your right.

5. The Great Lawn. Helene (Anne Bancroft) loved books but had trouble finding them in New York's bookshops. Luckily, there was a bookstore at *84 Charing Cross Road* in London that had a better selection and was able to send her whatever books she desired. One of Helene's favorite pastimes was to walk along portions of the Great Lawn and read the books she received.

Continue along the same path and, at your earliest opportunity, take a path to the right that leads into the center of the park and toward the Great Lawn. When you reach the Great Lawn, look to the south and west at Belvedere Castle, nestled on a hill above the small body of water known as Turtle Pond. There is a path just north of Turtle Pond.

6. Path north of Turtle Pond. Learning that the responsibility of caring for an infant also came with incredible benefits, perennial bachelors Jack (Ted Danson), Michael (Steve Guttenberg), and Peter (Tom Selleck) threw Frisbees and collected women's phone numbers one pleasant afternoon along this spot in *Three Men and a Baby*.

Look up at the Castle.

7. Belvedere Castle. She wasn't their mom, but Isabel (Julia Roberts) should have been paying closer attention, especially since she would soon be their *Stepmom*. While Isabel filmed an ad at

Belvedere Castle, the kids waited nearby. But soon they had trouble locating Ben (Liam Aiken), and Isabel searched frantically in and around the castle. Luckily for Isabel and her future with Ben's father, Luke (Ed Harris), Ben was finally found.

———•·•———

Turn left and follow the path, keeping Turtle Pond to your right. You should pass the statue of King Jagiello (which will be on your left as you follow the path first up the hill, then down to Park Drive East). When you reach the road, turn to the right and follow it as it curves down and around to the Loeb Boathouse Café.

8. Loeb Boathouse Cafe. Park Drive East at 74th Street. Sally (Meg Ryan) was newly single, which she somehow let slip to her friend Marie

(Carrie Fisher) over lunch at an outdoor table at this restaurant. Only too happy to help, Marie pulled out her Rolodex and looked to see who might prove a worthy setup for Sally in *When Harry Met Sally....*

———•·•———

The Boathouse sits upon the Lake, where rowboats can often be spotted.

9. Rowboat on the Lake. Their first meeting had ended in disaster, with each sneaking out of the restaurant when the other wasn't looking. But on a particular *Sunday in New York*, when Eileen (Jane Fonda) and Mike (Rod Taylor) ran into each other a short time later, they realized that maybe they should give it another shot. So the two of them came here and took a boat out onto the Lake, starting the getting-acquainted process for real.

But while Mike did the rowing for Eileen, Hubbell Gardner (Robert Redford) made no such pretense at chivalry. While he relaxed at one end of the boat, Katie (Barbra Streisand) did the rowing. For Katie and Hubbell, that was the way they were in *The Way We Were*.

Early in their relationship, New York restaurateur Will (Richard Gere) and the much younger Charlotte (Winona Ryder) strolled along Bow Bridge, which crosses over the Lake. By the end of the film, much had changed, and seasons had come and gone. A lonelier but more mature Will sat in a rowboat on this Lake with his daughter and grandchild and glanced at the bridge, remembering his *Autumn in New York* with Charlotte.

Look up the hill on the far side of the Lake from where you stand.

10. Cherry Hill. Overlooking the Lake. Not really sure why, literary agent Martha Marie Talridge (Demi Moore) accepted the invitation of Aaron Riley (William Fichtner) to join him at nine o'clock on a Sunday morning. He supplied the coffee, and they sat on the grass overlooking the Lake. He told her he was interested in her and in who she was, but Martha wasn't even sure which of her two lives—the high-powered New York literary agent or the single mother in a tranquil European town—was real and which was a dream in *Passion of Mind*.

Spotting Layla (Joey Lauren Adams) near the Lake, Sonny (Adam Sandler) enlisted the help of young Julian (Cole and Dylan Sprouse) to win a date with her in *Big Daddy*.

Walk along the path, keeping the Lake on your right. Stop at the first staircase you come to, with the stairs leading to the left away from the Lake.

11. Staircase near Boathouse Café. George (Jack Lemmon) had come to New York to interview for a job. After the hotel had given away their room, George and Gwen (Sandy Dennis), his wife, spent a harrowing night in Central Park, battling the elements, as well as a shoe thief. The next morning, famished, they still had one more battle to wage: fighting off a stray dog for the few remaining morsels in a box of Cracker Jacks they

had found. Savoring their victory over the hungry canine, George and Gwen sat at the base of these stairs and ate the few pieces of candy–coated popcorn. For *The Out-of-Towners*, it was time to go home to Ohio.

———•—•———

Walk down the stairs and pass through Trefoil Arch. When you reach the other side, turn and note the arch.

12. Trefoil Arch. Just East of Boathouse Café. In unfamiliar territory, psychiatrist Dr. Sam Rice (Roy Scheider) followed someone he thought was Brooke Reynolds (Meryl Streep) and got mugged underneath this arch. Knowing that a mugger was the least of his worries in *Still of the Night*, Dr. Rice asked the mugger to look out for him until he got safely out of the park, but the man did not honor the request, and Dr. Rice lost his coat in the process.

———•—•———

Continue along the path, leaving the arch at your back until you reach the Sailboat Pond.

13. Sailboat Pond. They attended the same school, but their friendship was just beginning. Their world was about to merge with *The World of Henry Orient*, but first they had to get to know each other. One Saturday morning, Marion

Gilbert (Merrie Spaeth) and Valerie Boyd (Tippy Walker) arranged to meet at the Sailboat Pond and go adventuring, which involved spying on people, usually from a safe perch.

Turn to the right and note the small building at the near end of the pond.

14. Sailboat Pond. Small Building. Fearing that he was being followed, Paul (George Peppard) walked along this pond and headed toward this building, hoping to draw out his pursuer, Fred (Buddy Ebsen), in *Breakfast at Tiffany's*.

Turn back the other way, keeping the pond on your right, and find the statue of Hans Christian Anderson.

15. Statue of Hans Christian Anderson. Old friends Midge (Ossie Davis) and Nat (Walter Matthau) spent a good deal of their free time in Central Park and on at least one occasion sat in front of the statue of this famed storyteller in *I'm Not Rappaport*.

Upon first learning that he had a son, options trader Michael Cromwell (Tim Allen) didn't think they would ever get along. While Cromwell made his living in the financial jungle, his son,

Mimi Siku (Sam Huntington), lived in a real jungle half a world away. But after spending some time together, Cromwell realized that having a son was pretty cool. In *Jungle 2 Jungle*, father and son joined a crowd and danced in front of this statue to the strains of live music, something Michael never would have done before.

Walk along, keeping the pond to your right. Stop when you reach the statue of Alice in Wonderland.

16. Alice in Wonderland Statue. Sailboat Pond. After inviting her so-called boyfriend for a birthday dinner with her and her mother, Hannah (Lauren Bacall), Rose (Barbra Streisand) strolled with Greg (Jeff Bridges) past this statue in *The Mirror Has Two Faces*.

Realizing that their relationship may have reached a crossroads, Lisa (Brooke Adams) and Phillip (Ben Masters) sat in front of this statue, discussing their future, in *Key Exchange*.

Turn to the right and see if anyone's sitting on the closest bench that you see.

17. Sailboat Pond. Bench near Northeast Corner of Pond. Sitting on a bench, Nina (Jennifer Aniston) told George (Paul Rudd), her roommate and best friend (and the real, though unrealistic, object of her affections), that she was pregnant in *The Object of My Affection*.

Walk along, still keeping the pond on your right, until you reach the building with the green roof on the east side of the pond.

18. Sailboat Pond. Alice and Edward Kerbs Memorial Building. Something had gone wrong with his assignment, and he sensed that something sinister was taking place. Rollie Tyler

(Bryan Brown) feared that he was to be the next victim of somebody's scam, so he hid in this building until his assistant, Andy (Martha Gehman), showed up with his bag of special effects. But when Rollie realized that Andy had

been followed, his only chance to escape was to push the man into the water and run off into the park, which he was only too happy to do in *F/X*.

Return to the side of the pond near the Hans Christian Andersen statue. Head up the path toward Trefoil Arch and ascend the staircase where *The Out-of-Towners* ate Cracker Jacks. When you reach the top, turn left and follow the path onto Bethesda Terrace.

19. Bethesda Terrace. Mel (Jack Lemmon) had taken as much as he could, and he wasn't going to take anymore. He had lost his job, had no air-conditioning in his apartment, and was just plain fed up. And after a man (future box-office superstar Sylvester Stallone) bumped into Mel on Fifth Avenue, Mel noticed his wallet was missing. Assuming that the man had lifted his wallet, Mel chased him here and then back out of the park, where he finally retrieved his wallet. Mel was a victim, *The Prisoner of Second Avenue*, but the wallet he recovered wasn't his: it belonged to the poor man he had chased. It was another example of how nothing was going his way.

The terrace was host to two very similar sounding movies: *It Should Happen to You* and *It Could Happen to You*. In the former, while filming scenes for his documentary around the terrace, Pete (Jack Lemmon) made an incredible discovery: Gladys Glover (Judy Holliday). In the latter, Charlie (Nicolas Cage) celebrated winning the lottery by going skating with Yvonne (Bridget Fonda), a waitress with whom he had agreed to share his winnings. But Charlie was a better cop than skater, and all Yvonne could do was watch as Charlie, unable to stop, skated through the terrace and into the Lake.

The serene beauty of the terrace was spoiled, first, by the congestion of the 10th Annual New York City Junior Science Fair and, second, by the kidnapping of young Sean Mullen (Brawley Nolte) at that fair in *Ransom*. While his wife, Kate (Rene Russo), the chairwoman of the science fair, presided over the proceedings, airline executive Tom Mullen (Mel Gibson) lost sight of his son for only an instant. But that was all it took.

———•◦•———

Note the fountain in the middle of the terrace.

20. Bethesda Fountain. As police commissioner, Anthony Russell (Henry Fonda) had taken an oath to defend and protect the citizens of New York. As part of his duties, Russell attended a meeting held near the fountain on behalf of the city and the Police Athletic League. After the meeting, in *Madigan*, Commissioner Russell offered to walk one of the meeting's attendees, Mrs. Bentley (Susan Clark), to her next destination, a nearby department store. But during their stroll, it became apparent that although Russell was keeping New York safe, he was aiding and abetting Mrs. Bentley in her commission of adultery.

In *Deconstructing Harry*, in one of the film's stories within the story, a crew was filming a scene by the fountain when they discovered that the star, Mel (Robin Williams), was literally out-of-focus, while the rest of the actors were clear.

The ragtag group of fun-loving disciples in *Godspell* dropped what they had been doing and converged on the fountain, where they splashed and sang to their hearts' content.

If you like, you can circle around the fountain and approach it from the other side (the west). If you do, you will be following in the footsteps of Georges (Gerard Depardieu) and Bronte (Andie MacDowell) as they wandered around, getting to know one another before taking the test to prove they were, in fact, married, so that Georges may qualify for a *Green Card*.

Walk through the terrace and stop when you see the archways between the staircases leading up to the 72nd Street Transverse.

21. Plaza outside Archways, off Bethesda Terrace. Their *One Fine Day* drawing to a close, Melanie Parker (Michelle Pfeiffer) and Jack Taylor (George Clooney) raced through the park to get their respective kids to a soccer game. They emerged from under these archways and took a few moments to splash joyfully in the puddles before heading over to the playing field.

But as you stand here, be careful. If you see Kevin McAllister (Macaulay Culkin) come running toward you, step aside. Although Kevin is small, he will be followed closely by those two big but bumbling menaces, Marv (Daniel Stern) and Harry (Joe Pesci), in *Home Alone 2: Lost in New York*.

———————

Look at the staircase to the left of the archways.

22. Eastern Staircase to Bethesda Terrace. At least Kevin's menaces took the very physical shape of Harry and Marv. The menaces that plagued Raymond Shaw (Laurence Harvey) were deep inside the recesses of his brain, as Ben Marco (Frank Sinatra) was beginning to learn. Ever since they had come back from the war, Raymond was a changed man, and Ben was intent on finding out how, and why. One day, Ben followed Raymond through the park and watched as Raymond descended this staircase and jumped into the Lake. Ben realized that such behavior did not bode well for the future, but it would still be a while before he learned exactly what that future was intended to be and that Raymond may be unwittingly casting his ballot for *The Manchurian Candidate*.

———•·•———

Ascend either staircase, carefully cross the 72nd Street Transverse, and continue south until you see the Bandshell come into view on your left.

23. Bandshell. They were vagabonds, hippies, flower children, practitioners of free love, products of the psychedelic 1960s who protested the war in Vietnam, and they did their best to spread love, cheer, and flowers, all the while singing and dancing their way through life. All that activity is exhausting, however, and the exuberant youth with their long, flowing *Hair* spent the night sprawled out onstage in the Bandshell, catching up on their sleep.

In *Mighty Aphrodite*, Lenny (Woody Allen) arranged a blind date for Linda (Mira Sorvino), the biological mother of his adopted son, and Kevin (Michael Rapaport). Their first meeting was in front of the Bandshell.

———•·•———

Find a bench nearby. Any bench will do.

24. Bench near the Bandshell. Trying to find ways to stop being *The Lonely Guy*, Larry (Steve Martin) rented a dog and sat with his lonely friend Warren (Charles Grodin) on one of these benches. Unfortunately, the move was a bust. Larry met nobody and was given a ticket because the rented dog pooped on the pathway.

In *Breakfast at Tiffany's*, Paul (George Peppard) sat on a bench and talked to Fred (Buddy Ebsen), the man who had been following him. Fred, who happened to be the husband of the beautiful Holly Golightly (Audrey Hepburn), wanted Paul's help to get his wife back, not knowing that Paul was falling in love with Holly, too.

In *I'm Not Rappaport*, adversarial companions Nat (Walter Matthau) and Midge (Ossie Davis) performed an old soft-shoe on the stage for the benefit of a very small audience.

———•••———

There is a staircase to the right of the Bandshell. If you like, ascend the staircase. If you prefer, remain where you are, and I will tell you what you are missing.

25. Walkway behind Bandshell. As they walked along here, Ted Kramer (Dustin Hoffman) had the unpleasant task of breaking the news to his son, Billy (Justin Henry), that Ted had lost the custody battle and that Billy had to go live with his mother in *Kramer vs. Kramer*.

———•••———

If you climbed the stairs, come back down and turn left. If you didn't, turn to the right (the Bandshell should be on your left) and walk along the tree-lined promenade between the long row of benches on each side, which is known as the Mall.

26. The Mall. After his talk with Billy, Ted was ready to make the transfer to Billy's mom. Having just spotted Joanna (Meryl Streep), Ted bent down to give Billy a pep talk in *Kramer vs. Kramer*.

Another father, or at least a father figure, and actually, not even a very good father fig- ure at that, was dealing with giving up custody of a small child along this stretch. Sonny (Adam Sandler) wasn't cut out to be a dad, though he had warmed to the idea as time went on. In *Big Daddy*, Sonny and his roommate, Kevin (Jon Stewart), who had just learned that he was the father of the boy, walked along the Mall. Kevin was getting parenting tips from Sonny: a scary thought indeed.

His wife, Patsy (Marcia Rodd), met with a violent death at the hand of a crazed gunman, just one of the *Little Murders* the city had endured, and eccentric photographer Alfred (Elliott Gould) tried hard to make sense of it all. At the end of the film, Alfred wandered around with his camera, taking many pictures, including some of people on the Mall.

———•◦•———

Continue heading south on the Mall (the Bandshell should be at your back). Where the Mall lets out, you will see a few statues. At the statue of Shakespeare (on your left), walk to the road. Cross the road by the two sets of traffic lights and turn left onto the path on the far side. Stay on the path (it runs to the north and parallel to the road) as it slopes down and to the right. You will come to the Statue of Balto.

27. Statue of Balto. East of Park Drive East. Not only is Balto the subject of the animated movie *Balto*, but the statue itself was shown in *Six Degrees of Separation*. Flanders (Donald Sutherland) and Ouise (Stockard Channing) were having a guest over for dinner when their hospitality was tested by a mysterious visitor, Paul (Will Smith), who appeared to be hurt. Paul revealed that he was standing in Central Park, looking at the statue of Balto (and wondering what a statue commemorating a dog from Alaska was doing in the middle of Central Park), when he was mugged. In a later scene, Paul sat by the statue with a young couple he befriended.

———•◦•———

Walk past the statue and follow the path around to the right. Walk through the underpass and emerge at the entrance to the Central Park Zoo. Turn around and look up at the clock.

28. Central Park Zoo. Delacorte Clock. Tired of being harassed and tortured, Babe (Dustin Hoffman) walked Mr. Szell (Sir Laurence Olivier) at gunpoint under this arch in *Marathon Man*. Things had clearly turned darker for Babe since his previous visit to the zoo, when he had come here on a date with the alluring Elsa (Marthe Keller).

One day she was an up-and-coming agent in the high-powered world of fashion models, the next she was trying to raise her sister's three kids. But that was no easy task, and the question kept coming up, if Helen (Kate Hudson) was going to raise the kids, who was going to be *Raising Helen*? Realizing that Helen needed a diversion, and maybe a hand, Pastor Dan (John Corbett), the head of the school where the kids were enrolled, took Helen and the kids, Audrey (Hayden Panettiere), Henry (Spencer Breslin), and Sarah (Abigail Breslin) here for an afternoon.

The zoo is a great place to while away an afternoon. Some find it very peaceful.

29. Central Park Zoo. Distraught that his wife was off in Reno with some playboy, business mogul Timothy Borden (Walter Connolly) came here to think and get away from the stress of his world. While sitting on a bench, Borden struck up a conversation with young Mary Grey (Ginger Rogers), who knew nothing of the finer things in life, which suited Borden just fine. He had had enough of that, and made this *Fifth Avenue Girl* a part of his family's life.

Mary was just what the doctor ordered for Timothy Borden. But when the animals in the zoo needed some attention, they got it from Tommy Donovan (Edward Herrmann), who worked here. And while Tommy was tending to his animal wards, his brother Michael (Tim

Matheson) was tending to most of the women in Manhattan in *A Little Sex*. On one occasion, Michael came here to ask for some brotherly advice.

Walk to the fence and look into the zoo.

30. Central Park Zoo. Outdoor Patio. Unhappy at home, but knowing that meeting another man in the middle of the day was a big step, *Alice* (Mia Farrow) stood on the patio, trying to decide what to do. While she waited outside, Joe (Joe Mantegna), with whom Alice was to have her rendezvous, stood nervously inside one of the buildings, waiting.

To your right is the Polar Bear Habitat.

31. Central Park Zoo. Polar Bear Habitat. Still trying to get his evil brothers back down to hell, but not sure of the form they had taken on Earth, *Little Nicky* (Adam Sandler) did his best to coax a polar bear into his magic flask. He failed, meeting his fate at the hands (or jaws) of the polar bear, and was sent back to hell, where he had to start all over again.

———•◦•———

Since you're in a zoo, you'll find animals all around.

32. Central Park Zoo. Animal Habitats. During a late-night transformation into a *Wolf*, book editor Will Randall (Jack Nicholson) stalked the caged animals in the zoo, sending them into a wild frenzy. When two police officers tried to apprehend him—one of them was played by David Schwimmer (Ross on the television comedy *Friends*)—Will leapt onto a nearby rock and disappeared into Central Park.

———•◦•———

If you've entered the zoo itself, exit and turn right at the turnstiles. If not, head south (away from the Delacorte Clock with the zoo to your right) and follow the path until you reach Park Drive East. Turn right and walk along the drive (you should now be walking in a northwesterly direction). When traffic allows, cross Park Drive East and follow the path until you are next to Wollman Rink.

33. Wollman Rink. While Jackie (Susan Sarandon) skated with her kids on the ice, soon-to-be *Stepmom* Isabel (Julia Roberts) snapped photographs so the kids would have a pictorial history of their time with their mother. Initially troubled by her ex-husband's relationship with the much younger woman, Jackie warmed to the woman who would soon take her place when she realized that her health would not let her take care of the kids much longer.

When I learn that my days are numbered, I am going to Costa Rica to do some whitewater rafting. If I'm not up for that, maybe I'll take one of those hot air balloons over the Grand Canyon. And if I'm in really rough shape, I'll settle for a three-day binge in Las Vegas. Anything but ice skating. What is it about the rink that makes people who are very sick want to fritter away so many of their dwindling supply of precious moments on the ice? Jackie did it in *Stepmom*. So did Charlotte (Winona Ryder) in *Autumn in New York* (see **Walking Tour 7: Midtown,** Location 47).

And in *Love Story*, Jenny (Ali MacGraw), weakened by her illness, sat on the bleachers and watched as her husband, Oliver (Ryan O'Neal), skated on this rink. When the skating was over, they sipped their hot chocolates in the little café inside and then headed straight for the hospital, where Jenny would spend her remaining days.

But the ice plays host to happy times as well. On a wondrous night, a night when New York never looked so good, a night that Jonathan (John Cusack) admitted was rapidly climbing up the charts on his list of best nights of his life, a long night filled with endless promise, a night that he and Sara (Kate Beckinsale) both wished could have gone on forever, the two of them came here to skate after meeting serendipitously and sharing scrumptious desserts (see **Walking Tour 6: The Eastern Seaboard,** Location 24). Jonathan hoped their night could turn into something more, but Sara preferred to leave it to *Serendipity*. It would be many years before they would learn whether such a gamble would pay off.

While revelers whizzed by on their skates, Marv (Daniel Stern) and Harry (Joe Pesci) plotted their next caper, unaware that their primary foil, Kevin McAllister (Macaulay Culkin), was near in *Home Alone 2: Lost in New York*.

Newly reinstated to the police department and assigned to the case of a serial killer terrorizing New York, Nick Starkey (Kevin Kline) followed Bernadette (Mary Elizabeth Mastrantonio) from her friend's funeral to this rink, where contact was made. Elizabeth was the mayor's daughter, but Nick was *The January Man*. It would prove to be a winning combination.

Leave Wollman Rink and head west, keeping the rink on your left. Walk through Driprock Arch and stop when you get to the path that leads to the Carousel, to the right. Before you take the path, turn and notice the playground to your left.

34. Heckscher Playground. Central Park. He had always had a pretty distant relationship with his son, who often addressed him as sir. But after the boy's mother passed away, Eddy Duchin (Tyrone Power) did his best to play a larger role in his life. Eddy made some headway, but he, too, was dying, and he knew the time had come to tell young Peter (Rex Thompson) that his father would be going away again, this time for good. In

The Eddy Duchin Story, father and son had that painful talk while Peter sat on one of the playground's swings.

Turn to the right and walk the path leading to the Carousel.

35. Central Park Carousel. Margaret (Barbra Streisand) had tried to tell her husband, Paul (David Selby), that she was pregnant when she visited him at work (see **Walking Tour 3: Uptown Broadway,** Location 1), but never got the chance. Subsequently, in *Up the Sandbox*, she found a note he left for her and came here to find him riding the Carousel with their kids. In a setting devoted to kids, she finally got to tell Paul that another child was heading their way.

Bright yet gullible Joe (Campbell Scott) was out to make sure he got what was coming to him for having invented "the Process" in *The Spanish Prisoner*. As instructed by the FBI, Joe waited at this Carousel for Jimmy Dell (Steve Martin), or Jimmy's contact, to arrive. It was a long wait and would be a while before Joe learned that people aren't always what they seem.

Usually intended for children, the Carousel was ridden by old codgers Midge (Ossie Davis) and Nat (Walter Matthau) while the Cowboy

(Craig T. Nelson) talked on his cell phone nearby in *I'm Not Rappaport*.

Two other men rode the ponies at a different time. Max Bialystock (Zero Mostel) and Leo Bloom (Gene Wilder) enjoyed the Carousel during an extended lunch break in which Max convinced Leo to become his partner, in *The Producers*.

Leave the Carousel to others, turn to the right, and walk up the path to the left of Playmates Arch. When you reach the road, turn left, walk a short distance until you reach the fence on the southern perimeter of Sheep Meadow, a large grassy area just north of the Carousel. Turn left on the path running the length of Sheep Meadow (the Carousel should be on your left) and stop when you get an unencumbered view of the grassy area on your right.

36. Central Park. Grass. Somewhere on the lawn, two ants, Z (voice of Woody Allen) and Princess Bala (voice of Sharon Stone), made their way to a veritable oasis a long distance (to ants, anyway) from their home somewhere out on the Central Park grass in *Antz*.

Now imagine lying out on the grass, stark naked, admiring the starlit night sky. That is what Perry (Robin Williams) and Jack (Jeff Bridges) did in *The Fisher King*.

And the magic lived on in another movie. Clearly filmed on a soundstage, there was no mistaking the fact that the setting was intended to be Central Park. In *The Band Wagon*, Tony (Fred Astaire) and Gabrielle (Cyd Charisse) started out as feuding co-stars, but gradually warmed to one another. In a magical and romantic scene that showcased the best New York has to offer and the wonder of Central Park, the two of them took a horse-drawn carriage ride. At some point, they got out of the carriage, strutted their stuff to the classic song "Dancing in the Dark," then gracefully got back in the carriage, and, holding hands, headed off into the night.

Continue along the path until you come to Park Drive West. Tavern on the Green will be right across the roadway from you.

37. Tavern on the Green. Central Park. In the original version of the movie, Jack Lemmon and Sandy Dennis spent a harrowing night in Central Park and were not feeling all that romantic at the end of the day. In the remake, Steve Martin and Goldie Hawn took a break from their "nightmare" to rekindle their passion, only to have it come back to haunt them. In *The Out-of-Towners*, Henry (Steve Martin) and Nancy (Goldie Hawn) got kicked out of a cab that was being used as a getaway car by some criminals. Abandoned in Central Park, they found a nice section of grass to spend a few quiet, romantic, "private" moments together. But they were grossly mistaken. The "isolated" area turned out to be right outside this restaurant, and the lights were off only until Mayor Rudy Guiliani gave the word to turn them on as part of a "Light up the City" campaign. The mayor and hundreds of prominent guests were inside Tavern on the Green, and

when the lights went on, those assembled got quite a glimpse of Henry and Nancy.

Ellen (Annabella Sciorra) lunched here with Lucy (Christine Baranski) and told her that she had taken an apartment in the city two days a week in which to do her painting, in *The Night We Never Met*. To see the building where that apartment is, see **Walking Tour 11: Greenwich Village,** Location 36.

In nice weather, many people enjoy eating out on the patio.

38. Tavern on the Green. Central Park. Outdoor Patio. Although the weather was nice enough to permit them to eat outside, Sheldon (Woody Allen) had to endure the entire lunch listening to his overbearing mother (Mae Questel) complain about having to sit outside in the "Oedipus Wrecks" segment of *New York Stories*.

Of course, Louis Tully (Rick Moranis) was not so much worried about eating out on the patio as he was about being eaten on the patio. His party had been interrupted by a beast, and the beast chased Louis out of his building (see **Walking Tour 2: Central Park West,** Location 7) and into the park, where Louis fell into the beast's clutches, as preoccupied diners looked on. It would be a while before Louis and the rest of New York would be saved by the *Ghostbusters*.

Cross the road when you can and walk along Tavern on the Green until you reach the front entrance.

39. Tavern on the Green. Entrance. Having just met with Gordon Gecko (Michael Douglas) in the park on an appropriately rainy day, the once promising Bud Fox (Charlie Sheen) walked toward this entrance and into a restroom within. There federal agents helped remove the tape recorder from his body and checked the tape. Bud had taped Gordon admitting his crimes, and it was clear that both Bud's and Gordon's high-flying days on *Wall Street* were numbered.

———————

Imagine this same area, half a century before.

40. The Central Park Casino. Back then, it was called the Central Park Casino, and it was a restaurant and nightclub all rolled into one. Musician Eddy Duchin (Tyrone Power) showed up for work at what was then the Central Park Casino only to learn that the job he expected to have with Leo Reisman's orchestra did not exist. But then Marjorie Oelrich (Kim Novak) stepped in, used her influence, and Eddy got the job and, as is so often the case, the girl. It was quite a story; it was *The Eddy Duchin Story*.

You have now reached the end of **Walking Tour 4: Central Park.**

Walking Tour 5
EAST OF THE PARK

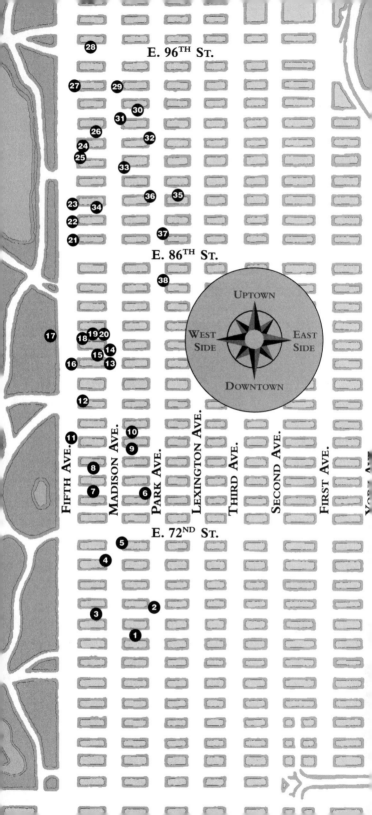

E. 96TH ST.

E. 86TH ST.

UPTOWN

WEST SIDE   EAST SIDE

DOWNTOWN

FIFTH AVE.

MADISON AVE.

PARK AVE.

LEXINGTON AVE.

THIRD AVE.

SECOND AVE.

FIRST AVE.

YORK AVE.

E. 72ND ST.

Walking Tour 5
EAST OF THE PARK

The Upper East Side has been synonymous with elegance and old money for a long time. Not surprisingly, many of the locations in **Walking Tour 5: East of the Park** consist of elegant buildings that adorn Fifth Avenue and Park Avenue, the homes of New York City's elite: the movers and shakers who live in apartments much larger than those most of us have ever seen. Throw in a mile of museums, upscale shopping, and even the city's largest sham castle, and you have all the ingredients for a neighborhood many people never want to leave.

Walking Tour 5: East of the Park begins at 67th Street and Madison Avenue. From the northeast corner of that intersection, head east the very short distance until you reach 27 East 67th.

1. 27 East 67th Street. Ronaldo Maia Flowers. After an overnight stakeout, New York City detective "Popeye" Doyle (Gene Hackman) followed the Frenchman (Fernando Rey) and waited outside this store while the man attended to business within in *The French Connection*.

Continue east on 67th and turn left on Park Avenue. Walk north one block and stop at the building on the northwest corner of Park and 68th Street.

2. 680 Park Avenue. The Americas Society. He didn't live nearby, but Jamal Wallace (Rob

Brown) had a skill that the administrators of the Mailor-Callow School hoped to capitalize on: his ability on the basketball court. But Jamal had another talent that gave him more in common with Pulitzer-Prize-winning author William Forrester (Sean Connery) than with most of the faculty or student body at the school, which was located here in *Finding Forrester.*

Cross 68th Street and turn left. Head west on 68th, cross Madison Avenue, and continue west until you are in front of 16 East 68th.

3. 16 East 68th Street. Money alone didn't make him happy. He liked art, and he loved the thrill of the chase. In *The Thomas Crown Affair*, billionaire industrialist Thomas Crown (Pierce Brosnan) got his hands on whatever pieces of art he liked, using legitimate or not-so-legitimate means. He lived with his artwork and his wealth in this grand home.

Return to Madison Avenue, turn left, and walk north to 71st Street. Walk west on 71st and stop at the entrance to 22 East 71st.

4. 22 East 71st Street. Not as famous as some of New York's other auction houses, this building was the location of Cromwell's Auctioneers and Appraisers, where Michael (Hugh Grant) worked and had to deal with everything from a meddling boss to a gangster who envisioned himself as the next Michelangelo in *Mickey Blue Eyes.*

Return to Madison, turn left, and walk north to 72nd Street. The Ralph Lauren store should be across Madison from you.

5. 867 Madison Avenue. Ralph Lauren Store. Thanks to the magic potion of Dr. Yang, Alice's herbalist, *Alice* (Mia Farrow), newly invisible, decided to follow two well-known gossips into this store. She overheard their conversation and realized that her affair with Joe (Joe Mantegna) was not as secret as she had hoped. She also learned that her husband Doug (William Hurt) had had his own infidelities, which everyone seemed to know about. Joe, also invisible, accompanied Alice into the store, but he had a different agenda. Spotting supermodel Elle MacPherson, Joe followed her into the dressing room. A few minutes later, Elle came out to complain to a salesclerk about "heavy breathing" coming from inside the changing room.

Continue north on Madison until you reach the north side of 74th Street. Stop at the first building north of 74th, number 800.

6. 800 Park Avenue. Sherman McCoy (Tom Hanks) had it all. A self-described "master of the universe," McCoy had a high-paying job on Wall Street, an expensive lifestyle, a beautiful mistress at his beck and call, a beautiful wife, and a child. McCoy and his family lived in a lavish apartment in this building. That is, before it all started to unravel in *The Bonfire of the Vanities*.

Return to 74th Street, turn right, and walk west until you are across from 4 East 74th.

7. 4 East 74th Street. His sister finally on the road to recovery, high school football coach Tom

Wingo (Nick Nolte) waited outside, across the street from this building, in *The Prince of Tides*. Inside was the office of Dr. Susan Lowenstein (Barbra Streisand), and as she emerged, Tom hesitated, knowing she would not want to hear the news. But Lowenstein was perceptive and knew that Tom had decided to return home to South Carolina and his family.

———◆———

Continue to Fifth Avenue, turn right, and walk north to the north side of 75th Street. Turn right on 75th and walk east until you reach 7 East 75th.

8. 7 East 75th Street. Familiar to ardent fans of television's *The Nanny*, this building was the home of Broadway producer Maxwell Sheffield (Charles O'Shaunessy), his children Maggie (Nicholle Tom), Brighton (Benjamin Salisbury), and Gracie (Madeline Zima), his nosey butler, Niles (Daniel Davis), and of course, his irrepressible nanny, Fran Fine (Fran Drescher).

———◆———

Continue east on 75th to Madison Avenue. Turn left on Madison and walk north to 76th Street. The Carlyle is across Madison on the northeast corner of Madison and 76th.

9. 35 East 76th Street. Café Carlyle. The movie is *Hannah and Her Sisters.* Mickey Sachs (Woody Allen) was in the middle of the worst date of his life, with former sister-in-law Holly (Dianne Wiest). Trying to infuse a little culture into the evening, Mickey took Holly to the Café Carlyle to hear Bobby Short sing. Holly was more at home in the world of punk rock, and the two clashed miserably. At least at the time.

Continue north on Madison to the north side of 77th Street. Cross Madison and walk east until you reach 55 East 77th.

10. 55 East 77th Street. Joe Turner (Robert Redford) left this building to get some lunch, and when he returned, he discovered that every one of his CIA colleagues had been brutally murdered in *Three Days of the Condor.*

Turn to the left and walk west on 77th. Continue to Fifth Avenue, turn left on Fifth, and stop in front of number 956, between 76th and 77th Streets.

11. 956 Fifth Avenue. Dr. Henry Harrison (William Hurt) lived in this building, and Beatrice (Juliette Binoche) lived in Paris, but they temporarily traded apartments, with Henry staying in Paris and Beatrice staying in Henry's apartment here, in *A Couch in New York*.

Turn and head north up Fifth Avenue (Central Park should be across Fifth on your left). When you reach 79th, turn right and stop in front of the entrance to the building on the corner.

12. 2 East 79th Street. The Ukranian Institute. It's not a private residence, but it served as such for Kathryn (Sarah Michelle Gellar) and her stepbrother, Sebastian (Ryan Phillippe), who lived here while their parents jetted around the world. The two of them had *Cruel Intentions* and used them to destroy the lives and reputations of many innocent people.

Continue east on 79th and turn left on Madison. Walk north past 80th Street until you reach E.A.T., between 80th and 81st.

13. E.A.T. 1064 Madison Avenue. Usually out of the city on weekends, Lane (Gaby Hoffmann) and Laura (Natalie Portman) spent a rare day in New York. They ventured into this eatery and spotted Jeffrey (John Griffin), on whom they both had a crush, in *Everyone Says I Love You*. The good news: Jeffrey was heir to the Vandermost millions, so he was quite a catch. The bad news: he could only choose one of them.

Walk north on Madison to the north side of 81st Street.

14. Frank E. Campbell Funeral Chapel. 1076 Madison Avenue. Little did they realize it at the time, but the suicide of their friend Cynthia (Stockard Channing) would reunite college friends Brenda (Bette Midler), Annie (Diane Keaton), and Elise (Goldie Hawn) and spur them

to action in *The First Wives Club*. Cynthia's funeral was held here.

Poor Goldie Hawn. That same year, she had to say good-bye to another family member at this funeral home. However, this other funeral ended on a more chipper note. In *Everyone Says I Love You*, the family gathered to pay their last respects to Grandpa (Patrick Cranshaw). While the family wondered about the frailty and meaning of life, Grandpa's ghost sat up in the coffin and broke into song and dance in an effort to perk up the mourners. He was joined by other ghosts, and the revelry even spilled out onto the street, right where you are now standing.

And while the actual location was not shown, it was Campbell's that Blake (Robert Downey, Jr.) called to make funeral arrangements for his mother in *Two Girls and a Guy*.

Turn left on 81st Street and walk west until you reach number 15.

15. 15 East 81st Street. Sidney (Alan Alda) and Constance (Allison Janney) lived here and one night threw a dinner party at which Sidney's daughter Nina (Jennifer Aniston) first met George (Paul Rudd). Though Nina had an interest in George, George was living with his boyfriend, Dr. Robert Joley (Tim Daly). In *The Object of My Affection*, George was about to be asked to find a new place to live, and he and Nina were about to become roommates.

Continue on to Fifth Avenue. Turn left and stop in front of the Stanhope Hotel.

16. Stanhope Hotel. 995 Fifth Avenue. While in New York to convince Sheriff (Vince Vaughn) and Tony (David Conrad) to *Return to Paradise* (Malaysia) and serve time in prison so that Lewis

(Joaquin Phoenix) would not be hanged, Beth (Anne Heche) stayed here.

Hotheaded superstar Brandon (Leonardo Di-Caprio) had the world at his fingertips and thought nothing of trashing his room in this hotel. Undeterred, writer Lee Simon (Kenneth Branagh) showed up to discuss his screenplay with the tempestuous *Celebrity*.

———◆·◆———

Turn back the other way and walk north on Fifth until you are across from the museum.

17. Metropolitan Museum of Art. Fifth Avenue and 82nd Street. Joe (Robert Walker) had only a few days leave, so *The Clock* was ticking, but he was lucky enough to meet the lovely and

friendly Alice (Judy Garland) almost as soon as he got off the train, when he rescued a piece of her shoe from a wayward escalator. Afterward, with his puppy dog look and just-off-the-farm sincerity, Joe convinced Alice to accom-pany him on a whirlwind tour of New York. This museum was one of the stops on that tour.

The museum is also where Rupert (Jeff Bridges) worked in *Kiss Me Goodbye*. He couldn't compete with Jolly (James Caan), the dead husband of Kay (Sally Field), his fiancée, who had been a memorable Broadway star, but Rupert hoped, eventually, he wouldn't have to.

Thomas Crown (Pierce Brosnan) spent a good deal of time admiring the artwork in the museum and only slightly less time swiping it off the walls. Near the end of *The Thomas Crown Affair*, Crown did the impossible: he returned a painting to the wall without anyone seeing—although a great many were watching—and without even entering the room where the painting was to be hung. The scene where Crown and dozens of look-alikes wearing overcoats and derbies out of a Magritte painting hustled through the museum's corridors in an attempt to obfuscate the view on the closed-circuit monitors is a work of art in and of itself, and not to be missed.

The museum was also the site of a gala affair that Steven Taylor (Michael Douglas) and his young wife, Emily (Gwyneth Paltrow), attended. Little did Steven know at the time that for the artist David Shaw (Viggo Mortensen), who was also there, the word "affair" had a very different meaning. Steven would soon start thinking about planning *A Perfect Murder*.

Kate Miller (Angie Dickinson) was *Dressed to Kill* as she wandered the rooms of this museum, playing cat-and-mouse with a mysterious man. She alternated between running from him and chasing him. But after she lost him and lost her glove, Kate left the museum and descended the front stairs, only to see a hand dangling her glove out the window of a waiting taxicab. Kate got into the cab, and she and the mysterious man treated the cabdriver and moviegoers to one of the most erotic scenes ever captured on film. It is a lesson for filmmakers of today. Often just the suggestion of sex is far more erotic than explicitness.

If you are lucky, you may see Holden (Edward Norton) singing to his beloved Skyler (Drew Barrymore) near a fountain in front of the museum in *Everyone Says I Love You*.

If you are not already there, walk to 82nd Street and turn right. Stop at the first building on the south side of the street.

18. 1009 Fifth Avenue (at 82nd Street). This elegant building was home to the Turner family in *Regarding Henry*: Henry (Harrison Ford), the high-powered attorney whose life was turned upside down when he was shot by a gunman (John Leguziamo) in a convenience store holdup, Sarah (Annette Bening), Henry's beleaguered wife, Rachel (Mikki Allen), their eleven-year-old daughter, and of course, Buddy the dog.

Elise (Goldie Hawn), Brenda (Bette Midler), and Annie (Diane Keaton) had founded *The First Wives Club,* and they enlisted the help of their friend, society doyenne Gunilla Goldberg (Maggie Smith), who lived here. Gunilla was only too happy to help other women take revenge on the male species, and she invited Shelly (Sarah Jessica Parker), the current girlfriend of Brenda's ex, Morty (Dan Hedaya), here for a society lunch.

Proving that this building has stood the test of time, the police tailed one of the suspects in a drug smuggling ring, trying to find *The French Connection*, to this building. In the movie, the police discussed the fact that Don Ameche, the actor, lived inside.

———•—•———

Walk east to the next building, 2 East 82nd Street.

19. 2 East 82nd Street. Although Brooke (Meryl Streep) was a suspect in the murder of one of his patients, psychiatrist Dr. Sam Rice (Roy Scheider) could not believe she was capable of any such

thing. But as he started getting a little too close, Dr. Rice began to lose his ability to figure out whether he could trust her or not. In *Still of the Night*, the mysterious Brooke lived here, and one night Dr. Rice came to see if his suspicions were correct.

———•—•———

Continue east on 82nd and stop in front of number 22.

20. 22 East 82nd Street. She found her live-in boyfriend in bed with a model and decided it was time to make other living arrangements. So Amanda (Monica Potter), who happened to work at the museum up the street, answered an ad and ended up moving into this building, where she would soon be *Head Over Heels* for Jim Winston (Freddie Prinze, Jr.), while sharing an apartment with the "last four nonsmoking models on the island of Manhattan."

Return to Fifth Avenue, turn right on Fifth, and walk north until you reach 87th Street.

21. 1056 Fifth Avenue. As part of their plan of revenge, Brenda (Bette Midler), Elise (Goldie Hawn), and Annie (Diane Keaton) had to break into the files of Brenda's ex-husband to get his phony books in *The First Wives Club*. While Morty (Dan Hedaya) and girlfriend Shelly (Sarah Jessica Parker) were kept busy by interior designer Duarte (Bronson Pinchot), the women did their digging. However, Morty and Shelly came back too soon, and the snoops made their escape out a window and onto a platform dangling outside Morty and Shelly's terrace.

Continue north on Fifth and stop between 87th and 88th Streets.

22. 1067 Fifth Avenue. This building was home to wealthy Tom Mullen (Mel Gibson), his wife, Kate (Rene Russo), and their son, Sean (Brawley Nolte), who was kidnapped in Central Park (see **Walking Tour 4: Central Park,** Location 19) and held for *Ransom*. As Tom sat sobbing on his terrace, the Guggenheim Museum was visible in the background.

The gullible Joe Ross (Campbell Scott) dropped off a book (*Budge on Tennis*) with the doorman at this building, having been told that this is where the sister of Jimmy Dell (Steve Martin) lived. On a later visit in *The Spanish Prisoner*, Joe learned the truth.

Continue north until you reach the Frank Lloyd Wright masterpiece the Guggenheim.

23. Guggenheim Museum. 1071 Fifth Avenue (between 88th and 89th Streets). Having just learned of their father's death, Ophelia (Julia Stiles) and Laertes (Liev Schreiber) confronted the wicked Claudius (Kyle MacLachlan) near the upper part of the Guggenheim in *Hamlet*. Ophelia screamed at the top of her lungs, and the echo can still be heard inside.

Responsible for the safety of the only witness in a murder case, Detective Mike Keegan (Tom Berenger) escorted the beautiful Claire Gregory (Mimi Rogers) to a function at the museum in *Someone to Watch Over Me*. Unfortunately, Detective Keegan, sidetracked by a chatty woman, lost sight of Claire, who went to the ladies' room

where she was threatened by the suspect, Joey Venza (Andreas Katsulas). Moments later, the two men faced off outside.

Walk north again on Fifth and turn right on 91st Street. Walk east and stop across from 1 East 91st.

24. 1 East 91st Street. His girlfriend, Ingrid (Dyan Cannon), lived in the building, which gave him the inside track, so Duke Anderson (Sean Connery) decided to target the entire building for a break-in, for which he served as the mastermind, in *The Anderson Tapes*.

Turn around and look at the building on the south side of the street.

25. National Design Museum. **2 East 91st Street**. Eddy Duchin (Tyrone Power) was used to playing the piano at parties as part of the musical entertainment, so when he was invited to be a guest at a fancy party given by the Wadsworths, who lived here, he not only jumped at the

chance, but even bought a used car to get him here. In *The Eddy Duchin Story*, he would go on to marry and have a son, and he would visit this home again and again over the years.

Like Eddy Duchin, Liz Hamilton (Jacqueline Bisset) became *Rich and Famous*. She came here for a meeting of the committee that selected the year's best piece of American fiction.

Unbeknownst to Jack Trainer (Harrison Ford), he and his *Working Girl,* Tess McGill (Melanie Griffith), had not been invited to the wedding they were about to attend, given by Mr. Trask (Philip Bosco) for his daughter. As Jack complained to Tess and wondered what she was up to, they walked along this fence and entered the building under this unique awning.

Although this building is actually a museum, it was suggested that it was the home of Martha (Geraldine Fitzgerald), the matriarch of the wealthy family of *Arthur* Bach.

Walk east on 91st and stop across from number 7.

26. 7 East 91st Street. This building was home to the lavish apartment that Steven (Michael Douglas) and Emily (Gwyneth Paltrow) Taylor called home, until Steven, angered over his wife's infidelity, planned what he thought would be *A Perfect Murder*.

Head back to Fifth Avenue, turn right, and head north past 94th Street until you reach number 1136.

27. 1136 Fifth Avenue. Struggling stand-up comic Lance Barton (Chris Rock) showed up at this building, and the doorman, mistaking him for a messenger, directed him around to the service entrance. Lance took offense at the doorman's putdown, but since he was, in fact, a messenger, he couldn't be too upset. But after his body was taken away by the "angels" before its time, Lance was temporarily given the body of a man who had lived in this building before his untimely demise, in *Down to Earth*. With the assistance of King (Chazz Palminteri), an otherworldly figure, Lance surveyed his options outside the building.

Continue walking to the north side of 96th Street. Turn right on 96th and stop in front of 9 East 96th Street.

28. 9 East 96th Street. After lunch with *Alice*, the unhappily married woman with whom he was having an affair, Joe (Joe Mantegna), still invisible thanks to a magic potion, came here to eavesdrop on his ex-wife's therapy session. What he heard made him glad, but was not music to Alice's ears.

Continue east on 96th Street. Turn right on Madison Avenue and walk south until you are across from the red brick "castle" between 94th and 95th Streets.

29. Madison Avenue. Playground Wall (between 94th and 95th Streets). In *The Fisher King*, Jack Lukas (Jeff Bridges) had to get the Holy Grail for Perry (Robin Williams) in order to restore Perry to sanity and, possibly, to atone for having indirectly led to the death of Perry's wife three years before. The Holy Grail was believed to be in the possession of Langdon Carmichael (Mel

Bourne), a reclusive billionaire who purportedly lived in this "castle," which we can now see is nothing more than the front to a playground. In the movie, Jack scales the outside of the castle wall to sneak in through one of its upper-level windows.

———————

Continue south on Madison and turn left on 93rd Street. Head east until you reach 55 East 93rd.

30. 55 East 93rd Street. Within this elegant-looking building loomed a growing menace. A war was on, and Nazi spies were using this building for purposes of espionage. Despite the title of this documentary-style film, *The House on 92nd Street* was actually located here on 93rd Street. Poetic license strikes again.

———————

Return to Madison, turn left, and cross to the south side of 93rd Street.

31. The Corner Bookstore. 1313 Madison Avenue. Helene (Anne Bancroft) loved old books, but was frustrated by her inability to find the precious volumes in New York. She came here during one of her searches, but to no avail. Eventually, she discovered a great supplier for her

Tour 5

habit: a well-stocked bookstore at *84 Charing Cross Road* in London.

Head east on 93rd Street and turn right on Park Avenue. Walk south on Park to the south side of 92nd Street and stop at number 1165.

32. 1165 Park Avenue. Ray (Woody Allen) and his wife, Frenchy (Tracey Ullman), had a tough time making ends meet. And then Ray came up with his brainstorm: they would open up a bakery next to a bank, and while Frenchy sold cookies out of the storefront, Ray and his gang of *Small Time Crooks* would dig through the store into the bank next door and steal millions from the bank's vault. Ray's scheme was a total bust, but when Frenchy's cookie business took off, they finally struck it rich and moved into this fancy building.

Walk south on Park and turn right on the north side of 90th Street. Walk west one block to Madison Avenue. Tom Mullen's bank is on the northeast corner of Madison and 90$^{th.}$

33. 1261 Madison Avenue (at 90th Street). Okay, it's not a bank, but it was, and it's where Tom Mullen (Mel Gibson) came to transfer the $4 million *Ransom* money to his son's kidnapper,

Jimmy (Gary Sinise). But Tom wasn't ready to give up without a fight, and a chase took place on this street.

Head south on Madison and turn right on the north side of 88th Street. Stop in front of Nineteen East 88th.

34. Nineteen East 88th Street. J. C. Wyatt (Diane Keaton) may not have had a perfect life, but she had a good life. Known as "the Tiger Lady" in business, she shared an apartment in this building with her equally successful boyfriend, Steven (Harold Ramis). But when a baby fell into their laps, Steven was not willing to get caught up in the *Baby Boom,* and he moved out, leaving the Tiger Lady to raise the child herself.

Return to Madison, turn left, and walk north to 89th Street. Cross Madison at 89th and walk east until you reach the Dalton School.

35. The Dalton School. 108 East 89th Street. In one of Woody Allen's older New York movies, *Manhattan*, forty-two-year-old Isaac (Woody Allen) was dating seventeen-year-old

Tracy (Mariel Hemingway). This is where Tracy was a high school student and where Isaac met her after school one day, got her a milkshake, and then broke off their relationship. But Mariel Hemingway surfaced in a later Woody Allen film (see **Walking Tour 3: Uptown Broadway,** Location 8).

Turn back and walk west to the west side of Park Avenue. Turn left and stop at 1088 Park.

36. 1088 Park Avenue (at 89th Street). At a luncheon where the acquisition of art was one of the topics of conversation, Ouise (Stockard Channing) stormed out on her friends, her colleagues, and her husband, Flanders (Donald Sutherland), in *Six Degrees of Separation*. Husband and wife argued in front of this building, where she told him they no longer had much in common.

Head south on Park to the south side of 87th Street. Look across Park at the building on the southeast corner of the intersection.

37. 1049 Park Avenue. Fans of the TV show *The Odd Couple* will recognize this building as the home of Oscar (Jack Klugman) and Felix (Tony Randall). In the show's familiar opening, as the two emerge from the building, Oscar throws down his cigar, and Felix picks it up with the point of his umbrella. In the movie of the same name, the mismatched roommates lived in a different building (see **Walking Tour 3: Uptown Broadway,** Location 11).

Continue south on Park until just south of 85th Street. Look for number 1009, on the east side of Park.

38. 1009 Park Avenue. He thought he was the luckiest man alive, with a successful musical career and Daniella (Nastassja Kinski), his young, beautiful wife. But then Claude Eastman (Dudley Moore) began to suspect adultery. In *Unfaithfully Yours*, they lived here.

————•—•————

You have now reached the end of **Walking Tour 5: East of the Park.**

UPTOWN

WEST SIDE

EAST SIDE

DOWNTOWN

2

3

1

EAST RIVER

E. 86TH ST.

4

5

6

EAST END AVE.

7

9

8

10

11

14

E. 72ND ST.

13

12

15

SECOND AVE.

FIRST AVE.

16

17

MADISON AVE.

PARK AVE.

LEXINGTON AVE.

THIRD AVE.

18

19

YORK AVE.

ROOSEVELT ISLAND

20

21

24

27

22

30

23

E. 59TH ST.

25

26

29

28

31

32

Walking Tour 6
THE EASTERN SEABOARD

The Eastern Seaboard boasts a cross-section of Manhattan. If offers homes of prominent people, and others who are not as well-known. It has hospitals, fine eating and drinking establishments, as well as a very photogenic bridge, and much of it comes with a water view: something people pay a premium for. The best place to begin **Walking Tour 6: The Eastern Seaboard** is at the home of the person who presides over this great city, at East End Avenue and 88th Street.

1. Gracie Mansion. East End Avenue and 88th Street. His office was in *City Hall* (see **Walking Tour 14: The Southern Tip,** Location 15), but Mayor John Pappas (Al Pacino) lived here. Early in the film, Deputy Mayor Kevin Calhoun (John Cusack) arrived late to a dinner hosted by his boss.

In *The Taking of Pelham One, Two, Three*, the mayor (Lee Wallace) was laid up with the flu, and the last thing he needed was a "situation," but that's what he got after a subway train was hijacked. He did what he could from his bed here inside his official residence.

Years later, in *Ghostbusters II*, the Ghostbusters paid a visit to the mayor (David Margulies) to tell him they had discovered a river of evil under the streets of Manhattan. The mayor was never happy to see this troublesome but necessary group of men, but he knew they represented his, and New York City's, best, if not only, hope.

Walk west on 88th Street until you reach Second Avenue. Look across Second to Elaine's, just north of the corner of 88th.

2. Elaine's. 1703 Second Avenue. For over thirty years a food and drink institution for New York's literary crowd, Elaine's has found its way into several movies. Isaac (Woody Allen), Tracy (Mariel Hemingway), Yale (Michael Murphy), and Emily (Anne Byrne) sat at a table here at the beginning of *Manhattan* and discussed the essence of life, art, and courage. Political pundits may note that in this scene Isaac remarked as he lit a cigarette that while he smoked, he didn't inhale. Years later, a presidential candidate from Arkansas was to make the same claim about another type of smoke.

In *Night and the City*, lawyer-turned-boxing-promoter Mr. Fabian (Robert De Niro) entered the restaurant and invited Regis Philbin and wife, Joy, who were peacefully enjoying a meal, to attend one of the boxing matches that Fabian hoped to promote.

Seeking a night of culture after many nights stuck inside with the kids, playwright Ivan Travalian (Al Pacino) and his new girlfriend, Alice Detroit (Dyan Cannon), went to a Romanian film, then stopped in here to mix and mingle with the literary world in *Author! Author!*

They worked together for the same television *Network*, and there was a mutual attraction, but when they came here for a late dinner, they both knew they were heading down a dangerous path, since Max Schumacher (William Holden) was married. And sure enough, Max's dinner with Diane Christensen (Faye Dunaway) led to a torrid yet short-lived affair.

Book parties are a frequent occurrence at Elaine's, and fittingly enough, a book party was held in *Celebrity* to celebrate "the best book ever written about the CIA."

———•—•———

Now note the large building on the west side of Second, between 87th and 88th Streets.

3. 245 East 87th Street. He could come and go as he pleased, but Mel (Jack Lemmon) felt like the *Prisoner of Second Avenue,* nonetheless. It was hot outside, he had lost his job, his apartment was

burglarized, and he never seemed to have exact change for the bus. Mel lived in this building with his wife, Edna (Anne Bancroft), who had her share of bad days, too.

———•—•———

Walk south on Second Avenue and stop at the southeast corner of Second and 85th Street.

4. 300 East 85th Street (at Second Avenue). Francis (Mike McGlone) was having an affair with his brother's ex-girlfriend Heather (Cameron Diaz), and even thought to himself that *She's the One* (despite the fact that he was already married to another). But when his brother Mickey (Ed Burns) told him how Heather had worked her way through college, Francis needed time to sort things out. When he made his decision, Francis raced to this building, and when

Heather emerged, they talked as her stretch limousine waited at the curb.

--- ♦ ---

Turn left and walk east on 85th Street. At First Avenue, turn right and walk south one block to 84th Street. Across from you on the northeast corner of the intersection is 401 East 84th.

5. 401 East 84th Street. He was *One Good Cop*, but when his partner was killed, leaving three kids without a dad, Artie Lewis (Michael Keaton) decided he had to take matters into his own hands. After following Grace (Rachel Ticotin) here, Artie donned a ski mask, tricked his way into a drug dealer's apartment, and took away the loot.

--- ♦ ---

Turn to the right and walk south on First Avenue. Turn left on the north side of 83rd Street and walk east until the very end of the block. Note the school across the street.

6. 610 East 83rd Street. Before they discovered concert pianist Henry Orient (Peter Sellers), the world of Marion (Merrie Spaeth) and Valerie (Tippy Walker) revolved around their school, which was located here, in *The World of Henry Orient*.

--- ♦ ---

Return to East End Avenue, turn left, and walk south to 81st Street. Turn right on the north side of 81st and walk west to number 539, between East End and York Avenues.

7. Le Boeuf à la Mode. 539 East 81st Street. After her suspension for using excessive force in the line of duty, police officer Megan (Jamie Lee Curtis) left her precinct and found herself in a sudden downpour. With cabs scarce, she agreed to share a cab with Eugene (Ron Silver), never realizing he was the city's newest serial killer, in *Blue Steel*. With so much traffic, they hardly moved, and Eugene suggested they wait it out over dinner. They got out of the cab and came to this restaurant. The chocolate mousse alone warrants a visit.

———•◦•———

Continue to York Avenue and turn left. Walk south and turn left onto 77th Street. Walk east until you are across from number 523.

8. 523 East 77th Street. Inside this elegant and majestic building, Lee Simon (Kenneth Branagh) attended a photo shoot, then stood out in the street polishing his snazzy car. When a supermodel (Charlize Theron) walked out of the building, Lee offered her a ride and then spent a pretty hectic evening cavorting with the glamorous set as if he were a real *Celebrity*, hoping it would give him an evening not to forget. It did, but not in the way he had hoped. By the end of the evening, his car was a wreck, and the supermodel had left Lee to fend for himself.

———•◦•———

Turn back and walk west on 77th Street. Stop at 325, between First and Second Avenues.

9. 325 East 77th Street. Five years after the ghosts, ghouls, and other slobbering demons had invaded her last apartment (see **Walking Tour 2: Central Park West,** Location 7), Dana Barrett (Sigourney Weaver) relocated to this building. At the beginning of *Ghostbusters II*, Dana was returning to her home when the demons struck again, propelling her baby carriage down the street and out into traffic. Dana gave chase onto First Avenue, and luckily, the baby was unhurt. But she knew that she had no choice but to reestablish contact with the zany Ghostbusters, as well as her past.

———•◦•———

Return to First Avenue and turn right. Walk south and turn right on the north side of 75th Street. Walk west until you reach number 333.

10. 333 East 75th Street. Lenny (Woody Allen) tracked down Linda (Mira Sorvino), the biological mother of his adopted son, and made an appointment to see her. Linda lived in this building, and Lenny visited her to learn all about her. She was a hooker, but that didn't stop the two of them from becoming good friends in *Mighty Aphrodite*.

Continue west on 75th and turn left on Second Avenue. Stop at the building on the southeast corner of Second and 74th Street.

11. 300 East 74th Street. A madman was on the loose, committing violent acts with a hammer. But Detective Ed Delaney (Frank Sinatra) was on

the case, and his research, his leads, and his hunches all led him to this building, where he convinced a doorman to give him access to the suspected serial killer's apartment, in *The First Deadly Sin*.

Continue south on Second and turn right on the south side of 72nd Street. Walk east until you reach number 242.

12. 242 East 72nd Street. He became well-known for the *Basketball Diaries* he kept, but life had its ups and downs. When things were going well, they went really well. During a visit to fun-loving twins who lived in this building, Jim (Leonardo DiCaprio) tasted the good life. But later when things turned sour, Winkie (Cynthia Daniel) and Blinkie (Brittany Daniel) pretended they didn't know Jim, and their father wouldn't let him back in the building.

Turn the other way on 72nd and walk east to the east side of York Avenue. Sotheby's auction house should be across 72nd Street from you on the southeast corner of York and 72nd.

13. Sotheby's. York Avenue and 72nd Street. Tom Logan (Robert Redford) and Laura J. Kelly (Debra Winger) were out to solve the murder of a well-known artist. The murder had occurred years before, but when Chelsea (Daryl Hannah), the artist's daughter, was implicated, the two *Legal Eagles* decided to determine what really hap-pened. Tom and Laura came here and interrupted an auction to talk to Victor Taft (Terrence Stamp).

Continue east on 72nd Street until you reach the low buildings on the left side, just before the end of the block.

14. 535-541 East 72nd Street. After running into Holly (Dianne Wiest), his former sister-in-

law, Mickey (Woody Allen) spent some time with her in *Hannah and Her Sisters*. Holly read Mickey her manuscript, which he loved. Afterward they emerged from a doorway in this building and went to get something to eat.

Walk to the end of the block. Look for the Promenade, to the east of the FDR Drive overlooking the East River.

15. East River Promenade. He lost his first wife and then fell in love with Chiquita (Victoria Shaw), the woman who cared for his young son. But knowing he didn't have much time to live, Eddy Duchin (Tyrone Power) came to this prom-

enade to clear his head. But Chiquita followed him here, and he revealed both his love for her and the fact that he was dying. Chiquita loved him too, and they agreed to marry, for however much time they had left together, in *The Eddy Duchin Story*.

Return to York, turn left, and walk south three blocks until you reach the hospital.

16. New York Hospital. 1300 York Avenue (at 69th Street). Connie (Kelly Lynch) worked here as a nurse. In *Three of Hearts*, she dreaded attending her younger sister's wedding without an escort until her patient suggested she rent one. And she did: Joe (William Baldwin).

———————

Continue south on York and turn right on the north side of 68th Street. Head west until just past First Avenue, to number 359.

17. 359 East 68th Street. Spurned mistress Dolores (Anjelica Huston) had become a bit of a problem, so Judah (Martin Landau) decided to do something about it. One night his brother Jack (Jerry Orbach) followed Dolores home to this building, where the problem was solved, once and for all, in *Crimes and Misdemeanors*.

———————

Continue west on 68th Street to the west side of Second Avenue. Turn left on Second and walk south to 66th Street. There is a sidewalk (with a stone wall alongside it) that runs in the middle of 66th, between Second and Third Avenues.

18. East 66th Street (between Second and Third Avenues). Alvie (Woody Allen) and Rob (Tony Roberts) walked along here and discussed life, anti-Semitism, and Alvie's relationship with *Annie Hall* (Diane Keaton). Alvie revealed the anti-Semitic remark someone had made at his office. Talking about lunch, someone asked Alvie if

he had eaten. But the man's question did not come across to Alvie as "Did you?" It came across as "Di-Jew?" Best friend Rob could only try to placate his paranoid friend as they walked along this street.

Turn back and return to Second Avenue. The Beekman Theatre should be across Second Avenue, at 66th.

19. Beekman Theatre. 1254 Second Avenue (at 66th Street). Certain that his wife, Daniella (Nastassja Kinski), was having an affair, symphony conductor Claude Eastman (Dudley Moore) followed her into this theater and searched for her in the dark in *Unfaithfully Yours*. Seeing an affectionate couple several rows up, Claude confronted them, but discovered it was not his wife. Claude found himself embarrassed and, a short time later, in the custody of the police.

Walk south on Second and turn right on 64th Street. Head west on 64th until you reach the hospital, at 210 East 64th Street.

20. Manhattan Eye, Ear and Throat Hospital. 210 East 64th Street. Having read about a surgeon who was performing some amazing surgeries to cure blindness, advertising-world hotshot Amy (Mira Sorvino) brought sight-challenged masseuse Virgil (Val Kilmer) here for experimental eye surgery. Thanks to a talented team of doctors, Virgil was able to see, although Amy turned out to be the one with blinders on in *At First Sight*.

Head back the other way on 64th until you reach First Avenue. Turn right on the east side of First and stop at the bar on the northeast corner of First and 63rd.

Tour 6

21. First Avenue and 63rd Street. Northeast Corner. After completing his military service, Brian Flanagan (Tom Cruise) came to New York to find a job. After failing to land something in

the worlds of finance and advertising, Brian responded to a HELP WANTED sign in the window of this place. Brian got the job, and under the tutelage of Douglas Coughlin (Bryan Brown), Brian learned that he really knew his way around a *Cocktail* and that when the two of them "poured, they reigned."

———•◦•———

Cross to the west side of First, then turn left and walk south on First to the north side of 60th Street. Turn right on 60th and stop in front of Scores.

22. Scores. 333 East 60th Street. One of their own was about to be married, and the cops who populated a town known as *Cop Land* came here for a bachelor party. After watching one of them get sick beside a parked car across the street, Murray (Michael Rapaport) headed home, only to get into trouble on the George Washington Bridge.

———•◦•———

Continue west on 60th and stop at Second Avenue. Look up to see if the Roosevelt Island Tramway is gliding overhead.

23. Roosevelt Island Tram. A band of terrorists, led by Rutger Hauer, had taken hostages aboard the tram as it dangled beside the 59th Street Bridge, high over the East River. But the terrorists were not monsters, or so they claimed. In a daring maneuver, as per the terrorists' in-

structions, Detective DaSilva (Sylvester Stallone), a New York City cop, was lowered from a helicopter to receive a released hostage, an infant, in *Nighthawks*.

Continue west on 60th until you reach Serendipity 3, at 225 East 60th Street.

24. Serendipity 3. 225 East 60th Street. Taking a pause during her extremely hectic, but *One Fine Day*, Melanie Parker (Michelle Pfeiffer) took her son, Sammy (Alex D. Linz), and his schoolmate Maggie (Mae Whitman), the daughter of flirtatious nemesis Jack Taylor (George Clooney), here for ice cream.

It means fortunate accident, fate, destiny, providence, kismet: In a word, *Serendipity*. And after their chance encounter, Jonathan (John Cusack) and Sara (Kate Beckinsale) came here, where they shared a wonderful dessert. Afterward, though Jonathan felt they had been meant to meet and get together, Sara decided they should leave their next encounter to fate, destiny, providence, and kismet. Because he was smitten with Sara, Jonathan had no choice but to agree to Sara's plan, however risky it appeared to be. Smitten guys will do that.

Return to Second Avenue and turn right. Walk south to 59th Street, then turn left on the south side of 59th and walk east until you reach number 346, just west of First Avenue.

25. 346 East 59th Street. After their misadventure in the Bronx, Sherman McCoy (Tom Hanks) and his mistress, Maria (Melanie Griffith), ended up here, where Maria had an apartment, in *The Bonfire of the Vanities*.

Even though New York City boasts thousands of buildings, restaurants, hotels, and stores, it does not seem unusual that some locations appear in more than one film (e.g., the Plaza, Tavern on the Green, the Metropolitan Museum of Art). But this building? It was home not only to Maria in

Bonfire, but also to Felix (George Segal) and Doris (Barbra Streisand), sometimes known as *The Owl and the Pussycat*, until Felix's complaining about Doris's nighttime habits got them evicted.

After getting kicked out of their respective apartments, Felix and Doris didn't walk far. Continue east, as they did, to the building on the southeast corner of 59th and First Avenue.

26. 400 East 59th Street. Felix (George Segal) and Doris (Barbra Streisand) came to this building and had the doorman ring up. Moments later, *The Owl and the Pussycat* were being welcomed into the apartment of Felix's friend and co-worker Barney (Robert Klein).

————

Head east on 59th Street and stop on the east side of Sutton Place (a continuation of York Avenue). From this vantage point, you should be under the 59th Street Bridge.

27. Under the 59th Street Bridge. He actually hailed from a prominent and well-to-do Boston family, but he found himself down on his luck. Plucked from this location, where he had made a transient home with other forgotten men, to serve as butler for the Bullock family, Godfrey (William Powell) learned that life among the well-heeled was no picnic either. In *My Man Godfrey*, Godfrey taught the Bullocks about life and taught the young Irene Bullock (Carole Lombard) about love. And when Godfrey opened a gentleman's club on this site at the end of the movie, Irene stopped by to show him what she had learned about the subject.

————

Turn right and head south on Sutton Place. Turn left on 57th Street and walk to the playground overlooking the East River.

28. Sutton Place and 57th Street. Playground. Feeling depressed and unhappy, and wondering why she was wasting her time with a married man, Ellen (Jane Fonda) ran from her apartment (see **Walking Tour 8: The UN and Beyond**, Location 4) and came here, a place she liked to visit when she needed to think. On one

occasion, Cass (Dean Jones), who had met her the previous day, followed Ellen and found her on the ledge. Fearing she would jump, Cass talked her into sitting on the swings instead. And on *Any Wednesday*, after the two of them had talked for a while, Ellen decided they should get married. Impulsive? Sure, but in New York, anything is possible.

The building doesn't exist, but if it did, it would be overlooking this playground.

29. 600 East 57th Street. His apartment overlooked the East River and offered an unparalleled view of the 59th Street Bridge. In it, happy-go-lucky playboy Charlie Reader (Frank Sinatra) entertained a bevy of beauties who battled for his affections. That is, until one of them, Julie Gillis (Debbie Reynolds), snared him in *The Tender Trap* that she had set for him.

Step back and take a look at the bridge.

30. 59th Street Bridge. Besides being immortalized in the song *Feeling Groovy* by Simon and Garfunkel, the bridge has had its share of the cinematic spotlight. In *Manhattan*, Isaac (Woody Allen) and Mary (Diane Keaton) sat on a bench and took in the bridge's splendor.

In *Home Alone 2: Lost in New York*, Kevin McAllister (Macaulay Culkin) took a cab from the airport and entered Manhattan this way, as have characters in many other movies.

Wesley Snipes has made his share of New York movies, and interestingly, many of them have had scenes located along the East River. In *New Jack City*, Nino Brown (Snipes) had his fingers in a lot of different pots, none of them legal. In the opening scene, Nino emerged from a car on the bridge and stood by as one of his associates held a man upside down by the ankles. The poor sap didn't have the money or the drugs that belonged to Nino, and he had to be taught a lesson. After Nino gave the word, the man was dropped into the waters of the East River.

Fans of the television show *Taxi* might be interested to know (if they don't already) that in the opening sequence of the show, a taxicab is also shown crossing this bridge.

Walk south until you reach 56th Street. If you look to the left, you will see a DEAD END sign. That should say it all.

31. Sutton Place and 56th Street. It was clearly a set, but intended to depict life in this part of Manhattan. Right around here, a cop walked his beat, the rich people lived in the houses up above and looked down upon the street urchins and poor working souls who inhabited the slums

below, overlooking the East River. This was the world of *Dead End*, inhabited by Dave (Joel Mc-Crae), an architect trying to earn a humble yet honest living, a young woman named Drina (Sylvia Sidney), who was doing her best to keep her kid brother from falling in with the wrong crowd, and Baby Face (Humphrey Bogart), who had no regard for decency, goodness, or the law. It was also the place where the Dead End Kids (Leo Gorcey, Huntz Hall, and Gabriel Dell, among others) got their start, and their name.

Continue south one block and note number 36, on the northwest corner at 55th Street.

32. 36 Sutton Place South (at 55th Street). It was an event that made every single man (and plenty of married men) in New York jump for joy: three beautiful women moving to Manhattan and throwing themselves into New York's social scene. Pooling their resources, Shotzy (Lauren Bacall), Paula (Marilyn Monroe), and Loco (Betty Grable) decided to share a furnished apartment in this elegant building, selling off pieces of furniture as needed to pay their expenses. But it was all for a good cause: figuring out *How to Marry a Millionaire*.

You have now reached the end of **Walking Tour 6: The Eastern Seaboard.**

Walking Tour 7
MIDTOWN

UPTOWN

WEST SIDE

EAST SIDE

DOWNTOWN

W. 54TH ST.

AVE. AMERICAS

FIFTH AVE.

MADISON AVE.

PARK AVE.

LEXINGTON AVE.

W. 46TH ST.

W. 42ND ST.

Walking Tour 7
MIDTOWN

Despite a skyline like that of no other city on Earth, Midtown Manhattan appears sterile and anonymous to some. However, that image is just a façade. To those who look closely, Midtown harbors the lifeblood of the city, as well as numerous locations that have won the affections of moviegoers for the past half-century. Contained within the parameters of Midtown are some of the city's best-known landmarks, a stunningly beautiful transportation hub, more world-famous hotels, and the world's best-known and best-loved ice-skating rink.

Walking Tour 7: Midtown begins on Park Avenue between 39th and 40th Streets. If you look up Park Avenue, you will see the grand façades of Grand Central Terminal and the MetLife Building. We'll get there, but for now, look at the building on your left.

1. 90 Park Avenue (between 39th and 40th Streets). New York City cop Leo McCarthy (Brian Dennehy) knew something was wrong. A federal agent—who had been using a borrowed social security number—was dead, and the agent's boss, Colonel Mason (Mason Adams), didn't seem curious about how the man died. In *F/X*, to get some answers, Leo paid Mason a visit here.

Look directly across Park Avenue to the large building on the east side of the street.

2. 99 Park Avenue. By night, Alice (Chloë Sevigny) and Charlotte (Kate Beckinsale) tripped the light fantastic at the hottest disco in town. By day, they trudged away as low-level workers in the publishing industry in this building in *The Last Days of Disco*.

———————

Walk to the corner of 40th Street and note the building diagonally across the intersection.

3. 101 Park Avenue. This large tower is one of those buildings that has found its way into numerous films over the years. In *Brewster's Millions*, baseball player Monty Brewster (Richard Pryor) stood to inherit $300 million if he could spend $30 million in a month with nothing to show for it. To get the details, he and a few others, including teammate Spike Nolan (John Candy), headed into this building to meet with the lawyers who had summoned him.

In *The Fisher King*, when Jack Lukas (Jeff Bridges) decided he was ready to get back to work as a radio talk show host, he and his agent Lou (David Hyde Pierce) headed into this building to discuss this step.

Fresh off the farm, Bradley Foster (Michael J. Fox) thought he would work here in *The Secret of My Success*. His success would have to start elsewhere, however, for on his first day at work, he learned that the company had slashed its workforce (including him), as the result of a hostile takeover.

Lastly, *Alice* (Mia Farrow) came here to visit her friend Nancy Brill (Cybill Shepherd) to toss around some ideas for a television series.

———•—•———

Before crossing 40th Street, note the ramp intersecting 40th and Park.

4. 40th Street and Park Avenue (Traffic Ramp). It was the 50th anniversary of the United Nations, a bad day to try to get to the airport, as Max (Wesley Snipes) discovered, fuming in the backseat of the taxi stalled at the foot of this ramp. Finally realizing he wasn't going anywhere, Max exited the cab and ended up having a *One Night Stand* with Karen (Nastassja Kinski). At least, at the time, they thought it would be a one night stand.

———•—•———

Before taking another step, note the grand MetLife Building, just ahead on Park.

5. MetLife Building. 200 Park Avenue. It looks fine now, but after *Godzilla* passed by, there was a gaping hole through the building from one side to the other.

———•—•———

Walk north on Park Avenue and stop at the corner of 41st Street. The next location is on the northwest corner of the intersection.

6. 120 Park Avenue (at 41st Street). Dressed as a clown, Grimm (Bill Murray) entered this building. Once inside, he pulled off a clever and daring bank heist, made a *Quick Change,* and emerged a normally dressed rich man. All he had to do was get to the airport to make his getaway. But that proved to be no small feat.

———•—•———

Continue north on Park Avenue and turn right on the south side of 42nd Street. Walk east and stop in front of 110 East 42nd.

7. 110 East 42nd Street. Always excited to accompany his "stern" father, Ben (Richard Portnow), into the city, a young Howard Stern (Bobby Borrello) came here with his dad. In this building, the elder Mr. Stern worked as a radio engineer, giving Howard his first taste of the world of radio, in Stern's semi-autobiographical film, *Private Parts*.

Head back the other way on 42nd Street and stop at the Barclay-Rex Pipe Shop at 70 East 42nd.

8. Barclay-Rex Pipe Shop. 70 East 42nd Street. Having escaped from the custody of federal agents, Mark Sheridan (Wesley Snipes) made his way to New York, intent on clearing his name. But doing so would not be easy. His first stop was here, to visit an acquaintance, but his reception was less than cordial. Thereafter Sheridan knew he would be on his own in his race with Deputy Sam Gerard (Tommy Lee Jones) and the rest of the *U.S. Marshals*.

Walk a few feet to the west. The Lincoln Building is at 60 East 42nd Street.

9. The Lincoln Building. 60 East 42nd Street. Jack Taylor (George Clooney) was a successful reporter for the *Daily News*, whose offices were located in this building, in the romantic comedy *One Fine Day*.

Look across 42nd at the Vanderbilt Avenue entrance to Grand Central Terminal.

10. 42nd Street and Vanderbilt Avenue. Northeast Intersection. Sent to the Earth's surface to bring his troublemaking brothers back down to hell, *Little Nicky* (Adam Sandler), Satan's childlike son, exited Grand Central and encountered a blind preacher (Quentin Tarentino) on this corner. Although the man was blind, or maybe because of that fact, he could sense that Nicky's appearance in this world could only mean trouble.

Turn left and walk west to Fifth Avenue. The New York Public Library stands majestically to your left. Turn left on Fifth and walk south until you're across from the entrance.

11. New York Public Library. Fifth Avenue and 41st Street. He discovered a piece of microfilm in a wallet he had lifted from a woman's purse while on the subway and then came here. In *Pickup on South Street*, Skip McCoy (Richard Widmark) put the microfilm into a machine in the library to see what he had stumbled onto.

When Skip walked into the building, he may have passed Murray Burns (Jason Robards), one of *A Thousand Clowns* out and about that day. But Murray was no longer a clown: He had quit the rat race. As he stood, binoculars in hand, beside his nephew Nick (Barry Gordon), he told the boy to watch for the horror he was about to witness: People going to work.

It was a job for the *Ghostbusters*. After an apparition appeared in one of the library's lower levels, Ray (Dan Aykroyd), Peter (Bill Murray), and Egon (Harold Ramis) were called in and after a none-too-friendly encounter with the ghost, came running out the library's front doors.

It is safe to say that the library provided no safe haven from the ghosts. But it did provide a safe haven from the cold. After global warming had wreaked havoc on the weather systems affecting the Earth's Northern Hemisphere, floodwaters converged on Manhattan and quickly turned to ice. A lucky few, including Sam Hall (Jake Gyllenhaal) and Laura Chapman (Emmy Rossum), managed to make it inside before the outside world froze. They burned books to keep warm until the ice melted in *The Day After Tomorrow*.

Turn left and walk south on Fifth Avenue until you are across from Lord & Taylor.

12. Lord & Taylor. 424 Fifth Avenue (between 37th and 38th Streets). Michael Chapman (Michael J. Fox) knew all about being a child star. With those days behind him, he and his brother, Ed (Nathan Lane), turned to representing other child stars. But life with their newest client, Angie (Christina Vidal), was proving to be a few tuna fish sandwiches short of a picnic. In *Life With Mikey*, Angie was picked up for shoplifting here after walking out on her agents, and possibly her career. In the spirit of the holiday season, the security guards let her go, especially after they saw the commercial she had made airing on TV.

Continue to 37th Street, then turn and cross Fifth Avenue.

13. Fifth Avenue and 37th Street. Northwest corner. Bus Stop. *The Cameraman* landed his dream date with Sally (Marceline Day), and they boarded a double-decker bus near this corner. But the crowd pushing onto the bus was so great that Buster (Buster Keaton) was forced to the upper deck while his date got a seat down below. And people say Romeo and Juliet had it rough.

Turn north on Fifth until you reach 40th Street. Turn left and walk west, with the library on your right, until you reach the entrance to Bryant Park. Feel free to enter.

14. Bryant Park. Between Fifth and Sixth Av-

enues (from 40th to 42nd Streets). During Fashion Week, enormous tents are erected here, and many designers hold their annual fashion shows to introduce their new clothing lines. Because *Head Over Heels* involved models, it should come as no surprise that Fashion Week and the park played a supporting role. The models were on the run from a Russian smuggler of illegal diamonds, but because the show must go on, Amanda (Monica Potter) and her model/roommates did their part to assist a designer, Mr. Alfredo (Stanley DeSantis), in showing his latest fashions.

Add a few thousand screaming fans to this small park, and you've got a full-fledged celebration. That's what Howard Stern did to celebrate his success in *Private Parts*.

If you can, walk further into the park and turn to the left. Look for the fountain.

15. Bryant Park. Fountain. If you look closely, you might be able to see Larry (Woody Allen) meet up with his wife, Carol (Diane Keaton), by the fountain. Suspecting their neighbor of having killed his wife, Carol broke into the man's apartment to snoop around, hoping to find a clue to this *Manhattan Murder Mystery*. She met Larry here to give him the update and to figure out their next step.

Walk through the park toward 42nd Street and stop at the walkway just south of 42nd.

16. Walkway inside Bryant Park, near 42nd Street. After getting fired from his job as a fact-checker for a magazine, Jamie Conway (Michael J. Fox) walked along here and sat on a bench, where he was approached by one of the park's more colorful characters (William Hickey), selling various wares, in *Bright Lights, Big City*. As a later scene revealed, one of the items Jamie purchased from the man was a ferret.

Along this walkway you might also find former Wall Street whiz kid Lewis (Christian Slater) and the object of his affections, Lisa (Mary Stuart Masterson), strolling during their day-long date, in *Bed of Roses*.

Exit the park onto 42nd Street, turn left, and walk to Avenue of the Americas (same as Sixth Avenue). Turn right and walk north on Sixth Avenue to 44th Street. Turn right on 44th and walk east until you are across from New York's legendary Algonquin Hotel.

17. The Algonquin. 59 West 44th Street. During their heyday, from here they reigned supreme, their words piercing and illuminating the literary scene of the 1930s. Holding court at the Algonquin's legendary "Round Table" were, among others, Alexander Woollcott (Tom McGowan), George S. Kaufman (David Thornton), Edna Ferber (Lili Taylor), Robert Benchley (Campbell Scott), and Dorothy Parker (Jennifer Jason Leigh), all vividly brought to life in *Mrs. Parker and the Vicious Circle*.

Still hot on the trail, not-quite supersleuths Charlie (John Ritter) and Arthur (Blaine Novak) followed the lovely subject of their surveillance, Dolores (Dorothy Stratten), here and waited to see whom she was meeting. But in *They All Laughed*, the sleuths were impatient and decided to take things into their own hands. They approached Dolores and engaged her in conversation.

If the sleuths had been better at their jobs, they might have noticed writer Liz Hamilton (Jacqueline Bisset), who stayed here on her trips to New York. Liz met her agent, Jules Levi (Steven Hill), in the lobby bar and gave him a new manuscript, but it wasn't hers. It was a novel that had been written by her good friend Merry (Candice Bergen), who, as a result, would soon become *Rich and Famous* herself.

Walk east until you are across from the beautiful building with the surreal window sills at 37 West 44th Street.

18. 37 West 44th Street. This building, with its windows that suggest a work by Salvador Dali, was an architectural site pointed out to Holly (Dianne Wiest) and April (Carrie Fisher) by David (Sam Waterston) on his tour in *Hannah and Her Sisters*.

Continue east. Pass Fifth Avenue, then Madison Avenue and turn right on Vanderbilt. Walk south one block, just past 43rd Street.

19. Vanderbilt Avenue, near 43rd Street (across from Grand Central Terminal). She liked to spend every *Sunday in New York*. Little did she know that on one such day she would meet the man of her dreams. Just off the train, Eileen (Jane Fonda) exited Grand Central and hailed a taxi on this spot. She was heading to her brother's apartment. Interestingly enough, Eileen gave the cabdriver the address of "120 East 65th Street," but when she got out of the cab, she entered a building that had number "184" on the awning. Let's call it a minor NitPick.

The time has come to enter the magnificence of Grand Central Terminal. At 43rd Street, cross Vanderbilt and enter Grand Central. Make your way to the marble railing overlooking the massive central room of the terminal.

20. Grand Central Terminal. Main Room. The lights dim, orchestral music fills the hall, and frenzied rush-hour commuters pair off to waltz for a few priceless moments. Hard to envision? Not for Perry (Robin Williams), who took part in those magic moments in *The Fisher King*. As he followed his beloved Lydia (Amanda Plummer) through the crowd, everyone began to waltz in one of the most magical moments captured on film in recent decades.

Would it be any easier to envision this great

room being bombarded by asteroids, like those that fell from the heavens in *Armageddon*? Let us hope not.

———•—•—•———

Walk down the staircase from the Vanderbilt Avenue entrance, but watch your step.

21. Grand Central Terminal. Staircase to West Balcony and Vanderbilt Avenue. Clark Kellogg (Matthew Broderick) didn't, and he tumbled down these stairs with all his luggage. Luckily for Clark, or so he thought at the time, he was helped to his feet by con man Victor Ray (Bruno Kirby) in *The Freshman*.

———•—•—•———

Turn your attention to the information booth in the center of the room.

22. Grand Central Terminal. Information Booth under the Big Clock. At the beginning of their *Midnight Run*, bounty hunter Jack Walsh (Robert De Niro) learned that "the Duke" (Charles Grodin), the fugitive Jack was to bring back to Los Angeles, was afraid of flying. As he was up against a deadline, a train became Jack's "Plan B." The two men passed through here as they headed for the train.

While you are standing near the information booth, keep an eye out for a beautiful young woman sleeping soundly with her back up against

163

the booth. After she missed her train, she must have felt like a *Loser*. But Dora (Mena Suvari) made the best of the situation. She called home from a pay phone and told her family that she was staying at her college dorm. With nowhere else to turn, she plopped down in the deserted room you are now in and spent the night trying to sleep, her back against the information booth.

Grand Central Terminal is a place of comings and goings. Commuters Frank (Robert De Niro) and Molly (Meryl Streep) passed through this room every day. Even though they rode the same train, their paths didn't cross at first. They even made phone calls from adjacent pay phones, not knowing that soon they would not only meet, but be *Falling in Love*. For a while, they spent a good deal of time together and waiting for each other in this room.

Boarding a train to leave town? First you must buy a ticket. Look for ticket window 15.

23. Grand Central Terminal. Ticket Window 15.

On the run for a murder he didn't commit, Roger Thornhill (Cary Grant) phoned his mother, telling her he was leaving town on a train. His destination? It wasn't clear, but it was obvious that he would be heading *North By Northwest*. After the phone call, he tried to buy a ticket at window 15. But knowing he had been spotted, Roger immediately boarded a train, and with the help of Eve Kendall (Eva Marie Saint), he was able to elude the police until the train pulled out of the station.

Turn toward the Vanderbilt Avenue entrance that you came through. There are two sets of staircases. Near the staircase on the right side is track 29.

24. Grand Central Terminal. Entrance to Track 29.

While Roger Thornhill hoped to

sneak onto a train unnoticed, accomplished violinist and struggling football player Bernard (Jason Gould) attracted a crowd as he waited to board his train. Bernard had been escorted here by his football mentor, Tom Wingo (Nick Nolte), and Bernard complied with Tom's wishes and treated Tom and a gathering crowd to a free concert in *The Prince of Tides*.

Truth be told, however, not everyone trying to leave here is treated as well as Bernard.

Turn right and walk until you reach the bank of escalators leading to and coming from the North Balcony and 45th Street.

25. Grand Central Terminal. Escalator Bank to North Balcony and 45th Street. Charlie (Al Pacino) was trying to flee from the men who were trying to kill him, as well as from the life of violence he had always lived. As his girlfriend, Gail (Penelope Ann Miller), waited by the train, Charlie (aka Carlito) tried to sneak down these escalators. But he was spotted, and a climactic shootout took place on and around this escalator bank, as the gunmen did their best to get in *Carlito's Way*.

Trains don't just leave Grand Central. They arrive, too.

26. Grand Central Terminal. After living through *The Incident*, the passengers on board the subway train that pulled into Grand Central late one night were not in the mood to sing. Two bad seeds out to cause trouble, Joe Ferrone (Tony Musante) and Artie Connors (Martin Sheen), terrorized innocent people onboard during a long, harrowing ride. The sheep-like passengers who endured the terrorizing and did nothing to stop it included Bill Wilks (Ed McMahon), Sam Beckerman (Jack Gilford), Alice Keenan (Donna Mills), Arnold Robinson (Brock Peters), and Joan

Robinson (Ruby Dee). Luckily, there was one passenger, Private First Class Felix Teflinger (Beau Bridges), who was willing to stand up to the hooligans, even with his arm in a cast. And he did, beating the two bullies to a pulp.

His movie career had all but faded, and former screen star Tony Hunter (Fred Astaire) decided to give Broadway a chance. Disembarking from a train into Grand Central, the soon-to-be Broad-

way star answered a few questions, but as he walked away, realized he was going his way, by himself, and so he sang, in *The Band Wagon*.

Most people pass through Grand Central en route to somewhere else. There is someone, however, who maintains his hideout and lair somewhere down below.

27. Grand Central Terminal. Underground Lair. Okay, maybe it's not really there, but it seemed real enough to Lex Luthor (Gene Hackman), the arch nemesis of *Superman*, who ran his criminal empire from somewhere in the bowels of this station. In the movie, Luthor's bumbling associate Otis (Ned Beatty) strolled through the station and entered the tracks to get to the lair, oblivious to the fact that he was being followed by the police.

There are lockers somewhere in Grand Central where people can store their belongings. At least back in the 1940s there were.

28. Grand Central Terminal. Lockers. The phone rang late at night, and a soothing yet firm voice instructed Briggsy (Woody Allen) to steal some jewels from the mansion of one of his firm's clients. Stealing was not something that Briggsy, an insurance investigator for the North Coast Fidelity and Casualty Company, would typically do, but because the man with the soothing voice, Voltan Polgar (David Ogden Stiers), had hypnotized him, Briggsy was under *The Curse of the Jade Scorpion* and therefore helpless to resist. As per Voltan Polgar's instructions, Briggsy swiped the jewels and placed them in a locker here.

And there came a time when it all changed, when humans battled apes for supremacy. Be-

neath Grand Central, as *Beneath the Planet of the Apes*, the humans didn't fare too well.

It is now time to leave the splendor of Grand Central Terminal and resume our trek through the streets of Midtown. Take the escalators up to the North Balcony and 45th Street, go through the revolving doors, and walk through the MetLife Building until you reach the entrance on the north side. After you exit on 45th Street, cross and walk through the East Walkway through the Helmsley Building. You will emerge on Park Avenue. Walk north on Park and stop across from number 270 Park, between 47th and 48th Streets.

29. 270 Park Avenue. Not interested in climbing the corporate ladder the conventional way, J. Pierpont Finch (Robert Morse) relied on a book to instruct him on *How to Succeed in Business Without Really Trying*. Starting as a window washer, Finch went from mail room to boardroom of the World Wide Wicket Company in record time, thanks to the help of his book and the love of Rosemary Pilkington (Michelle Lee), who believed in him.

Continue north until you reach the Waldorf-Astoria, between 49th and 50th Streets.

30. The Waldorf-Astoria. 301 Park Avenue. The Waldorf has probably played host to a greater variety of film characters over a longer period of time than any other hotel in the world. This is where Hazel Flagg (Carole Lombard) was brought for a last fling before succumbing to her mortal illness. She got her whirlwind New York adventure, but the public who followed her poignant story never got to see Hazel's suffering, because her illness proved to be not as life-threatening as originally believed, demonstrating that there is *Nothing Sacred*.

The Waldorf is where syndicated columnist Randy Morton (Robert Benchley) lived in *Week-End at the Waldorf*. Morton wrote a column entitled "Randy Morton's New York" and narrated the story that began with the arrival of a young honeymoon couple who found that there were no rooms available. Taking pity on them, a hotel resident who was going to his country house for the weekend permitted the hotel to give them his room. And that's when the trouble started. And the adventure began.

George (Jack Lemmon) and Gwen (Sandy Dennis) did not fare as well when the hotel gave away their room. They had no place to stay, and no kindly benefactor offered them his room. In the course of one very long night, *The Out-of-Towners* were mugged, rode along on a police chase, slept in Central Park, and battled a stray dog for a few morsels of Cracker Jacks.

They were good friends, and both were *Rich and Famous*, but while Liz (Jacqueline Bisset) stayed at the Algonquin Hotel (see Location 17) on trips to New York, Merry Noel Blake (Candice Bergen) opted to stay here.

On a wild Thanksgiving weekend in Manhattan, Lieutenant Colonel Frank Slade (Al Pacino), with his naïve protégé, Charlie (Chris O'Donnell), stayed here in *Scent of a Woman*. The weekend turned out to be a wild ride that changed the lives of the two of them forever.

It seemed as if every member of the royal family of Zamunda was *Coming to America*. First, Prince Akeem (Eddie Murphy) came to find a bride. Then, learning that Akeem and sidekick Semmi (Arsenio Hall) were spending money far too quickly, Akeem's parents, King Jaffe Joffer (James Earl Jones) and Queen Aoleon (Madge Sinclair), came and took up temporary residence here until they could find Akeem and bring him home to the suitable bride that had been selected for him.

The Waldorf is also where Sonny (Kiefer Sutherland) and Pepper (Woody Harrelson) stayed after deciding to find themselves a "motel" in *The Cowboy Way*.

While glove shopping, Jonathan (John Cusack) and Sara (Kate Beckinsale) crossed paths. By the end of the evening, both were convinced there could be something great between them, but Sara wanted to leave things up to fate. They came here, with Jonathan thinking his fortunes had suddenly taken a huge leap forward, but Sara had other ideas. Standing in the deserted lobby, they boarded separate elevators, and each had to select a floor. If they selected the same floor, Sara would see it as a sign that they were meant to be together. When Sara reached the twenty-third floor, she waited as long as she could, saw Jonathan's failure to appear as a bad sign, and left moments before his elevator arrived. It would be years before they would learn whether they were right to rest their future on *Serendipity*.

And after chauffeuring her around town in his limousine and flirting shamelessly with her, *Alfie* (Jude Law) dropped Liz (Susan Sarandon) and one of her many romantic partners off here, realizing that he had met the female, older version of himself.

Walk north until you reach the church at Park Avenue (between 50th and 51st Streets).

31. St. Bartholomew's Church. Park Avenue (between 50th and 51st Streets). *Arthur,* the immature but fun-loving millionaire playboy (Dudley Moore), was supposed to marry Susan (Jill Eikenberry) in a marriage arranged by their two families. Arthur had different ideas. He wanted to marry Linda (Liza Minnelli), a girl from the wrong side of the tracks. At the wedding

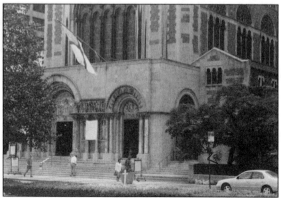

ceremony being held here, Arthur announced that he wouldn't marry Susan. Afterward he descended these steps, where Martha (Geraldine Fitzgerald), the matriarch of the Bach family, sat at the curb in her Rolls-Royce. To be with Linda, Arthur gave up his claim to the family fortune. And then he thought better of it and found a way to keep both.

Barney Martin played Linda's father, Morty. Fans of the television show *Seinfeld* may or may not remember that he went on to play Jerry's dad.

Walk north on Park and stop at number 375 (between 52nd and 53rd Streets).

32. 375 Park Avenue. "Tiger Lady" J. C. Wyatt (Diane Keaton) was at the top of her field at the ad agency Sloane, Curtis & Co. until she got caught up, unexpectedly, in the *Baby Boom*. And, suddenly, the upward-climbing Ken (James Spader) was gunning for her job. The agency where the "Tiger Lady" and the "snake" worked was located in this building.

This building is also where the studios of IB, the Scrooge-like network that wanted to air a live version of Charles Dickens's *A Christmas Carol* on Christmas Eve, was located. No wonder, since the show was being overseen by the grinch-like studio head Frank Cross (Bill Murray) in the movie *Scrooged*.

During the filming of a movie within a movie, actress Nicole Oliver (Melanie Griffith), a bona fide *Celebrity*, ran from a car parked at the curb, up these plaza steps, and looked up at the word HELP being spelled out by a skywriting plane, while the rest of the cast, crew, and writer Lee Simon (Kenneth Branagh, essentially playing Woody Allen with straighter hair) looked on. The scene was repeated when, at the end of the movie, the story written by Lee was being made into a movie. Or something like that.

Continue north and stop at number 399, between 53rd and 54th Streets.

33. 399 Park Avenue (between 53rd and 54th Streets). The Larrabees lived in a huge mansion on the North Shore of Long Island on a very large estate. But they—or at least the older of the two sons, Linus (Harrison Ford)—spent a good deal of time here in *Sabrina*.

After the bank officer had been hypnotized, John Dortmunder (Robert Redford) had only to utter the phrase "Afghanistan Bananistan" to get the man to show him to the safe deposit box that held *The Hot Rock*. After taking possession of the priceless jewel, Dortmunder left the bank, which was located here, and got into a waiting car, where he celebrated the success of the caper with his jubilant colleagues.

Continue north on Park Avenue. There is a deli on the east side of the street between 54th and 55th Streets.

34. Deli/Café. 407 Park Avenue (between 54th and 55th Streets). Alone on Christmas Eve, Jack (Nicolas Cage) went into this deli to buy eggnog, which was the extent of his planned holiday celebration. Inside, he diffused a tense situation involving a lottery ticket and wound up

being given a special gift by Cash (Don Cheadle), the lottery ticket holder. The gift, as Cash explained to Jack outside the deli, was a "glimpse" of what Jack's life would have been had he taken the route of *The Family Man* rather than that of high-powered finance.

———◆———

If you walked to the deli, return to 54th Street and turn right. If you did not, turn left on 54th, and in either case walk west on the south side of 54th Street until you reach The Monkey Bar, at 60 East 54th Street.

35. The Monkey Bar. 60 East 54th Street. Having given up on attractive women, Professor Greg Larkin (Jeff Bridges) placed a personal ad in which he declared that looks are not important. Among the responses was one from Professor Rose Morgan (Barbra Streisand). Although Rose's sister had answered the ad on Rose's behalf, Rose agreed to go out with Greg, and on their first date they dined here in *The Mirror Has Two Faces*.

———◆———

Continue west on 54th Street, but keep your eyes peeled for an available cab.

36. 54th Street, between Park and Madison Avenues. It was just before the start of the Thanksgiving holiday, and in the search for available taxicabs, it was every man for himself, as Neal Page (Steve Martin) quickly learned in *Planes, Trains and Automobiles*. Standing on the corner of 54th and Madison, Neal eyed one of those scarce resources on 54th, toward Park Avenue. But on the other side of the street, another man (Kevin Bacon) spied the same cab, and the race was on. Avoiding obstacles as if running a steeplechase, the two men vied for the cab, but Neal tripped and fell. He was lucky he didn't get run over, but Kevin Bacon won the prize.

Walk west on 54th and stop across from the plaza just east of Madison Avenue.

37. 535 Madison Avenue (at 54th Street). After his friends tried to set him up on a date, *Jeffrey* (Steven Weber) fled their apartment and raced up Madison Avenue. They finally caught up with him at the plaza of this building where, to the delight of onlookers, Jeffrey agreed to give the date a try. One of the onlookers was Camryn Manheim, who went on to play Eleanor Frutt on television's *The Practice*.

Cross Madison and stop at the first doorway on the north side of 54th Street.

38. 25 East 54th Street (same as 532 Madison Avenue). Staking out a gift shop across the street (which is no longer there), Detective Buddy Manucci (Roy Scheider) stood just inside this doorway, waiting for the proper moment to strike, at the beginning of *The Seven-Ups*. After a few minutes, Buddy crossed the street, entered the store, and the sting operation was under way.

Walk west on 54th and turn left on Fifth Avenue. Stop at the building on the southeast corner of 53rd and Fifth.

39. HarperCollins Building. 10 East 53rd Street. Attorney Dan Gallagher (Michael Douglas) attended a Saturday meeting here while his wife and daughter were out of town. At the meeting, he met Alex Forrest (Glenn Close), with whom he later had dinner. Anyone who has seen the movie will never forget the *Fatal Attraction* that evolved from this encounter.

The building also housed the office of Larry (Woody Allen), who was an editor for Marsha (Anjelica Huston) in *Manhattan Murder Mystery*.

Continue south on Fifth Avenue and turn right on the north side of 52nd Street. Walk west and stop in front of the famed 21 Club (with the horse jockeys lining the front steps).

40. The 21 Club. 21 West 52nd Street. This cinematic regular has seemingly been around forever. In *Sweet Smell of Success*, ruthless tabloid columnist J. J. Hunsecker (Burt Lancaster) held court at his usual table inside with the likes of senators, aspiring singers, and sleazy press agent Sidney Falco (Tony Curtis).

Fresh from the success of his first "tip" to *Wall Street* powerhouse Gordon Gecko (Michael Douglas), Bud Fox (Charlie Sheen) met Gordon for a power lunch here. After recommending the steak tartare, Gordon gave Bud a check for $1 million to invest, in what looked like the beginning of a beautiful friendship.

In the lounge area near the front of the restaurant, another power meeting was taking place. Melanie Parker (Michelle Pfeiffer) sat having drinks with her boss and clients in *One Fine Day*. But Melanie grew increasingly anxious, knowing that the longer she sat there, the less likely she would be able to get the kids to their end-of-the-season soccer game in Central Park.

As the 21 Club is a popular place for meetings and celebrations, Laurel Ayres (Whoopi Goldberg) set up a meeting here involving her partner, the fictional Robert S. Cutty, in *The Associate*.

Carol (Diane Keaton) and Larry (Woody Allen) took a break from solving their *Manhattan Murder Mystery* to celebrate the birthday of their son, Nick (Zach Braff), here.

They were old beyond their years, although not necessarily any wiser for it. In *Metropolitan*, two confirmed city dwellers from families of means, Serena (Elizabeth Thompson) and Tommy (Edward Clements), had drinks here, a place more accustomed to serving an earlier generation. Among other things, they discussed how Tommy had saved every letter that Serena had sent him.

———•◆•———

Return to Fifth Avenue, turn right, and walk south until you reach the statue of Atlas holding up the world, between 50th and 51st Streets.

41. 630 Fifth Avenue. The Atlas Statue. Journalist Phil Green (Gregory Peck) stood before this statue with his son, Tom (Dean Stockwell), in *Gentleman's Agreement*. Phil explained that Atlas was holding the world up on his shoulders, something Phil knew a little something about, as he was pretty much doing the same.

Peter Fallow (Bruce Willis) and Albert Fox (Clifton James) exited this building discussing the story of the hit-and-run incident in the Bronx. By time they reached the statue of Atlas, Fox had pretty much convinced Peter that there was a great book in the incident, and that the book could salvage Peter's career. Fox was right on both counts. The movie was *The Bonfire of the Vanities*.

Most people stand at the foot of this statue and can't help but admire Atlas, his physique and his strength. But Hercules (Arnold Schwarzenegger) was not like most people. In *Hercules in New York* (a must-see for fans of the bodybuilder-turned-actor-turned-politician), Hercules noted that the statue was not a very good likeness of Atlas. Hercules was in a position to know.

———•◆•———

St. Patrick's Cathedral is right across Fifth Avenue from you. Many parades pass this landmark, but only one gets people to don their Easter bonnets.

42. In front of St. Patrick's Cathedral. Fifth Avenue. Easter is traditionally the day when people put on their very best clothes, adorn themselves with the most lavish of bonnets, and saunter along with their loved ones, friends, and strangers, passing this spot. Among the throngs marching in the *Easter Parade* were Don Hewes (Fred Astaire) and Hannah Brown (Judy Garland).

———•◆•———

Turn right and head south one block. Saks, the large department store, will be directly across Fifth Avenue from you.

43. Saks Fifth Avenue. 611 Fifth Avenue. It was the night before Christmas, and neither Frank (Robert De Niro) nor Molly (Meryl Streep) had finished their holiday shopping. Along with thousands of others who waited until the last minute, Frank and Molly came here to shop. They didn't know each other, and their paths hadn't yet crossed, but there were a few near misses, and it was only a matter of time before they were *Falling in Love*.

Professor Alcott (Greg Kinnear) was bringing Dora (Mena Suvari) to meet his parents, but first he insisted on buying her some new clothes. While shopping at Saks, Dora realized that Alcott didn't like her for who she was, but rather for what he wanted her to be. Once he lost Dora, Alcott became the *Loser*.

———•◆•———

Behind you is a city landmark, but before turning, imagine that a car pulls up to the curb.

44. Fifth Avenue, in front of Rockefeller Center. After an acting audition, Marjorie (Natalie Wood) stepped from the curb into a car driven by David (Martin Balsam). He wasn't Noel Airman (Gene Kelly), on whom Marjorie had once had a crush, but a lot of time had passed since then. At least for a while, not being with Noel was a good thing for *Marjorie Morningstar*.

———•◆•———

Now turn around and take in the splendor that is Rockefeller Center. If it is the Christmas holiday season, you may be treated to one of the most spectacular Christmas trees in all the world, as well as numerous other wonderful holiday decorations.

45. Rockefeller Center. Fifth Avenue (between 49th 50th Streets). Kevin (Macaulay Culkin) had just endured another battle with Marv (Daniel Stern) and Harry (Joe Pesci). As he stood here gazing at the Christmas tree (which won't be there if it isn't the season) and the skating rink below, Kevin prayed for the only thing

he wanted that Christmas—to be reunited with his family, in *Home Alone 2: Lost in New York*. As you can see, Kevin's wish was granted.

———◦•◦———

Note the building in front of you: the tallest structure around.

46. 30 Rockefeller Plaza. In this building were the offices of the Federal Broadcasting Company, where efficiency expert Richard Sumner (Spencer Tracy) and reference department head Miss Watson (Katharine Hepburn) first battled, then fell in love, in *Desk Set*.

Stan "King" Kaiser (Joseph Bologna) hosted *The Comedy Cavalcade*, which was filmed in this building. Benjy Stone (Mark Linn-Baker), a writer for the show, narrated, in *My Favorite Year*, his experiences the week that screen legend Alan Swann (Peter O'Toole) was the show's guest.

Another television show, *Twenty-One*, the focus of the *Quiz Show* scandals of the 1950s, was televised from studios within this building.

It is no longer the elite venue it was then, but in 1940, it was the place to go, and in *The Curse of the Jade Scorpion*, this is where George Bond (Wallace Shawn) was taken to celebrate his fiftieth birthday. During dinner, George and his colleagues were entertained by hypnotist Voltan Polgar (David Ogden Stiers). But his hypnotism of C. W. Briggs (Woody Allen) and Betty Ann Fitzgerald (Helen Hunt), two of George's colleagues, hid Voltan's criminal intent.

———

Find a safe vantage point from which to view the skating rink.

47. Rockefeller Center Skating Rink. A popular location that finds its way into movies time and again, the rink is at its most magical during the cold winter months, when skaters glide gracefully across the slick, glistening surface. When her brother, Adam (Cliff Robertson), told her he was going ice-skating with his "virtuous" friend Mona, Eileen (Jane Fonda) came here to find him, never imagining that, as intended by Adam, ice-skating was a euphemism. On one *Sunday in New York*, Eileen met a stranger on a bus who gallantly offered to help her find her brother. They came here, but, of course, couldn't find him. So Eileen and the stranger, Mike (Rod Taylor), decided to get acquainted at a table overlooking the skating rink.

His uncle wanted him to dump his girlfriend, Elizabeth (Margaux Hemingway), but Alby (Elliott Gould) hoped to borrow money from Uncle Benjamin (Sid Caesar) to open a Manhattan restaurant without giving in to that one demand. During a night on the town, Alby and Elizabeth came *Over the Brooklyn Bridge* and skated here.

Clearly a popular place for a date, this rink is also where Ann (Liv Ullman) and Peter (Edward Albert) came to discuss their relationship. In *40 Carats*, it had started in an idyllic overseas setting, and Ann thought it should end there, because she was so much older than Peter. But when they met up again in New York, Peter wanted things to continue and even confessed his love for her. Ann denied having the same feelings for him, but they both knew she was lying.

A few years later, another May-December romance seemed to be blossoming on the ice. In *Autumn in New York*, Will (Richard Gere) had almost put aside his bachelor ways to devote himself to Charlotte (Winona Ryder), his much younger girlfriend. As the weather turned colder and autumn inched toward winter, Will walked alongside as Charlotte skated, but when she collapsed on the ice, they knew their autumn was almost over.

———•·•———

Keeping the rink on your left, walk to the right and exit the plaza on 50th Street. If you look west, you will see an entrance to NBC Studios, near Sixth Avenue.

48. NBC Studios. Rockefeller Center. 50th Street Entrance. Having just gotten his sidekick fired for an antic that backfired, Howard Stern followed a furious Robin Quivers (both playing themselves) outside this NBC entrance onto 50th Street in *Private Parts*. Robin wanted Howard to quit in protest, but Howard argued that he could be more effective at winning her back her job by staying at the station.

———•·•———

Across the street from the NBC Studios is Radio City Music Hall.

49. Radio City Music Hall. 1260 Avenue of the Americas. One of his fondest and most vivid memories of childhood was when Aunt Bee (Dianne Wiest) and her boyfriend took Joe (Seth Green) to Radio City Music Hall. Such an outing was a rare occurrence for Joe and his family, and it happened in *Radio Days*.

Poor Joe. He had to attend a show at Radio City along with everyone else who had a ticket for that evening's performance. Not so for little orphan *Annie*. Thanks to her extreme great fortune in falling into the lap of the ultra-wealthy Oliver "Daddy" Warbucks (Albert Finney), Annie (Aileen Quinn) was treated to a command performance here, along with the beautiful Grace (Ann Reinking), after Daddy Warbucks rented out the place.

Look across 50th to the parking garage, just west of where you are.

50. Rockefeller Center Garage. 41 West 50th Street. There was a *Saboteur* on the loose, and Barry Kane (Robert Cummings) was the primary suspect. He was taken by car into this garage and then upstairs to the offices of American Newsreel, Inc. But then the shooting started, and Barry fled, free to find the real criminal (Norman Lloyd) before it was too late.

Walk north one block. The Time Warner building will rise before you.

51. 75 Rockefeller Plaza. He was doing okay, but with the expenses piling up, Tommy (Gregory Peck), *The Man in the Gray Flannel Suit*, knew that he had to do better. Tommy came here for an interview with the United Broadcasting Corporation and got the job, but soon learned that a part of his past was about to catch up to him.

You have now reached the end of **Walking Tour 7: Midtown.**

THE UN AND BEYOND

E. 72ND ST.

LEXINGTON AVE.

THIRD AVE.

SECOND AVE.

FIRST AVE.

YORK AVE.

E. 59TH ST.

MADISON AVE.

PARK AVE.

EAST RIVER

E. 42ND ST.

Walking Tour 8
THE UN AND BEYOND

Walking Tour 8: The UN and Beyond threads its way through several neighborhoods, covering just enough locations in each to give TourWalkers a taste of what each has to offer. From the elegance of the lower portion of the Upper East Side, to the hidden serenity of Beekman Place, to the city-within-a-city named for the Tudor-style architecture that predominates its structures, **Walking Tour 8: The UN and Beyond** will not fail to deliver.

The first stop on **Walking Tour 8: The UN and Beyond** is located at 769 Madison, just south of 66th Street.

1. Krizia. 769 Madison Avenue. Two killers were out for their *15 Minutes* of fame, and Daphne (Vera Farmiga), a witness to the first murder, worked here at the fictional Ludwig's Hair Salon. Minutes before Detective Eddie

Flemming (Robert De Niro) and arson investigator Jordy Warsaw (Ed Burns) showed up to question her, the killers, Emil (Karel Roden) and Oleg (Oleg Taktarov), had paid her a visit and warned her not to talk. Or else.

Walk south on Madison and stop across from La Goulue, just south of 65th Street.

2. La Goulue. 746 Madison Avenue. Her marriage failed, but Judith (Holly Hunter) did her best to get on with her life. She came here for dinner by herself, reading Edith Wharton's *The House of Mirth*. Noticing the people around her enjoying themselves, she realized the gaping hole that existed in her life and resolved that soon she, too, would be *Living Out Loud*.

Continue south on Madison and turn left on the north side of 64th Street. Walk east until you are in front of the Plaza Athénée Hotel.

3. Plaza Athénée Hotel. 37 East 64th Street. Renamed the Grand Mark, this is where Mr. Mersault (John Cleese), the hotel concierge, made life miserable for *The Out-of-Towners,* Henry (Steve Martin) and Nancy (Goldie Hawn), during their stay in New York, and vice versa.

Continue east on 64th past Lexington Avenue and stop at 165 East 64th Street.

4. 165 East 64th Street. She was young, beautiful, and more than a little naïve. And much to her dismay, she became involved with a smooth-talking married man, John (Jason Robards), who convinced her to let him pay for her apartment here as long as he could stay *Any Wednesday*, while his wife thought he was traveling. It was the perfect arrangement for John. But eventually Ellen (Jane Fonda) realized she was missing out on something, and she had to choose between the married man and Cass (Dean Jones), an available suitor.

Return to Lexington, turn left, and walk south to 63rd Street. The Barbizon Hotel is on the southeast corner.

5. Barbizon Hotel. 140 East 63rd Street (at Lexington Avenue).

With his days of boxing behind him, Jake LaMotta (Robert De Niro), the now pudgy *Raging Bull*, sat in his dressing room in this hotel, where he was the featured performer in "An Evening With Jake LaMotta," reading the works of famous authors like Shakespeare and Tennessee Williams. In a poignant scene, we see that nothing lasts forever. Except the works of the authors, perhaps.

Turn right on 63rd and walk west to the west side of Park Avenue. Turn left on Park and walk south until you reach the Regency Hotel, between 61st and 62nd Streets.

6. Regency Hotel. 540 Park Avenue.

Things weren't easy for Frankie (Ed Harris). While trying to manage his illicit business operations, he had to deal with a bad seed like Terry (Sean Penn), who was dating his daughter Kathleen (Robin Wright). Frankie came to talk to Kathleen, who worked here, in hopes of convincing her to choose another guy, in *State of Grace*.

Continue south to 60th Street and turn left. Walk east to Lexington Avenue. Bloomingdale's covers the entire block, beginning at Lexington and 60th.

7. Bloomingdale's. 1000 Third Avenue.

It was the night before Christmas, and both Jonathan (John Cusack) and Sara (Kate Beckinsale) had left some shopping to the last minute. They found themselves vying for the same pair of gloves at a counter in this store, but had no idea how that chance encounter would soon have them thinking about things other than Christmas: things like fate, chance, destiny, and *Serendipity*.

Fed up with life in the Soviet Union, Vladimir (Robin Williams), a musician with a Russian circus that came here for a quick shopping trip before returning to Moscow, decided to defect in the store. Vladimir decided to make New York City his *Moscow on the Hudson*.

Fans of the television show *Friends* will remember that Rachel (Jennifer Aniston) worked here at Bloomingdale's for a while.

Turn and walk south on Lexington until you reach 53rd Street. On the southeast corner is 599 Lexington.

8. 599 Lexington Avenue (at southeast corner of 53rd Street). The offices of Moramax, the corporation run by two scions of *Big Business*, Sadie (Bette Midler) and Rose (Lily Tomlin), who were also, remarkably, twins, were located in this building.

Walk south one more block and look for a subway grating near the northwest corner of Lexington and 52nd Street.

9. Lexington Avenue and 52nd Street. Subway Grating. Legend has it that this scene was reshot in Hollywood because the original filming caused too great a commotion. On this corner, The Girl (Marilyn Monroe) stood on a subway grating in a sexy white skirt, and a gust of air from beneath the grating did the rest, creating an image that charmed Richard (Tom Ewell), the man with *The Seven Year Itch*, as well as filmgoers ever since.

Head east on 52nd Street until you reach Second Avenue. Look for Clancy's on the east side of Second, between 51st and 52nd Streets.

10. Clancy's. 978 Second Avenue. Still trying to figure him out, Amanda (Monica Potter) went to dinner with mystery man Jim (Freddie Prinze, Jr.). But because she had already fallen *Head Over Heels*, her roommates kept an eye on things from a safe corner of the bar.

Return to 52nd Street and turn right. Walk east on 52nd to First Avenue. Walk north on First until you reach the Metropolitan Café, at 959 First Avenue, just south of 53rd Street.

11. Metropolitan Café. 959 First Avenue. Alby (Elliot Gould) owned a small place in Brooklyn, but he aspired to make his mark in Manhattan's restaurant world. With the help of his sophisticated, opinionated, and meddling Uncle Benjamin (Sid Caesar), Alby had a chance to buy the restaurant that was located here, but his uncle's assistance came with significant strings attached. If Alby played by his uncle's rules, he would get his restaurant, in *Over the Brooklyn Bridge*, but he would have to dump his non-Jewish girlfriend, a heavy price indeed.

Turn and walk south on First to 51st Street. Turn left on 51st and cross First Avenue. Continue east as 51st Street becomes Beekman Place North. Turn right on Beekman Place and stop at number 3, on your left, just before Mitchell Place.

12. 3 Beekman Place. She coaxed the blues right out of the horn. She charmed the husk right off of the corn. To her nephew Dennis (Bruce Davison), who moved in with her, she was Auntie Mame (Lucille Ball). To the rest of us, she will always be *Mame*, and she lived here.

Continue to Mitchell Place and turn right. Walk down the hill and cross to the west side of First Avenue. Turn left and walk south on First until you are across from the United Nations.

13. United Nations. General Assembly Building. First Avenue and 45th Street. He fled the clutches of the men who mistook him for a man named George Kaplan yet again, and came here to find Lester Townsend, who worked for Unipol. Roger Thornhill (Cary Grant) had reason to believe that Townsend was connected to his kidnapping, but a few minutes later Townsend (Philip Ober) lay dead with a knife in his back, and Roger was the chief suspect in the murder. Heading *North By Northwest*, he was on the run again.

In the first film to actually use the UN's interior locations, Silvia Broome (Nicole Kidman), *The Interpreter*, overheard an assassination plot, and FBI agent Tobin Keller (Sean Penn) was assigned to protect her.

Continue south on First until you reach 43rd Street. The United Nations Secretariat Building rises high above the East River, just across First.

14. United Nations. Secretariat Building. The home of diplomacy and intrigue, often exist-

ing side by side, the United Nations was presided over by Sec-retary-General Dou-glas Thomas (Donald Sutherland) and his assistant, Eleanor (Anne Archer), in *The Art of War*. Inside, some people wanted to bring about a trade agreement with China, while others wanted to prevent it. And it fell to Neil Shaw (Wesley Snipes), who of-ficially didn't exist, to figure out who was on which side and to keep things running smoothly.

Turn from the Secretariat and climb the stairs that lead from Ralph Bunche Park. At the top of the stairs, turn and observe the street at the end of Ralph Bunche Park.

15. Tudor Place at 43rd Street, overlooking First Avenue. From this vantage point, artist David Shaw (Viggo Mortensen) watched Emily Taylor (Gwyneth Paltrow), with whom he was having an affair, standing with her husband, Steven (Michael Douglas), and sharing more ap-parent affection than David had expected to see, in *A Perfect Murder*.

Turn to the right and walk south on Tudor Place. Stop when you reach number 45.

16. 45 Tudor Place. While evading *U.S. Mar-shals*, who were hot on his trail, Mark Sheridan (Wesley Snipes) rented an apartment in this building, which afforded him an unimpeded view of the United Nations across the street.

Continue south on Tudor Place and stop on the bridge that crosses 42nd Street.

17. Tudor Place, above 42nd Street. Atop this overpass, Rollie Tyler (Bryan Brown) stood with Colonel Mason (Mason Adams) and discussed whether Rollie would participate in the "fictitious" murder of DiFranco (Jerry Orbach), an organized crime kingpin, in *F/X*.

Continue in the same direction a short distance. Tudor Tower will be on your left.

18. Tudor Tower. 25 Tudor Place. Allen Bauer (Tom Hanks) had a thriving produce business but lacked a meaningful relationship with anyone except his brother, Freddie (John Candy). Then along

came Madison (Daryl Hannah), who made a big *Splash* in Allen's life. Allen's apartment was in this building, and for a while Madison lived with him.

Return to the bridge that crosses 42nd Street and look east, beyond First Avenue.

19. Robert Moses Playground. 42nd Street and FDR Drive. In her case, having *Love With* *the Proper Stranger* left Angela (Natalie Wood) pregnant. Not cut out to be a father, Rocky (Steve McQueen) still wanted to do the right thing, which meant borrowing money from his parents to help Angela "take care of" the problem. He brought her to this park, where his parents were spending the afternoon with friends, but when Angela's father and brothers showed up, Rocky grabbed her, and they fled to the relative safety of a nearby building.

Walk on either side of the bridge that spans 42nd Street, west, and descend the staircase that leads down to 42nd. Continue east on 42nd and stop at the News Building, at 220 East 42nd Street, just west of Second Avenue.

20. The News Building. 220 East 42nd Street. In *Superman*, this building housed the "Daily Planet," the paper that employed Clark Kent (Christopher Reeve), Lois Lane (Margot Kidder), cub reporter Jimmy Olson (Marc McClure), and editor Perry White (Jackie Cooper).

You have now reached the end of **Walking Tour 8: The UN and Beyond.**

Walking Tour 9
THE THEATER DISTRICT

UPTOWN

WEST SIDE

EAST SIDE

DOWNTOWN

W. 57TH ST.

TENTH AVE.

NINTH AVE.

EIGHTH AVE.

BROADWAY

SEVENTH AVE.

AVE. AMERICAS

27 28

29 30 33 34

26 31

32

25
24

23 22

19 18 21
20
17
16 15
12 13 14 3
9 10 11 4
6 5
1

8 W. 42ND ST. 2
7

Walking Tour 9
THE THEATER DISTRICT

Many cities have a street named Broadway, but only New York has BROADWAY. On any given night, the buzz and excitement that electrify this area thirty minutes before curtains go up in the theaters has to be experienced to be believed. A great cross-section of New York City's cultural offerings can be found within the confines of **Walking Tour 9: The Theater District**. From the thrill of a Broadway show to the underbelly of some of the less reputable dance clubs, from restaurants where the glitterati mingle to the home of the best overstuffed pastrami sandwiches money can buy. Whatever your tastes, whatever your inclinations, **Walking Tour 9: The Theater District** should entertain you during the next two hours.

Walking Tour 9: The Theater District begins at the intersection of 42nd Street and Seventh Avenue, smack in the middle of what is known throughout the world as Times Square. Find the southwest corner of Seventh Avenue and 42nd Street. Then before you go anywhere else, look all around and take in the splendor that is Times Square. Not quite as colorful as it was before the so-called Disneyfication in the 1990s, the area still exemplifies the startling cultural diversity that can be found by walking a block in any direction.

1. Times Square. Sky Masterson (Marlon Brando), Nathan Detroit (Frank Sinatra), Nicely

Nicely Johnson (Stubby Kaye), Sister Sarah Brown (Jean Simmons), Miss Adelaide (Vivian Blaine), along with the Hot Box Girls, Benny Southstreet, Harry the Horse—even the names evoke a different era: a time of shady charmers, irreverent gamblers, and irrepressible dreamers. They wore bright-colored suits, spit-shined shoes, and bet on everything from sales of cheesecake to whether a certain guy could take a certain doll to Havana. This was the world created by Damon Runyon, and Times Square was where the people who gave life to *Guys and Dolls* spent their long days and endless nights.

Just west of the southwest corner of Seventh and 42nd is the New Amsterdam Theatre.

2. New Amsterdam Theatre. 214 West 42nd Street.

In Broadway's earlier days, when great showmen and impresarios ruled the night, the original New Amsterdam Theatre was where Flo Ziegfeld (William Powell), known as *The Great Ziegfeld*, staged many of his great "Follies."

From this corner, look east to the intersection of Broadway and 43rd Street.

3. Broadway and 43rd Street.

He was far from home, and his English was nonexistent, which makes sense, since he hailed from Olympus, and his voice was dubbed, but when Hercules (Arnold Strong, aka Mr. Universe, aka Arnold Schwarzenegger) was set loose in New York, anything was possible. In *Hercules in New York*, Hercules commandeered a horse-drawn carriage, turned it into a chariot, and the chase was on, past this intersection.

Towering above the same intersection is 1500 Broadway.

4. 1500 Broadway. Northeast Corner of Broadway and 43rd Street. Tabloid TV has always flirted with crossing the line of decency, but Robert Hawkins (Kelsey Grammar) went way over it. From his studio, which was located in this building, Hawkins aired his exclusive footage of the torture and subsequent execution of Detective Eddie Flemming (Robert De Niro) at the hands of camera-toting terrorists seeking their *15 Minutes* of fame. Irate over the airing of the tragedy, police stormed the building.

Walk north until you reach 1501 Broadway, between 43rd and 44th Streets.

5. 1501 Broadway. In *The Muppets Take Manhattan*, the fuzzy critters approached Broadway producer Martin Price (Dabney Coleman), hoping he would want to produce their show, "Manhattan Melodies." Mr. Price's offices were located in this building.

Turn back and walk south to the south side of 43rd. Turn right and walk west until you reach the Hotel Carter at 250 West 43rd Street.

6. Hotel Carter. 250 West 43rd Street. A far cry from the dilapidated mansion in Florida, this is where Finn (Ethan Hawke) nursed his *Great Expectations* after moving to New York.

Walk west to Eighth Avenue and turn left. The Port Authority Bus Terminal is one block to the south.

7. Port Authority Terminal. Eighth Avenue and 42nd Street. One of the major transportation hubs in Manhattan and one of the busiest bus stations in the world, this is where Florence Keefer (Judy Holliday) came with her daughter in

The Marrying Kind. The two of them boarded a bus bound for the town of Brewster, New York.

Fresh off the farm and eager to make his way in the big city, young Bradley Foster (Michael J.

Fox) took his first steps on the streets of New York when he exited the Port Authority bus terminal and emerged from this entrance in *The Secret of My Success.*

If you want to see where the soap opera "Southwest General" was taped in *Tootsie,* head south to 42nd Street, turn right, and walk west until you are between Tenth and Eleventh Avenues. If you don't wish to make the trip, you may be lucky to see stars walking on the street.

8. 460 West 42nd Street. National Video Center. They had become friends when Dorothy (Dustin Hoffman) joined the cast of "Southwest General," but after the truth was revealed, Julie (Jessica Lange) wanted nothing to do with Dorothy's creator. But even though Dorothy was not real, the feelings for Julie were. At the end of *Tootsie,* Michael (Dustin Hoffman) waited for Julie to emerge from the studio and convinced her to give their relationship a shot.

If you made the trip, return to Eighth Avenue and turn left. If not, turn back and walk north on Eighth Avenue. Stop at 44th Street and look at the northwest corner of Eighth and 44th.

9. Eighth Avenue and 44th Street. Northwest corner. It was just another crazy night in the life of paramedic Frank Pierce (Nicolas Cage). Responding to a call in *Bringing Out the Dead*, Frank showed up here and found a crazy man named

Noel (Marc Anthony) threatening to shove a broken bottle into his own neck. Luckily for all, Frank talked him out of it.

Turn right on 44th and walk east. Stop across from the Majestic Theater, at 247 West 44th Street.

10. Majestic Theater. 247 West 44th Street. Things had been going so well for C. C. "Bud" Baxter (Jack Lemmon). By letting his bosses use *The Apartment* he called home for their indiscretions, Bud was rising fast in the company. However, he hit a snag when his big boss, Mr. Sheldrake (Fred MacMurray), wanted to use the apartment for a rendezvous with Fran (Shirley MacLaine), on whom Bud had developed a huge crush. One evening Bud waited in front of this theater (*The Music Man* was playing) for Fran to show up for their date.

Continue east until you reach the Times Square institution Sardi's, at 234 West 44th.

11. Sardi's. 234 West 44th Street. Sardi's has traditionally been the place where those involved in Broadway opening nights come to party and wait for the first reviews to hit the newsstands. In *Forever Female*, that is exactly what people did while waiting for word on what the critics thought of the new show "No Laughing Matter." Sardi's was

used several times in the movie, and in one scene, after the show, aging star Beatrice Page (Ginger Rogers) was ushered into the restaurant to enjoy dinner with both her ex-husband and her current boyfriend, George, played by George Reeves (Superman in the classic television series).

Several decades later, playwright Ivan Travalian (Al Pacino) came here with his kids, as well as the producer, cast, and crew, to await the reviews of his new show "English With Tears." It was worth the wait, for the reviews made them all smile in *Author! Author!*

In another scene from *The Muppets Take Manhattan*, Kermit the Frog sneaked a framed picture of himself onto the wall. Then he sat at a table and waited for his friends to point out to the other restaurant patrons that he, Kermit, was among them.

———————

Look across the street to the Broadhurst Theater, at 235 West 44th.

12. Broadhurst Theater. 235 West 44th Street.

He thought it was just a typical day until some bizarre things started happening to him. Before long, he was uttering thoughts that weren't his own and doing things he didn't want to do. He was John Malkovich, and in *Being John Malkovich*, countless others were paying good money to live his life. There was a bright side to all the disruption, however. During a rehearsal at this theater for the play in which John was appearing, Maxine (Catherine Keener) showed up and took John into his dressing room, where they engaged in a little afternoon delight.

———————

A short distance to the east, and across the street, is the famed Shubert Theatre.

13. Shubert Theatre. 225 West 44th Street.

Every Broadway star wants fans, but nobody

wants *The Fan*. And that's exactly what Sally Ross (Lauren Bacall) had. She was starring in a play called "Never Say Never," and Douglas Breen (Michael Biehn) was making his move. He had wounded and killed to get close to her, and after the curtain had come down and the theater had emptied, it was just the two of them in a game of cat and mouse. But Sally was tough, and her number-one fan would soon learn who was the mouse and who was the cat.

Continue east until you reach Broadway. Look at the median between Broadway and Seventh Avenue.

14. 44th Street Median (between Broadway and Seventh). Their trip to Yankee Stadium having gone horribly wrong, the patients from Cedarbrook Hospital, Billy (Michael Keaton), Jack (Peter Boyle), Henry (Christopher Lloyd), and Albert (Stephen Furst), not what most people would consider *The Dream Team*, found themselves lost in New York without their chaperone. Caught in the rain, they made their way across this intersection, with an empty refrigerator carton over their collective heads.

Walk north to 45th Street and turn left. Walk west until you are across from the Booth Theatre, at 222 West 45th Street.

15. Booth Theatre. 222 West 45th Street. During a performance of *Carousel* here, Mayor John Pappas (Al Pacino) and powerful politico Frank Anselmo (Danny Aiello) met privately to discuss the shooting death of a small child and its larger ramifications in *City Hall*.

Walk slightly further to the west and stop at the Plymouth Theatre at 236 West 45th Street.

16. Plymouth Theatre. 236 West 45th Street.
Finally agreeing to play the role of a mother, Elise
Eliot (Goldie Hawn) appeared in the play "Of a
Certain Age" in *The First Wives Club*. The show,
which proved to be a hit, was staged at this the-
ater.

Across the street is the Music Box Theatre.

17. Music Box Theatre. 239 West 45th Street.
They were sleuths, not very good ones, but they
gave it their all. During a matinee performance,
Charlie (John Ritter) and Arthur (Blaine Novak)
staked out the front of this theater, waiting for the
people they had been hired to follow to exit the
building in *They All Laughed*.

Continue on to Eighth Avenue. Turn right
and walk north to the northeast corner of
Eighth and 46th Street. McHale's tavern should
be in front of you.

**18. McHale's. Eighth Avenue and 46th
Street**. In many cop movies, the officers often
unwind after their shifts at a local bar. This place
was frequented by Charlie (Woody Harrelson),
John (Wesley Snipes), Grace (Jennifer Lopez), and
other transit cops in *Money Train*.

Their lives had been changed forever: first, by a mischievous prank that went wrong, precipitating their being sent to reform school, and, second, by the brutality of Sean Nokes (Kevin Bacon), a reform school guard. When they found Nokes dining alone here one night, John (Ron Eldard) and Tommy (Billy Crudup) recognized him and exacted their revenge. After reminding him of his transgressions, they shot him dead in *Sleepers*.

Turn left, cross Eighth Avenue, and walk west until you reach Barbetta, at 321 West 46th.

19. Barbetta. 321 West 46th Street. Their affair in full swing, *Alice* (Mia Farrow) and Joe (Joe Mantegna) shared a late lunch here, with no other patrons in sight. After the meal, Alice shared her secret potion with Joe, and they both became invisible.

Behind you should be one of the Theater District's most popular eateries, Joe Allen.

20. Joe Allen Restaurant. 326 West 46th Street. Fresh out of rehab, Georgia (Marsha Mason) was hoping to make a new beginning, having finally put her alcoholic days behind her. But things got off to a rocky start when her ex, David (David Dukes), called her and asked her to meet him here. Over what both of them hoped would be a pleasant dinner, David revealed that the play he had written about their life together was going to be produced and that David wanted Georgia to play herself. Georgia was less than thrilled in *Only When I Laugh*.

Turn back and head east on 46th Street. Cross Eighth Avenue and continue east until you reach the Lunt-Fontanne Theatre, just west of Broadway.

21. Lunt-Fontanne Theatre. 205 West 46th Street. Frank White (Christopher Walken) was inside to see a show, but the police had other ideas. Confronting Frank in the lobby, several cops (including those played by Wesley Snipes and David Caruso) took the *King of New York* outside for a "talking to."

Walk to Broadway and turn left. Walk north until you reach Paramount Plaza, between 50th and 51st Streets.

22. Paramount Plaza. 1633 Broadway. He called a number of times, but never got Jerry Langford (Jerry Lewis) on the phone. Not appreciating such treatment from his idol, zealous fan Rupert Pupkin (Robert De Niro) stopped by to see Jerry, whose studio was in this building, claiming that he was "in the neighborhood." Although that tactic didn't work, when he left the building, he ran into fellow Langford fan Masha (Sandra Bernhard), and, together, in *The King of Comedy*, they began to hatch a plot they thought would satisfy them both.

Continue north to 51st Street and turn left. Walk west until you reach the Hotel Washington-Jefferson, between Eighth and Ninth Avenues.

23. Hotel Washington–Jefferson. 318 West 51st Street. The last of the *Small Time Crooks*, Ray (Woody Allen) had a brilliant moneymaking scheme: buy a store, dig from its basement into the bank two doors down, and remove all the cash. But Ray's plan had one major hitch: the store had just been purchased by a woman named Nettie Goldberg. After learning that Nettie lived here, Ray went to make her an offer. But when he arrived, he found an even bigger surprise: Nettie was none other than Benny (Jon Lovitz), another small-timer Ray

had known in prison. After hearing Ray's plan, Benny agreed to join Ray's gang.

Return to Eighth Avenue, turn left, and walk north to 52nd Street. Turn right and walk east on the south side of 52nd. Stop at 240 West 52nd Street.

24. 240 West 52nd Street. The band was Stillwater, and the members were *Almost Famous*. At the conclusion of their cross-country tour, the band had a celebratory dinner here, at a place called Max's Kansas City. During the dinner, William (Patrick Fugit) informed the members of the band that they were going to be on the cover of *Rolling Stone*. It was great news, but the news was not as good for one of the band's most loyal followers, Penny Lane (Kate Hudson). She would soon learn that all good things must come to an end.

Across the street is Roseland, a landmark in the world of music and dance.

25. Roseland. 239 West 52nd Street. Not every nightspot has a movie named for it, but this one does. In *Roseland*, a movie that took place almost entirely within this building, people gathered night after night, hoping to find someone to dance with, perhaps someone to love, and at the very least, just a little bit of happiness to help them through their humdrum lives.

———◆———

Turn back the other way and walk west on 52nd to Eighth Avenue. Turn right on Eighth, walk north, then turn right on the south side of 54th Street. Stop at Studio 54.

26. Studio 54. 254 West 54th Street. This is where it all happened on those boogie nights and last days of disco during the high-flying 1980s of flying-high New York. Here, Steve Rubell (Mike Myers) ruled with an iron fist, and bouncers decided whether an aspiring denizen of the night would be welcomed into the inner sanctum of paradise or left to pine away in the street, all brought to life in the movie *54*.

They went somewhere else earlier in the evening, but quickly learned that the punk scene wasn't for them. And with good reason, for these were the 1970s, when disco reigned supreme, and nowhere more so than here. Newly married, Vinnie (John Leguziamo) and Dionna (Mira Sorvino) came here to be with fellow lovers of the disco beat, but during the *Summer of Sam*, things didn't always work out the way it was hoped. The young couple was selected to join a group that was heading to an even more decadent New York scene, Plato's Retreat.

———◆———

Return to Eighth Avenue, turn right, and walk north to 55th Street. Turn right and stop across the street from Soup Kitchen International.

27. Soup Kitchen International. 259–A West 55th Street. Immortalized by a classic episode of the television show *Seinfeld*, this popular eatery is the real-life location of the "soup nazi" depicted on the show. If it's open, feel free to get on line

and enjoy the soup. But have your money ready, order, and quickly step to the left, and don't mention *Seinfeld*. Word has it the owner is not a fan, despite the publicity the show has generated for this storefront business.

Continue east to Broadway. Note the MONY Building on the east side of Broadway, between 55th and 56th Streets.

28. MONY Building. 1740 Broadway. Sheldon (Woody Allen) waited for Lisa (Mia Farrow) outside this building before bringing her to meet his overbearing, intrusive mother in the "Oedipus Wrecks" segment of *New York Stories*.

Continue east on 55th Street to Seventh Avenue. Turn right on Seventh and stop at the Carnegie Deli.

29. Carnegie Deli. 854 Seventh Avenue. In *Broadway Danny Rose*, a number of comedians (including Sandy Baron, Corbett Monica, Morty Gunty, and Jackie Gayle) sat around a table in this restaurant and told stories about hard-luck talent manager Danny Rose (Woody Allen). One of the comedians told the definitive Danny Rose story, which became the film's plot. At the end of the film, Danny caught up with Tina (Mia Farrow) in front of Carnegie Deli on a cold and bleak Thanksgiving Day.

In *One Fine Day*, Melanie Parker (Michelle Pfeiffer) and Jack Taylor (George Clooney) were rushing to get Melanie's son, Sammy (Alex D. Linz), and Jack's daughter, Maggie (Mae Whitman), to a soccer game in Central Park. If the kids didn't play in the game, they didn't get trophies. As they ran up Avenue of the Americas, having just left the 21 Club (see **Walking Tour 7: Midtown,** Location 40), little Maggie said she had to use the bathroom. As the next exterior shot clearly showed, Jack and young Sammy waited outside this restaurant while Melanie and Maggie were in the bathroom, presumably inside.

Across Seventh Avenue is an apartment building called the Wyoming.

30. The Wyoming. 853 Seventh Avenue. Linda (Andie MacDowell) lived here, where she enjoyed an occasional respite from the shenanigans and schemes of her on-again, off-again boyfriend, Gary (Andy Garcia), who thought he had *Just the Ticket* for making a quick buck.

Walk south on Seventh and stop at the Stage Deli, halfway between 53rd and 54th Streets.

31. Stage Deli. 834 Seventh Avenue. Jeffrey Anderson (Kevin Kline) had been brought back to New York and into the cast of the soap opera "The Sun Also Sets" in order to drive his old flame Celeste (Sally Field) insane in *Soapdish*. While on the set, Jeffrey asked out the aspiring young starlet Lori Craven (Elisabeth Shue) and then took her here for dinner.

———•—•———

Across Seventh and one block south is the Sheraton New York Hotel.

32. Sheraton New York Hotel. 811 Seventh Avenue. High-priced call girl Elizabeth Black (Nancy Allen) had just left a customer at this hotel and, as she exited, found herself being followed by someone who looked eerily like the platinum blonde she had seen standing over the body of Kate Miller (Angie Dickinson) in the elevator in *Dressed to Kill*. The ensuing chase led to the subway. Fans of Dennis Franz (Detective Andy Sipowicz in television's *NYPD Blue)* will find him playing a familiar role in this movie— that of a cop.

———•—•———

Return to 54th Street and turn right. Cross Seventh Avenue and walk east until you reach the Ziegfeld Theater, at 151 West 54th.

33. Ziegfeld Theater. 141 West 54th Street. Named for the famed Broadway showman, this theater is the site of many movie premieres, including one for the film "The Liquidator," starring Nicole Oliver (Melanie Griffith), in the movie *Celebrity*.

———•—•———

Continue east on 54th until you reach the Hilton Hotel, just west of Sixth Avenue.

34. Hilton Hotel. Sixth Avenue and 54ᵗʰ Street. Much to the dismay of his friends and followers, *Malcolm X* (Denzel Washington), whose life was believed to be in danger, took a room here to get some work done.

———•—•———

You have now reached the end of **Walking Tour 9: The Theater District.**

Walking Tour 10
THE CHELSEA CIRCLE

W. 42ND ST.

W. 34TH ST.

W. 23RD ST.

W. 14TH ST.

NINTH AVE.

EIGHTH AVE.

SEVENTH AVE.

AVE. AMERICAS

BROADWAY

FIFTH AVE.

MADISON AVE.

PARK AVE. SO.

LEXINGTON AVE.

THIRD AVE.

Walking Tour 10
THE CHELSEA CIRCLE

Walking **Tour 10: The Chelsea Circle** weaves through several distinct neighborhoods, so a few words about each is probably warranted. It begins in Chelsea, a culturally diverse neighborhood with a thriving nightlife, blends into the bustling areas of Union Square, Irving Place, and Gramercy Park, each hosting a unique blend of residents and visitors, and emerges at the foot of the city's, and possibly the world's, most famous building, which gives New York State its nickname: the Empire State.

Walking Tour 10: The Chelsea Circle begins on Eighth Avenue and 21st Street in an area of Manhattan known as Chelsea. When you reach the intersection, note the Bright Food Shop on the northeast corner, at 216 Eighth Avenue.

1. Bright Food Shop. 216 Eighth Avenue. After getting flowers from an anonymous suitor and then spotting the florist Lewis (Christian Slater) standing beneath her window one night, Lisa (Mary Stuart Masterson) was understandably jumpy. She went to the flower shop to confront Lewis, but they ended up sharing a meal here in *Bed of Roses*.

Get to the northwest corner of the intersection and head west on 21st Street. Stop when you reach number 303.

2. 303 West 21st Street. Things were going well for Kate (Jennifer Aniston), but everything wasn't

Picture Perfect. In the eyes of her boss, Mr. Mercer (Kevin Dunn), they would go a lot better if Kate were in a stable relationship and more grounded. Rising to the challenge, she arranged to have Nick (Jay Mohr) pose as her fiancé for an important business dinner. Nick, who was from Boston, stayed with Kate in her apartment in this building. Unfortunately for Nick, however, he slept on the couch.

<hr />

Return to Eighth Avenue, turn left, and walk north. Turn right on the south side of 23rd Street and stop in front of the Chelsea Hotel.

3. Chelsea Hotel. 222 West 23rd Street. He may not have been to everyone's taste, but Elizabeth (Kim Basinger) was attracted to John (Mickey Rourke) and his sexual games and fetishes—until he crossed over the line. They were together *Nine 1/2 Weeks*, but after Elizabeth met John here, as per his instructions, for a tryst with another woman, Elizabeth realized it was time to rethink the relationship.

This legendary bohemian haunt played host over the years to such literary and musical luminaries as Eugene O'Neill, Dylan Thomas, Janis Joplin, Bob Dylan, and, at least until tragedy befell them, *Sid and Nancy*. Late one morning the desk clerk received a call about trouble in room

218

100. That morning the life of Nancy Spungen (Chloe Webb) had come to an end, and the life of punk rocker Sid Vicious (Gary Oldman) changed forever. The incident was real, and the film captured it all.

***

Continue east on 23rd Street. Stop at number 32, between Sixth and Fifth Avenues.

4. 32 West 23rd Street. Within this building were the corporate offices of MacMillan Toys, the company in which young Josh Baskin (Tom Hanks) climbed the corporate ladder pretty quickly for a thirteen-year-old boy, much to the delight of Mr. MacMillan (Robert Loggia) and Susan (Elizabeth Perkins), and much to the chagrin of Paul (John Heard), in *Big*.

***

Continue on to the intersection of 23rd Street and Fifth Avenue.

5. Intersection of 23rd Street and Fifth Avenue. In this intersection, biologist Niko Tatopoulos (Matthew Broderick) had a plan to lure the monster to this spot by dumping truckloads of fish into a huge pile. The plan worked, and *Godzilla* took the bait. However, he then moved destructively on, leaving Niko to come up with another plan.

In an odd twist that I can only presume was intended, in the movie *Armageddon*, a vendor stood along this very same intersection peddling small Godzilla toys, as the first wave of meteorites fell to Earth.

***

Turn left, cross 23rd Street, and stop in front of 200 Fifth Avenue.

6. 200 Fifth Avenue. The International Toy Center. He had torn up the private detective's report on the supposed infidelity of his younger wife (Nastassja Kinski) without even reading it, but then Claude Eastman (Dudley Moore) had second thoughts and paid an agitated visit to the private detective (Richard B. Shull), whose office was in this building, to request another copy in *Unfaithfully Yours*.

This building also housed the offices of the "New York Globe," the paper for which J. J. Hunsecker (Burt Lancaster) wrote his column in *Sweet Smell of Success*.

The lobby of this building is beautiful. I should know. I got married inside.

Look across Fifth Avenue to Madison Square Park.

7. Madison Square Park. Fifth Avenue and 23rd Street. The government was cracking down, and the likelihood of putting on a show was diminishing with each passing day. But in *Cradle Will Rock*, the playwright Marc Blitzstein (Hank Azaria) refused to give up. One hectic afternoon, he sat on a bench in this park, imagining the musical he was writing, while police rode by on horseback and hit people with their nightsticks. It was a surreal scene, indeed.

Turn right and walk south on Fifth Avenue. Turn right on the south side of 22nd Street and walk west until you reach Lola, at 30 West 22nd.

8. Lola. 30 West 22nd Street. After the pre-wedding celebratory dinner that was held here, the wedding was still on, because the groom, Lance (Morris Chestnut), had not yet learned that his fiancée, Mia (Monica Calhoun), had a somewhat romantic past with *The Best Man*, Harper (Taye Diggs). Meanwhile, Julian (Harold Perrineau, Jr.) and Shelby (Melissa De Sousa) had their own problems to discuss.

Return to Fifth Avenue and continue east one block to Broadway. Turn right on Broadway and walk south to the southwest corner of Broadway and 21st Street.

9. Metronome. 915 Broadway (at 21st Street). It started with an insult and embarrassment, then escalated all the way to murder. After a friendly dinner inside this restaurant turned deadly, John *Shaft* (Samuel L. Jackson) took up the case and pursued it even after giving up his police shield.

Dressed to the nines in white formal wear, thirteen-year-old Josh Baskin (Tom Hanks) attended his company's holiday party here. In a memorable scene, Josh, whose typical party had probably involved potato chips and "pin the tail on the donkey," could be forgiven for picking up baby corns and trying to eat the kernels the way one would eat corn on the cob. Josh may have been thirteen, but he had gotten *Big*. He left the party with Susan (Elizabeth Perkins).

Continue south on Fifth Avenue and stop across from number 85, between 16th and 17th Streets.

10. 85 Fifth Avenue (between 16th and 17th Streets). This building is where Lenny (Woody Allen) worked as a sportswriter in *Mighty Aphrodite.*

Head back north to 17th Street and turn right. Walk east on 17th (you will see Union Square Park to your right). Continue east on 17th and stop across from Barnes & Noble.

11. Barnes & Noble. 33 East 17th Street. Was Jerry (Mel Gibson) crazy, or was everyone really out to get him? Jerry had his own *Conspiracy Theory*, and after his purchase of *The Catcher in the*

Rye at this bookstore set off an alarm that had him quickly chased by men on motorcycles and in helicopters, it appeared that he may have been right.

Continue east on 17th (you will cross Park Avenue South) and walk east until you reach Irving Place. Turn left on the east side of Irving Place and walk north to 18th Street. Pete's Tavern is on the northeast corner of Irving Place and 18th.

12. Pete's Tavern. 129 East 18th Street (at Irving Place). One of the oldest pubs in Manhattan, dating back to when Abraham Lincoln

was president, Pete's is where Jerry Ryan (Robert Mitchum) stopped in to have a drink in *Two For the Seesaw* after spending a long day walking around the city. He had come to New York to practice law after his marriage had fallen apart, but it was going to take more than a couple of drinks to ease his pain.

———•◆•———

Walk north on Irving Place and turn right on 19th Street. Stop at the entrance to the first building off the corner.

13. 78 Irving Place. Having just moved down from Boston to head up the mergers and acquisitions department of Petty Marsh, Katharine Parker (Sigourney Weaver) stayed in the home of her parents, located here, in *Working Girl*.

———•◆•———

Continue north to Gramercy Park South (same as 20th Street) and turn left. Walk west until you reach the National Arts Club, at 15 Gramercy Park South.

14. National Arts Club. 15 Gramercy Park South. A valuable painting had already been stolen from the Metropolitan Museum of Art, and insurance investigator Catherine Banning (Rene Russo) was on the case. At a fundraiser here, she introduced herself to billionaire businessman Thomas Crown (Pierce Brosnan) and told him

she knew far more about him than he would have expected, including his suspected involvement in the museum theft. All this piqued his interest, and their affair was not far off on the horizon in *The Thomas Crown Affair*.

Certain that her neighbor Paul House (Jerry Adler) had killed his wife, Lillian (Lynn Cohen), bored housewife Carol (Diane Keaton) sat in the window facing this street, discussing this *Manhattan Murder Mystery* with Ted (Alan Alda). Moments after Ted left, Carol was certain she saw the supposedly deceased Mrs. House pass by the window on a public bus. The revelation convinced her husband, Larry (Woody Allen), to join her in a stakeout.

Walk west the short distance to Gramercy Park West, and north on Gramercy Park West to Gramercy Park North (the same as 21st Street). Gramercy Park will be on your right as you walk. Turn right on Gramercy Park North and stop across from the Gramercy Park Hotel, at 52 Gramercy Park North and Lexington Avenue.

15. Gramercy Park Hotel. 52 Gramercy Park North. Their tour ended in New York, and the members of the band Stillwater checked in here in *Almost Famous*.

Walk north on Lexington Avenue and turn left on 24th Street. Walk west one block to Park Avenue South. Look at the massive building on the northwest corner.

16. 330 Park Avenue South (at 24th Street). This building is where Daryll (William Hurt) worked as a janitor in *Eyewitness*. After he discovered a corpse one night, people starting paying attention to him, and one in particular, television reporter Tony Sokalow (Sigourney Weaver), caught his fancy. Tony showed up to court a story of murder. Daryll turned the tables and courted her.

Perry (Robin Williams) suffered a horrible tragedy: his wife was gunned down in a trendy

restaurant right before his eyes. Since that time, he lived a nomadic life and had little reason to live. The only thing that kept him going was Lydia (Amanda Plummer), who worked behind the gates of this building. Every day like clockwork, Perry staked out the front of the building to watch his beloved Lydia leave for lunch. One day Jack Lukas (Jeff Bridges), his newfound friend and possible savior, waited with him in *The Fisher King*.

Turn right and walk north on Park Avenue South. At 28th Street, turn left and cross to the west side of the street.

17. Park Avenue South and 28th Street. Subway entrance on Southwest Corner. A subway train had been hijacked, and the cops raced to get the ransom money before it was too late. In *The Taking of Pelham One, Two, Three*, they took the money and descended this staircase to the subway and the hijackers somewhere down below.

———◆◆———

Walk west on 28th Street and turn right on Madison Avenue. Walk north on Madison and stop when you reach 33rd Street, or sooner if you get a good view of the Empire State Building towering overhead on your left.

18. Empire State Building. 350 Fifth Avenue. Once but no longer the tallest building in the world, the Empire State Building still reigns as one of the most impressive structures in Manhattan. As you admire this proud structure, make sure that you remain safely on the curb. Terry McKay (Irene Dunne) didn't, and she paid a heavy price for her lapse. Rushing to keep her rendezvous with Michel Marnay (Charles Boyer) on the pre-arranged day (July 1) at the pre-arranged time, Terry was looking up when the car hit her. In *Love Affair*, an increasingly despondent Michel waited on the observation deck high atop the building. As the day turned increasingly stormy, Michel wondered aloud if the woman he loved would ever show. And when she didn't, he finally left alone, not understanding what could possibly have gone wrong.

Had he been there years later, he could have waited with playboy Nicky Ferranti (Cary Grant), who similarly waited in vain for his shipboard paramour, also named Terry McKay (Deborah Kerr), to show up in *An Affair to Remember*.

For Terry, reaching the observation deck would have taken a Herculean effort that day, but for Hercules (Arnold Strong, aka Arnold

Schwarzenegger), such efforts came with the territory. With his new friend Pretzel (Arnold Stang), he came up here to admire the view at the end of *Hercules in New York*. But while Pretzel enjoyed his first visit to this spot, he lost sight of his friend, and when he went to find him, could not. Pretzel didn't know that "Herc" had been summoned back home to Olympus, his New York adventure at an end.

Years later, a planned rendezvous finally took place on the observation deck. Widower Sam Baldwin (Tom Hanks) flew from Seattle to New York to find his son, Jonah (Ross Malinger), who had set up a meeting between Sam and Annie Reed (Meg Ryan) atop this famed structure. Sam found Jonah, they hugged, they left. Luckily, Jonah had forgotten his backpack, and when they returned to retrieve it, Annie was standing on the deck, clutching the item. It looked like Sam's days of being *Sleepless in Seattle* had come to an end.

And speaking of coming to an end, *King Kong* came to his after climbing to the top of this building, clutching Ann Darrow (Fay Wray) in one paw and swatting at planes with the other.

Continue north on Madison and stop at number 211, between 35th and 36th Streets.

19. 211 Madison Avenue between 35th and 36th Streets. Morgan Court. This towering structure, which seems to cut the sky like a *Sliver*, was home to Carly (Sharon Stone), Jack (Tom Berenger), and the

building's Peeping Tom/owner, Zeke (Billy Baldwin).

Walk north to 36th Street and turn right. The Morgan Library will be slightly to the east, across 36th Street.

20. Morgan Library. 29 East 36th Street.

Coalhouse Walker, Jr. (Howard E. Rollins, Jr.), had been wronged by the New Rochelle Fire Department, and especially by Fire Chief Willie Conklin (Kenneth McMillan). Demanding justice—in truth, his only demand was that his car be cleaned and returned to him—Walker and some friends muscled their way in here and

waged a standoff, with the police covering the building, in *Ragtime*.

Return to Madison Avenue, turn left on Madison, and walk south to 34th Street. Turn right on 34th and walk west to the east side of Avenue of the Americas. Look across the avenue and south one block. The Manhattan Mall sits before you.

21. Manhattan Mall. 100 West 33rd Street.

Gary (Andy Garcia) came to pay a surprise visit to his ex-girlfriend Linda (Andie MacDowell) at the mall, where she worked in an electronics store. But she wasn't interested in talking, having all but given up on their relationship. Being a gambling man, Gary made Linda a wager. If he could convince a very cheap potential customer to buy a giant television set, Linda had to listen to what Gary had to say. A skillful salesman with the gift of gab, Gary made the sale and then his pitch to Linda. In *Just the Ticket*, their relationship had many such ups and downs.

Look across Avenue of the Americas to Macy's, once billed as the largest department store in the world. For all I know, it might still be.

22. Macy's. Herald Square. 151 West 34th Street.

In *Love With the Proper Stranger*, this is where Angela (Natalie Wood) worked, on the fifth floor, in the pet department. When her father and brothers came to pick her up in their fruit truck, she was embarrassed, but put such feelings aside, for that is what one does with family. Later Rocky (Steve McQueen), trying to make amends for his boorish behavior, greeted Angela out front, banjo in hand, with a sign that said BETTER WED THAN DEAD. Poor Angela was embarrassed yet again, but again she put such feelings aside, for that is what one does with one's future spouse.

Walk west on 34th Street and stop at Seventh Avenue. One block to your left, on the west side of Seventh, is one of the premiere sports and entertainment venues in the world.

23. Madison Square Garden. Seventh Avenue between 33rd and 31st Streets.

Eddie (Whoopi Goldberg) was an avid fan of the New York Knicks and came here to watch every home basketball game. During a promotional event sponsored by the team's new owner, Wild Bill Burgess (Frank Langella), Eddie sank a basket during halftime and was made the team's honorary coach for the second half of the game. But after the real coach, John Bailey (Dennis Farina),

had her thrown out of the arena, Wild Bill decided to get his revenge and made Eddie the coach on a full-time basis—a dream come true for any sports fan, and a reality for *Eddie*.

The Knicks were again the subject when Jamal Wallace (Rob Brown) convinced recluse William Forrester (Sean Connery) to leave his apartment to celebrate his birthday by attending a basketball game in *Finding Forrester*. But when they got separated on the way into the Garden, William became scared and disoriented, and experienced a vivid reminder of why he had stopped leaving his home. The anxiety attack sent the two from the Garden without watching the game. A few weeks later, Jamal was back here playing in a basketball tournament.

———

You may walk there if you wish, or if you squint, you may be able to see the main branch of the United States Post Office one long block to the west, at Eighth Avenue, and one block to the south, at 33rd Street. The building takes up an entire city block.

24. Post Office. Main Branch. Eighth Avenue and 33rd Street. He met his wife-to-be in Central Park and honeymooned in Atlantic City, but eventually had to return to his job here. Chet

Keefer (Aldo Ray) took a lot of ribbing from his colleagues for tying the knot, but because he was *The Marrying Kind*, he knew his days as a single man had been numbered, anyway.

You have now reached the end of **Walking Tour 10: The Chelsea Circle.**

Walking Tour 11
GREENWICH VILLAGE

Walking Tour 11
GREENWICH VILLAGE

Long considered the habitat for New Yorkers with the funkiest and most bohemian lifestyles, Greenwich Village is rich with winding streets, beautiful brownstones, and endless outdoor cafés that can satisfy the most diverse tastes from anywhere in the world. Home to thousands of college students, one of New York's premier outdoor gathering places, and the birthplace of the Gay Rights movement, the Village has it all. Even on long weekends when the rest of the city seems to clear out, the Village is always hopping, no matter the time of day or night.

Walking Tour 11: Greenwich Village begins at the northeast corner of Broadway and 12th Street.

1. The Strand. 828 Broadway (at 12th Street).

Ouise (Stockard Channing), Flanders (Donald Sutherland), and friends headed to this bookstore

looking for an autobiography of Sidney Poitier to find out if their mysterious visitor, Paul (Will Smith), was really the famed actor's son in *Six Degrees of Separation*.

———————

Walk south on Broadway and turn right on 10th Street. Walk west until you are across from the Devonshire House, at 28 East 10th.

2. Devonshire House. 28 East 10th Street. Newspaper editor Henry (Michael Keaton) returned home to this building one night to find emergency medical personnel tending to Martha (Marisa Tomei), his very pregnant wife, in *The Paper*.

———————

Continue west on 10th Street and turn right on Fifth Avenue. Walk north to the building on the right, just south of 12th Street.

3. 51 Fifth Avenue (at 12th Street). Fans of television's *Mad About You* might recognize this

building, with its distinctive colonnade outside each corner window on the second floor, as the home of Paul (Paul Reiser) and Jamie (Helen Hunt) Buchman.

———————

Walk to the corner of 12th Street and turn left. Cross Fifth Avenue and walk west until you are across from 31–33 West 12th Street, maybe a third of the way up the block.

4. 31–33 West 12th Street. Perhaps the secret to winning both an Emmy and an Oscar in the same year is to keep the location-shooting for your movie and television show close together. While husband Paul (Paul Reiser) was working on one of his many documentaries, Jamie Buchman (Helen Hunt) might have been sneaking out of their apartment, in the building we just left, to visit obsessive-compulsive Melvin Udall (Jack Nicholson) in the building before you now. In one memorable scene, Carol Connelly (Hunt) showed up at Melvin's apartment in a very wet, tight-fitting T-shirt. For the two damaged souls, the other was *As Good as it Gets*. And as it turned out, that wasn't half bad.

Walk back the other way to Fifth Avenue. Cross Fifth, turn right, and walk south on Fifth to the building on the northeast corner of Fifth and 11th Street.

5. 43 Fifth Avenue (at 11th Street). He lived in this building and did his best to teach Frenchy (Tracey Ullman) how to fit into high society. His name was David (Hugh Grant), but he wasn't all he claimed to be. Frenchy and her husband, Ray (Woody Allen), may have been *Small Time Crooks*, but David was a big-time crook.

Continue south on Fifth Avenue and make a left on 9th Street. Walk east on 9th to University Place. The Knickerbocker Bar & Grill should be across University Place, on the southeast corner of University and 9th.

6. Knickerbocker Bar & Grill. 33 University Place (at 9th Street). From high society scam artist to mobster wannabe, Hugh Grant knows this part of town pretty well. He was doing his best to impress and fit in with Frank (James Caan), his future father-in-law. Walking the walk and talking the talk (although his attempts at "fuhgeddaboutit" left a lot to be desired), Michael (Hugh Grant) came here for a "sit down" with a couple of tough characters. But for *Mickey Blue Eyes,* as he was sometimes known, something always seemed to be going wrong. When Michael saw his auction-house boss in the restaurant and his cover was about to be blown, he had no choice but to scream at the man and forcibly push him outdoors.

———

Continue south on University until you are half a block south of 8th Street. On your right should be a gated entrance to the Washington Mews. Assuming the gate is open, walk into the short, picturesque street and stop in front of number 14, on the left side of the street.

7. 14 Washington Mews. He had been given a glimpse of how his life would have turned out, had he married his college sweetheart. Realizing that having a loving wife and kids would have made him happier than all the wealth that his career brought him, Jack Campbell (Nicolas Cage) decided to find his old flame and see if his life could still take the correct turn. Tracking down Kate (Tea Leoni) to her office, which was located in this building, Jack showed up as she was about to move. He hoped to rekindle their love and become *The Family Man.*

———

Exit Washington Mews the same way you entered, turn right, and walk south to Washington Square North. Washington Square Park sits before you. Just south of you and to your left, across from the park, sits 100 Washington Square East.

8. 100 Washington Square East (between Waverly and Washington Place). Frank Serpico (Al Pacino) had a job—he was a cop—but took classes to better himself. One day after class,

Tour 11

Frank waited outside this building for Laurie (Barbara Eda-Young), then gave her a ride on his motorcycle. It wasn't long before *Serpico* and Laurie were an item.

Look across to the south side of Washington Square Park. You can see the tall, red brick building that is the Elmer Holmes Bobst Library jutting up above the trees.

9. Elmer Holmes Bobst Library. 70 Washington Square South. One of the mainstays of the prestigious New York University, this library is a good place to study. And study is what Kathleen Conklin (Lili Taylor) did in *The Addiction*. For one of her courses on human suffering, Kathleen spent many nights researching the subject, until she actually became a vampire and added to the suffering by killing people. Hey, don't blame me. I didn't write the script: I'm just telling you where it was filmed.

Turn right and walk west on Washington Square North. Stop in front of number 7.

10. 7 Washington Square North. Virgil (Val Kilmer) had been given the gift of sight, thanks to the devotion and urging of Amy (Mira Sorvino), but his sight, in *At First Sight*, was fleeting. Eventually reverting to blindness, Virgil still considered himself luckier than most and decided to do what he could to help others in need. Under the tutelage of Dr. Phil Webster (Nathan Lane), Virgil worked as a social worker in this building.

Continue west and stop across from the Washington Square Park Arch, at Fifth Avenue.

11. Washington Square Park. Fifth Avenue Entrance (the Arch). After driving together to New York City, Harry Burns (Billy Crystal) and Sally Albright (Meg Ryan) parted ways under the shadow of the Arch. Harry had said that men and women can't be friends, because sex always gets in the way. Sally told him how unfortunate that was, since Harry was the only person Sally knew in New York, where she was about to begin law school. They went their separate ways, and it would be five years before their paths crossed again, in *When Harry Met Sally...*.

It was back in the days before the park was closed to vehicular traffic, and cars could actually flow through what is now open only to pedestrians. His name was Harold Swift, his nickname was Speedy (Harold Lloyd), and his goal was to save the last horse-drawn trolley in New York from extinction. *Speedy* drove the trolley down Fifth Avenue and under the Arch, doing his best to stay one step ahead of the stereotypical bad guys, who were in hot pursuit.

Before you cross and enter the park, walk the

short distance west on Washington Square North until you reach number 21.

12. 21 Washington Square North (between Fifth Avenue and Washington Square West).

This elegant brownstone was home to the Sloper family: the strict, yet well-meaning Dr. Sloper (Albert Finney); the plain Jane of a patsy for unscrupulous suitors, Catherine (Jennifer Jason Leigh); and the kindly old Aunt Lavinia (Maggie Smith). In *Washington Square*, the Slopers lived here, and it was here that Morris Townsend (Ben Chaplin) did his best to win the heart (and the bank account) of Catherine. Protected from such a cad by her father, Catherine was destined to live a wealthy, but lonely, life.

———————

Cross Washington Square North and enter the park. Walk through or around the Arch and find the Performance Pit, just to the south.

13. Washington Square Park. Performance Pit.

It would be five years before Sally (Meg Ryan) was to see Harry (Billy Crystal) again, and eight years until Meg Ryan, playing Maggie, a jilted lover in *Addicted to Love*, would sit here and plot revenge with fellow jilted lover Sam (Matthew Broderick). A favorite of street performers, the circular Performance Pit is crowded

most weekends with magicians, jugglers, and the like. Among the dirty tricks that Sam and Maggie plotted were putting lipstick on a performing monkey and having him kiss the collar of Anton (Tcheky Karyo), for whom Sam's girlfriend, Linda (Kelly Preston), had jilted Sam. Another plot involved having kids squirt Anton with perfume from their water guns.

Interestingly enough, Meg Ryan wasn't the only one of the two to appear twice in a Washington Square Park movie scene. Years earlier, in *The Freshman*, Matthew Broderick, as Clark Kellogg, spotted Victor Ray (Bruno Kirby), the man who had stolen his luggage a few days before, nearby. Clark climbed out of a window and chased Victor through this park.

If you look hard enough, you may even see Steven Taylor (Michael Douglas) near the Performance Pit making a payoff of $400,000 to David Shaw (Viggo Mortensen), in return for David's silence about the attempted murder of Steven's wife, Emily (Gwyneth Paltrow), in *A Perfect Murder*.

In *Three of Hearts*, after her girlfriend, Ellen (Sherilyn Fenn), broke up with her, Connie (Kelly Lynch) was so distraught that she stood up and screamed aloud to the world what had just occurred. Ellen had hoped to avoid just such a scene, and it wasn't what those nearby were expecting to see, but it just went to prove that anything can happen in New York, and often does.

Not all scenes in and around the Performance Pit are verbal, and not all events are entertaining. In the stark film *Kids*, which depicted life among a reckless group of poorly supervised New York City kids, this area was a popular hangout for the gang that was the focus of the movie. In one particularly chilling scene, the kids beat a man within an inch of his life after only the slightest provocation, while onlookers did their best to pretend not to see.

In *The Butcher's Wife*, Marina (Demi Moore) tried to teach the affable yet uncoordinated Doc (Jeff Daniels) how to roller-skate inside the Performance Pit.

—————•◆•—————

As you turn, leaving the Performance Pit to others, look along the path that leads west from the Performance Pit, and you may find a bare-footed man, walking on the grass, showing the effects of having had a little too much to drink. Of course, you may see many such men. But look for one in particular.

14. Washington Square Park. Grass along Path. The honeymoon was clearly over, as Paul (Robert Redford) and his new wife, Corie (Jane Fonda), were fighting like cats and dogs. The snow was falling through the skylight in their fifth-floor walk-up, and Paul had a "big case in the morning," as he liked to remind Corie. Pushed to the brink, Paul got drunk and walked along here, *Barefoot in the Park*, until Corie came to retrieve him.

—————•◆•—————

With the Performance Pit behind you, you should be facing west. Start walking and bear left at the statue of Alexander Lyman Holley. Three asphalt mounds should be on your left. Continue until you reach Chess Table Alley.

15. Washington Square Park. Chess Table Alley (off MacDougal and West 4ᵗʰ). By watching Vinnie (Laurence Fishburn) and others play chess at these tables, young Josh Waitzkin (Max Pomeranc) developed both an understanding of, and a genuine flair for, the game. In *Searching for Bobby Fischer*, Josh's parents, Bonnie and Fred (Joan Allen and Joe Mantegna), were wary at first of their son's hanging around here, but eventually warmed up to the players and the area,

once they realized that all looked upon Josh as the next great chess phenomenon.

——•◦•——

Continue through Chess Table Alley and exit Washington Square Park onto MacDougal Street. Turn left and walk south on MacDougal until you are across from Caffe Reggio.

16. Caffe Reggio. 119 MacDougal Street. It was a tough day for John Shaft (Richard Roundtree), and it was going to get tougher. While sitting in this café sipping his espresso, a man came in and told him they had to go see a lady. But for *Shaft*, nothing was ever easy. A few minutes later, guns were blazing, and Shaft was hit.

Sometime after Shaft vacated his table near the back of the café, it was occupied by Larry (Lenny Baker), his girlfriend Sarah (Ellen Greene), Robert (Christopher Walken), and the rest of their gang, who made this place a frequent stop in *Next Stop, Greenwich Village*.

——•◦•——

Continue south on MacDougal and stop at Minetta Lane (across from Minetta Tavern).

17. Minetta Tavern. 113 MacDougal Street. He got his childhood friends acquitted of murder charges (no simple task, considering that he was the prosecuting attorney), and afterward

244

Michael (Brad Pitt) came here for a secret re-union with the defendants, John (Ron Eldard) and Tommy (Billy Crudup), reporter Shakes (Jason Patric), and childhood friend Carol (Minnie Driver) in *Sleepers*.

Although it was called "The La Trattoria," this was the place owned by Frank (James Caan) in *Mickey Blue Eyes*. And although it was a far cry from what he was used to in his world of auction houses and fine pieces of art, Frank's future son-in-law, Michael (Hugh Grant), did his best to fit in as one of the gang. Literally.

Jonathan Elliot (Jonathan Silverman) and his friends also frequented this establishment in the television show *The Single Guy*. I watched it, even if nobody else did.

Turn right on Minetta Lane and stop a short way down the street (Minetta Tavern will be on your left).

18. Minetta Lane (West of MacDougal Street). Adam Sandler has cornered the market on this little stretch of Manhattan. At a loss for how to entertain young Julian (Cole and Dylan Sprouse), with whose care he had been saddled, Sonny (Adam Sandler) finally hit on a surefire plan: while Julian looked on in delight, Sonny ran in to a moving car on this street and pretended to get hit. In *Big Daddy*, Sonny fell to the ground as Julian broke into laughter.

He had lost his magic flask (the one in which he was to capture his errant satanic brothers), but thanks to the intervention of Valerie (Patricia Arquette), flask and owner were together once

again. Soon afterward *Little Nicky* (Adam Sandler) and Valerie walked down this street, eating ice cream cones and getting to know each other.

———•◦•———

Return to MacDougal, turn right, and walk south to Bleecker Street. Le Figaro Café is on the southeast corner of Bleecker and MacDougal.

19. Le Figaro Café. Bleecker and MacDougal Streets. His conviction having finally been overturned after he had spent five years in prison, Carlito Grigante (Al Pacino) was anxious to pick up where his life had left off. That included getting re-involved with his onetime girlfriend Gail (Penelope Ann Miller) in *Carlito's Way*. They sat here, at a table near the window along MacDougal Street, and caught up.

———•◦•———

Turn right and walk west on Bleecker. When you reach Avenue of the Americas (same as Sixth Avenue), cross (carefully), and walk along Bleecker until you reach Carmine Street.

20. Bleecker and Carmine Streets. Northwest Corner. While he walked near this corner, bemoaning his rock-bottom social life, but admitting he was not yet ready for a relationship, Sam (Matthew Broderick) fantasized about his dream woman: a Norwegian who spoke no English, was in town for only two weeks, and was then flying to Burma to do relief work for the next five years. And as so often happens in the movies, and especially in *The Night We Never Met*, she appeared, in the guise of the lovely Inga (Dana Wheeler-Nicholson).

Turn right on Carmine and walk in a northerly direction until you reconnect with Sixth Avenue. Turn left on Sixth Avenue and walk north to 3rd Street and the Waverly Theatre.

Tour 11

21. Waverly Theatre. 323 Avenue of the Americas. Their mysterious visitor, Paul (Will Smith), had finally agreed to turn himself in to the police, in *Six Degrees of Separation*, but only if Ouise (Stockard Channing) promised to meet him at the Waverly and accompany him. But Ouise and her husband, Flanders (Donald Sutherland), delayed by traffic, got to the movie house too late: the police had already apprehended Paul.

This theater was also visible in the background of *Carlito's Way*. While Gail (Penelope Ann Miller) waited in the car across the street, Charlie (Al Pacino) went to a travel agency to buy the train tickets that would get them out of New York to finally start a new life. Of course, most people buy their train tickets at the train station, but who am I to argue with Al Pacino?

Continue north on Sixth Avenue. Stop when you are across from the basketball courts on the east side of the avenue.

22. Basketball Courts. Sixth Avenue, near West 4th Street. While riding around in a stretch limo, basketball superstar Stacy Patton (Malik Sealy) noticed a pickup game on these courts and decided to get in on the action. Because his new coach, Eddie Franklin (Whoopi Goldberg), had given him limited playing time for the Knicks, Patton got some practice by playing one-on-one here, until his mother came by to break up the game, in *Eddie*.

If there is not a pay phone just off the courts, at the curb, imagine there is one.

23. Sixth Avenue, just north of Basketball Courts. At another pay phone that doesn't exist in real life, hard-luck boxing promoter Harry Fabian (Robert De Niro) made a call to a Mr. Feldman around this spot in *Night and the City*. The purpose of Harry's call was to get boxing gloves for use in the matches he was promoting.

Continue north on Sixth Avenue and turn left on Waverly Place. Walk west and stop at Gus's Place, on the north side of the street.

24. Gus's Place. 149 Waverly Place. Late as usual and working on a story with a fast-approaching deadline, Henry (Michael Keaton) met his pregnant wife, Martha (Marisa Tomei), and her parents here for dinner. Distracted by the deadline and the cacophony caused by kids at a nearby table, Henry decided to skip dinner, leaving his wife quite unhappy with him, in *The Paper*.

Retrace your steps on Waverly and make a left onto Gay Street. Walk the short distance up Gay Street until you reach the white building on the right, just before the large "10" on the window.

25. 17 Gay Street. Carlito (Al Pacino) liked to do things his way. He followed ex-girlfriend Gail (Penelope Ann Miller) and found that she

lived in this building, down the steps leading from the curb. Pretty soon they were doing things *Carlito's Way*.

Continue on to 13 Gay Street.

26. 13 Gay Street. In the movie, the building looked much different, which makes it quite unlikely that the movie was actually filmed here, but the address is unmistakable. In *A Night to Remember*, 13 Gay Street is the building where the Troys (Loretta Young and Brian Aherne) came to live, only to uncover a murder plot.

Continue to the end of Gay Street and make a left on Christopher Street. Follow Christopher (it bears to the right) until you reach the Stonewall (the bar where the gay rights movement is said to have been born) on the right. Facing Stonewall, look at the building to the left and the steps leading down to a bar.

27. 55 Christopher Street. In *Jeffrey*, at this bar, which had a large "M" on its façade, Jeffrey (Steven Weber) ran into his friends Sterling (Patrick Stewart) and Darius (Bryan Batt), who had joined the Pink Panthers to prevent gay-bashing.

Continue on Christopher the short distance to Seventh Avenue South. Turn left and note the entrance to the subway station at Sheridan Square.

28. Sheridan Square. Seventh Avenue and West 4th Street. Subway Entrance. Things had not been going well for Jamie Conway (Michael J. Fox) in *Bright Lights, Big City*. His wife, Amanda (Phoebe Cates), had dumped him, and he had lost his job as a fact-checker at a prestigious magazine. Now, to top it off, he showed up at his apartment building to find his brother Michael (Charlie Schlatter) waiting for him. Panicking, Jamie headed for the relative safety of the subway and ran down these stairs.

He started out in Brooklyn, but it was *Next Stop, Greenwich Village*. Suitcases in hand, Larry (Lenny Baker) emerged from the subway, up these stairs, and crossed Seventh Avenue South. For Larry, the subway ride was the start of a new life in a new home.

Look across Seventh Avenue South to Village Cigars.

29. Village Cigars. 110 Seventh Avenue South. Later that night, or sometime soon after, Larry may have seen actress Alice Detroit (Dyan Cannon) standing on that corner, waiting for her late-night rendezvous with playwright Ivan Travalian (Al Pacino) in *Author! Author!* Alice was going to star in Ivan's play, but decided that they might be able to share more than just a professional relationship. Ivan apparently agreed, for when he received Alice's call, giving him only a few minutes to meet her on this corner, he dropped everything and ran. Guys will do that.

There is a doorway to the left of Village Cigars, leading up to a second-floor office.

30. 110 Seventh Avenue South. He may not have been the most successful attorney in the world, but somehow he still believed in doing the honorable thing. And thanks to Roger Baron (Robert Downey, Jr.), who was a *True Believer*, Edward J. Dodd (James Woods) was able to fight for what was right. His office was upstairs behind the door, to the left of Village Cigars.

Cross Seventh Avenue South (toward Village Cigars), turn left on the west side of the street, and head south. Turn right on Grove Street and stop at the restaurant on your left, on the corner of Grove and Bleecker.

31. Grove. 314 Bleecker Street. Harry (Woody Allen) walked along the red brick sidewall and into this restaurant. He sat down at a table with ex-girlfriend Fay (Elisabeth Shue) and suggested that they try again, but Fay had other ideas. She told him that she was getting married to Harry's onetime friend Larry (Billy Crystal) in *Deconstructing Harry*.

Look at the storefront diagonally across the intersection.

32. Storefront, Grove and Bleecker. This storefront served as the modest office of Laura J. Kelly (Debra Winger) in *Legal Eagles*. And when Tom Logan (Robert Redford) joined forces with her to solve a murder mystery, they spent a lot of time together here.

Continue along Grove Street and walk until you reach number 16, on the left, just past Bedford Street.

33. 16 Grove Street. Although her school was way up on the Upper East Side of Manhattan (see **Walking Tour 6: The Eastern Seaboard,** Location 6), and she wished her world would overlap with the world of concert pianist Henry Orient (Peter Sellers), Valerie Boyd (Tippy Walker) lived here with Isabel (Angela Lansbury) and Frank (Tom Bosley), who happened to be her parents, but not very good ones, as they were almost never home, in *The World of Henry Orient*.

━━━━◆◆━━━━

Turn to the left and look back up Grove Street. The building on the corner should look familiar.

34. 90 Bedford Street (at Grove). This exterior should be familiar to anyone who is a fan of

Friends, the hit television show. The apartments of Rachel (Jennifer Aniston), Monica (Courtney Cox), Chandler (Matthew Perry), and Joey (Matt LeBlanc) were located here.

━━━━◆◆━━━━

Walk to Bedford Street and turn right. You'll be heading in a southeasterly direction. Cross Barrow Street and turn left on Commerce Street. If you walk a few feet, you'll see the Cherry Lane Theatre.

35. Cherry Lane Theatre. 38 Commerce Street. *Godspell* was a movie, a rock opera, an inspirational anthem to a decade in America and to an era long since gone. It also contained scenes filmed all over New York. In one scene, the cast from the movie put on a skit, complete with piano music and film footage, inside this theater.

In *Mo' Better Blues*, this entire street was reconstructed to reflect a jazzier time in our history. The music venue Beneath the Underdog, where trumpeter Bleek Gilliam (Denzel Washington) was one of the featured performers, was located in what is now the Cherry Lane.

Return to Bedford Street, turn left, and walk one block to Morton Street. Turn right on Morton and walk until you reach number 66. It will be on your left, near the end of the block.

36. 66 Morton Street. It seemed like a great arrangement at the time, although one that only New Yorkers may fully understand. About to get married but unwilling to give up his rent-controlled apartment, real estate man Brian (Kevin Anderson) decided to rent out his apartment to two other people for two nights each. As with all well-laid plans, this one went awry. The movie is *The Night We Never Met*,

and the apartment was located upstairs in this building. A nosy neighbor often watched the goings-on from the window closest to the front door.

You have now reached the end of **Walking Tour 11: Greenwich Village.**

Walking Tour 12

THE LOWER EAST SIDE MELTING POT

Walking Tour 12
THE LOWER EAST SIDE MELTING POT

Walking Tour 12: The Lower East Side **Melting Pot** covers a part of New York that harbors a great confluence of lifestyles, from bohemian to grunge, from heavy metal to punk. Known for comparatively cheap eats and bars that cater to every whim imaginable, the Lower East Side has something for everyone. Be it pizza topped with crayfish, hot pastrami at midnight, or pickles by the barrel, the Lower East Side is where you can come to scratch such itches. **Walking Tour 12: The Lower East Side Melting Pot** doesn't have as many locations as some others, but this part of Manhattan has provided locations to a vast diversity of films.

Walking Tour 12: The Lower East Side Melting Pot begins at the northeast corner of Fourth Avenue and 9th Street.

1. Astor Place Subway Entrance. Although the movie ostensibly took place in Hell's Kitchen (Manhattan's far west side, in the 40s and 50s), the pivotal scene in *Sleepers* took place right here. Four young boys had a scheme where one of them would order a hot dog from a vendor and then run off without paying. The vendor would then give chase, leaving his hot-dog cart unattended, allowing the others to help themselves to the waiting hot dogs. Everything worked fine, but the boys decided to run off with the cart itself and left it dangling at the top of these subway stairs. When they lost their grip, the cart plum-

meted down the steps, injuring a man and changing all of their lives forever.

Finally trying to be more self-assertive, standing near this subway entrance, Paul (Jason Biggs) got up the nerve to ask Dora (Mena Suvari) to go with him to a rock concert. Although he had had a crush on her for a while, he knew he was considered something of a *Loser* and was surprised when she agreed to meet him at the concert after her job interviews.

Turn from the subway entrance and head north on the east side of Fourth Avenue. Turn right on 10th Street and walk east until you reach Second Avenue. The church known as St. Mark's in the Bowery should be on your left, and if you're lucky, some street vendors might be peddling their wares in front of the church in Abe Lebewohl Park.

2. 10th Street, west of Second Avenue. After his flask had been stolen, one of the devil's children, *Little Nicky* (Adam Sandler), found it being sold by an indignant street vendor (John Witherspoon) and tried to get it back. But he needed help, which he found in the person of Valerie (Patricia Arquette), who happened to come along at the right moment and worked her charm on the vendor. Nicky regained the flask and found a friend at the same time.

Turn right and head south on Second Avenue until you are across from 148 Second Avenue.

3. 148 Second Avenue. Up the few steps in this nondescript building, *Out-of-Towners* Henry (Steve Martin) and Nancy (Goldie Hawn) went to see if their daughter, who lived here, was home. But she wasn't, so their quest to find a place to stay continued.

Continue south until you reach the Ottendor-fer Branch of the New York Public Library.

4. New York Public Library: Ottendorfer Branch. 135 Second Avenue. This is where Lewis (Christian Slater) came to read to children and to watch as the children were read to in *Bed of Roses*.

Walk south to St. Mark's Place and turn right. Walk west a short distance on St. Mark's until you reach the building to the right of St. Mark's Deli (number 31).

5. Just to the Right of 31 St. Mark's Place. Five years after their heyday, the Ghostbusters were all off doing different things, as the crisis that had plagued New York dissipated. Ray (Dan Aykroyd) owned a bookstore called Ray's Occult Books on this spot in *Ghostbusters II*. But after the demons returned, Peter (Bill Murray) and Egon (Harold Ramis) paid a visit to Ray and convinced him the time had come to resume their ghost-busting heroics.

Return again to Second Avenue and turn right. Head south until you are across from the Orpheum Theatre, at 126 Second Avenue.

6. Orpheum Theatre. 126 Second Avenue.
He was still trying to balance his love life, which
he left behind in Connecticut, with his career
ambitions. His play, "Master of My Emotions,"
was opening here, thanks to the enthusiasm of
producer Carl Fisher (Tony Curtis), but playwright Jake (Eric Stoltz) only made things more
complicated by getting *Naked in New York* with
the play's leading lady, Dana (Kathleen Turner).

Turn back north and walk to St. Mark's Place.
Turn right on St. Mark's and walk east to First
Avenue. Turn north on First and stop at Coyote
Ugly, at 153 First Avenue.

**7. Coyote Ugly. 153 First Avenue (between
9th and 10th Streets).** This is the true location of
Coyote Ugly, the focus of the movie of the same
name. However, in *Coyote Ugly*, the bar's location

was moved to the meat-packing district in and
around 14th Street, Gansevoort Street, and Washington Street, many blocks west of here.

Continue north on First Avenue and make a
right on 11th Street. Head east on 11th until you
are across from the large school, halfway down
the block, on the north side of the street.

8. Junior High School 60. 11th Street (between First Avenue and Avenue A). The front of the school is actually on 12th Street, but Michael (Hugh Grant), or *Mickey Blue Eyes,* as he would soon be known, showed up here, where Gina (Jeanne Tripplehorn) was a teacher. With big plans for that night, Michael was anxious to get started.

Continue east on 11th Street and turn right on Avenue A. Head south on Avenue A until you reach 9th Street. At 9th, cross Avenue A and enter Tompkins Square Park. Follow the path as it curves to the right. You will soon come to a large sculpture adorning a water fountain.

9. Sculpture and Water Fountain. Tompkins Square Park. Off 9th Street and Avenue A. Finn (Ethan Hawke) had just arrived in New York and was taking a break from the sketching he was doing in this park. As he stooped to drink from the fountain, he was elated to learn that the tongue licking his face belonged to his lifelong

friend Estella (Gwyneth Paltrow) and not an aggressive squirrel. He would have done well to keep his *Great Expectations* in check, however, as he would learn later after accompanying Estella and her friends for drinks.

Continue south along the path and exit the park. Walk south on Avenue A and stop just before you reach 7ᵗʰ Street. Imagine a fountain in this corner of the park.

10. Tompkins Square Park (Avenue A and 7ᵗʰ Street). In order to prevent the detonation of a bomb, John McClain (Bruce Willis) and Zeus

(Samuel L. Jackson) struggled to solve a riddle involving jugs and water from the fountain that is not there in real life, in *Die Hard With a Vengeance*.

Turn left on 7ᵗʰ Street and walk east until you reach the near corner of Avenue B.

11. Avenue B and 7ᵗʰ Street. Corner Bar. Mick Dundee (Paul Hogan) was out for a night on the town, and he and a cabdriver who had just gotten off duty came here to hoist a few in *"Crocodile" Dundee*. Outside the bar, Mick defended the honor of two ladies. Unbeknownst to Mick, however, the ladies were hookers, and the man he belted was their pimp.

Return to Avenue A and turn left. Walk south until you are across from Two Boots Pizza, between 3ʳᵈ and 4ᵗʰ Streets.

12. Two Boots Pizza. 37 Avenue A. The movie was *Hi-Life,* and bartender Ray (Campbell Scott) was walking around the neighborhood collecting money other bartenders had borrowed from him. He ended up here, engaged in a heated discussion with a grumpy Santa Claus (Dean Cameron), and the two of them spilled out onto the street, fighting. However, no matter how much I like the pizza here (it is terrific), I must nominate this location for a NitPick. Why? Because the neighborhood Ray worked in was the Upper West Side (see **Walking Tour 2: Central Park West,** Location 26), and how he ended up down here remains a mystery. In fact, when the police broke up the fight, they reported it as occurring on Amsterdam Avenue at 84th Street. Unfortunately, poetic license provides no protection against the NitPick label.

Continue south on Avenue A until you reach East Houston Street. Turn left and walk east on East Houston until you reach Suffolk Street. Cross East Houston. Meow Mix should be on the corner of East Houston and Suffolk.

13. Meow Mix. East Houston and Suffolk Streets. Comic book creator Holden McNeil (Ben Affleck) thought he had finally met the ideal woman. She invited him here one night to hear her sing. Holden was smitten, but he didn't yet have all the facts. That all changed at this bar, where Holden learned that Alyssa (Joey Lauren Adams), the object of his crush, was already involved: with another woman. Holden was *Chasing Amy*, but his prey was elusive.

Turn right and head west on East Houston Street. Stop at Katz's Deli, on the corner of East Houston and Ludlow Streets.

14. Katz's Delicatessen. 205 East Houston (at Ludlow Street). This deli is the home of some very tasty food, not to mention one of the more memorable scenes in recent movie history. Harry (Billy Crystal) just wanted corned beef, but Sally (Meg Ryan) gave him and the rest of the restaurant patrons a whole lot more—a simulated orgasm, prompting a nearby diner (director Rob Reiner's real-life mom) to tell a passing waiter, "I'll have what she's having." The line is a classic, and the movie is *When Harry Met Sally...*, but I suspect I didn't have to tell you that.

A few people who may have missed Sally's performance were sitting around the corner, to the right, in the back of the restaurant. There undercover FBI agent Joey Pistone, also known as *Donnie Brasco* (Johnny Depp), met with fellow agents to discuss the progress and status of his infiltration of local mobs.

If you go inside, you will no doubt enjoy the food. Please feel free to point out to them the similarity between my name and the restaurant's. It may not get you any free food, but it may sell a book or two. And, after all, isn't that what this is all about?

Head back the other way, east on East Houston for one block, and turn right on Essex Street. Walk south on Essex. At Rivington Street, turn to the left and look for the Williamsburg Bridge. Imagine the neighborhood just north of the bridge, back in times when New York was younger and wilder.

15. Neighborhood in the Shadow of the Williamsburg Bridge. Most gangs have a turf they consider their own, and the young friends who grew up *Once Upon a Time in America* considered this neighborhood theirs. When they grew into the likes of Noodles (Robert De Niro) and Max (James Woods), they ran things with fists of steel.

Continue south on Essex until you reach Guss's Pickles, at 35 Essex.

16. Guss's Pickles. 35 Essex Street. This is where Sam (Peter Riegert) worked. Occasionally, he humored Hannah the Matchmaker (Sylvia

Miles), who was known to come by with pictures of eligible young women. One such woman, Isabel (Amy Irving), really caught Sam's fancy, and she would soon have Sam *Crossing Delancey*.

Turn around and look at the handball courts on the other side of Essex.

17. Essex Street. Handball Courts. This time it was Isabel (Amy Irving) who was *Crossing Delancey*. She showed up where Sam (Peter Riegert)

was playing a game of handball to thank him for the new hat he had sent her.

* * *

Walk back north on Essex Street and turn left on Delancey. Walk west until you reach The Bowery Ballroom, on the north side of Delancey, past Chrystie Street, but before Bowery.

18. The Bowery Ballroom. 6 Delancey Street. The owners of this club loved her tape and decided to give her a chance to sing here. En route, she had second thoughts, but showed up anyway, with all her friends in the crowd. It was a far cry from *Coyote Ugly*, where she tended bar, but here Violet (Piper Perabo) made her musical debut.

* * *

Turn back the other way on Delancey and make a left on Chrystie Street. Head north on Chrystie a short distance until you reach Sammy's Roumanian, on your left, at number 157.

19. Sammy's Roumanian Restaurant. 157 Chrystie Street. He owned a greasy spoon in an outer borough, but Alby (Elliott Gould) wanted to make his future *Over the Brooklyn Bridge*. After getting his Uncle Benjamin (Sid Caesar) to agree to lend him the money to buy a restaurant in Manhattan, Alby and his entire family came here to celebrate the new venture. But, for Alby, his uncle's involvement came with a heavy price: dumping Elizabeth (Margaux Hemingway), his non-Jewish girlfriend. The dinner started amicably, but Alby finally decided to stand up for what he believed in, and what was in his heart, and he set the family straight about a whole host of issues. After the dirty laundry was exposed, much to the chagrin of the restaurant's other patrons, it seemed like the family was finally heading in the right direction, and Alby would get to keep his restaurant, and his girlfriend.

Continue north on Chrystie Street. When you reach East Houston, continue north. You should now be on Second Avenue. Stop at Provenzano Funeral Home, which is on the west side of Second, between 2nd and 3rd Streets.

20. Provenzano Funeral Home. 43 Second Avenue. He was a good cop. In fact, some considered Danny Ciello (Treat Williams) the *Prince of the City*. But not some of his fellow officers. When Danny came here to attend the funeral of

a murdered relative, he was turned away at the door. Some of the other cops believed that by agreeing to cooperate with the commission that was investigating police corruption, Danny had turned against them.

Turn back, walk south to 2nd Street, and turn right. Walk west on 2nd and turn right on Bowery. Stop at the venerable music venue CBGB, at 315 Bowery (between 2nd and Bleecker).

21. CBGB (OMFUG). 315 Bowery. It was the summer of 1977, and a madman was on the loose, killing people as they sat in parked cars. But during the *Summer of Sam*, people could feel the beat, and they had to keep dancing, so they went out and tried to maintain a normal life as best they could. On a typically hot night, a nervous Vinnie (John Leguziamo) and his wife, Dionna (Mira Sorvino), came here to see their friend Richie (Adrien Brody), one of the musical acts on the bill. But they lived in the world of disco, and as this, the heart of the punk scene, was just a little too weird for them, they got in their car and headed for greener pastures (see **Walking Tour 9: The Theater District,** Location 26).

Walk north on Bowery and turn left on 4th Street. Walk west until you are across from 23 East 4th Street.

22. 23 East 4th Street (between Bowery and Lafayette). Jane (Ashley Judd) and Ray (Greg Kinnear) both worked for the Diane Roberts Show, which starred Diane Roberts (Ellen Barkin) and taped in the studio located here, in *Someone Like You.* Against her better judgment and despite all her studying of the male animal, Jane found herself in an amorous relationship with Ray. And when it soured, she still had to see him every day at work.

Return to the east side of Bowery. Turn left and walk north. Around 5th Street, Bowery forks into Fourth Avenue and Third Avenue. Take the Third Avenue prong and walk north to 7th Street. Turn right on 7th and walk east to McSorley's Old Ale House, one of the oldest pubs in New York, on your left.

23. McSorley's Old Ale House. 15 East 7th Street. He went on a date with Susan (Annabella Sciorra) and her daughter, Bonnie (Christina Ricci), and afterward Lieutenant John Moss (James Woods) did what any self-respecting male would do: he went to a bar to drink away his sorrows and lick his wounds. And in his downtrodden state, the last person he wanted to see was

actor Nick Lang (Michael J. Fox), who had been tagging along to learn about police work for an upcoming movie role, in *The Hard Way*. But Nick showed that, although he was all thumbs when it came to police work, he did know a little bit about women.

You have now reached the end of **Walking Tour 12: The Lower East Side Melting Pot.**

Walking Tour 13
TRIBECA TO SOHO

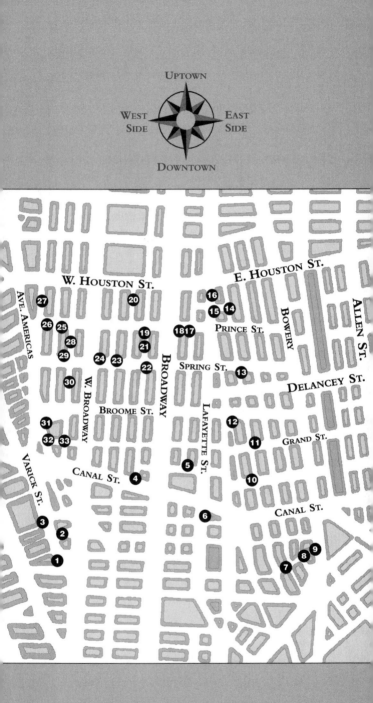

Walking Tour 13
TriBeCa to SoHo

Walking Tour 13: TriBeCa to SoHo covers the greatest diversity of cultures, ethnicities, lifestyles, and tastes, all within a relatively small geographical area. One neighborhood literally begins where another leaves off, giving this part of Manhattan the feel of a real-life Disneyland, where you turn the corner from Chinatown and find yourself in Little Italy. Unlike Disneyland, however, the attractions here are real.

Walking Tour 13: TriBeCa to SoHo starts at the intersection of Franklin Street and Varick Street. Find the beautiful and ornate subway entrance that looks as if it were airlifted from the streets of Paris and dropped here. Stand near the entrance without getting in the way of rushing commuters.

1. Franklin Street Subway Entrance (at Varick). They were both involved with others, but nothing was going to get in the way of true love.

Or at least, true passion. Or maybe it was simply lust. They were used to traveling in a world peopled by celebrities, so they decided to do as those around them did. In *Celebrity*, Lee Simon (Kenneth Branagh) and Nola (Winona Ryder) threw caution to the wind and had a rendezvous late one night in front of these stairs.

Walk north on Varick and turn right on the north side of North Moore Street. The fire station on the south side of the street should look mighty familiar.

2. Hook & Ladder 8. Varick and North Moore Streets. If you can picture the *Ghostbusters* logo over the entranceway, you've figured this one out. Thanks to the generosity of Ray (Dan Aykroyd) and the banks that let him take

out multiple mortgages on his family's home, Ray, Peter (Bill Murray), and Egon (Harold Ramis) moved their operation into this building after their funding from Columbia University (**Walking Tour 3: Uptown Broadway,** Location 1) was cut.

Turn right on Varick and walk north one block, to Ericsson Place. You will find the 1st Police Precinct located on the southwest corner of Varick and Ericsson Place.

3. 1st Police Precinct. Varick Street and Ericsson Place. Madmen were on the loose, terrorizing the city, capturing it all on video, and hoping to get their *15 Minutes* of fame. But the authorities were hot on their trail. Arson Investigator Jordy Warsaw (Ed Burns) brought Daphne (Vera Farmiga), the only witness to a double homicide, here and traded ideas with Detective Eddie Flemming (Robert De Niro). Afterward, to avoid the frenzy-feeding media outside the front door, they left through a side door.

———————

Turn right and head east on Beach Street. Turn left on West Broadway. Walk north on West Broadway and turn right on the south side of Canal Street. Walk east on Canal and stop when you are across from Pearl Paint (at Mercer Street).

4. Across from Pearl Paint. 308 Canal Street (at Mercer Street). Each day can be a struggle for an aspiring actor and playwright, what with trips to the copy store, the stationery store, and the post office. But on one particular day for Wallace Shawn (portraying himself), his typical activities seemed like a vacation compared to what his evening held: dinner with old friend and mentor Andre Gregory (also playing himself). Worrying about whether it would be among the most boring evenings he had ever spent, Shawn crossed Canal Street here and headed for the subway and his dinner date in *My Dinner With André*.

———————

Continue east on Canal, turn left on Broadway, and head north one block. Make a right on Howard Street and stop at 28 Howard, at the northeast corner of Howard and Crosby Streets.

5. 28 Howard Street (northeast corner at

Crosby). Mild-mannered word processor Paul Hackett (Griffin Dunne) led a pretty boring existence, so when he met the beautiful and alluring Marcy (Rosanna Arquette) at a coffee shop, he decided a change in routine might do him some good. How wrong he turned out to be. Later in the evening he called Marcy and arranged to meet her downtown, *After Hours*, for what can only be described as a wild and bizarre evening of paranoia, mayhem, and death. The nightmare began innocently enough in Marcy's loft, which was inside this building, where she lived with Kiki Bridges (Linda Fiorentino). By morning, Paul was happy to return to his boring job in his boring world uptown.

——— ⋅◆⋅ ———

Turn right and continue east on Howard Street. Make a right on Lafayette Street and walk south to the south side of Canal Street. Stand near the entrance to the subway station on the southeast corner of Canal and Lafayette Streets.

6. Canal Street Subway Entrance. Southeast corner of Canal and Lafayette Streets. It was not the Thanksgiving Day Dr. Nathan Conrad (Michael Douglas) had been hoping for, having begun with the kidnapping of his daughter. A few hours later, Dr. Conrad had whisked his greatly troubled pro bono patient, eighteen-year-old Elisabeth Burrows (Brittany Murphy), out of the Bridgeview Psychiatric Hospital, and the two of them paused at the top of these stairs, anticipating with dread what lay below. For Elisabeth, it was the prospect of reliving the horror she had witnessed ten years before, and for Dr. Conrad, in *Don't Say a Word*, it was a necessary step toward getting his daughter back unharmed. Knowing the enormity of the stakes for both of them, they worked their way down the steps and onto the platform of the subway station below.

——— ⋅◆⋅ ———

Continue east on Canal and turn right on Mott Street. Walk south on Mott and turn left on Pell Street. Stop in front of the restaurant to the left of 22 Pell Street.

7. Restaurant to Left of 22 Pell Street. Edward J. Dodd (James Woods) was defending a man accused of murder. In *True Believer*, the murder took place on this spot.

———•—•———

Turn right on Doyers Street. Walk until you get to number 15-17 Doyers, on your right.

8. 15-17 Doyers Street. Proving that *Small Time Crooks* will always be small-time, Ray (Woody Allen) hatched a scheme to steal a priceless piece of jewelry from one of his high-society acquaintances, have a copy made, and swap the copy for the original. Ray came here to pick up the replica, but for Ray nothing worked out quite the way he planned.

———•—•———

Turn around and find 18 Doyers.

9. 18 Doyers Street. *Alice* (Mia Farrow) had it all—a beautiful New York City home, complete with domestic staff, a good-looking, successful husband, and adoring children. Or so it seemed to the outside world. But she still was not happy.

Alice came here on a regular basis to visit her herbalist, Dr. Yang (Keye Luke), who gave her magical potions.

———•+•———

Now turn right and admire one of the most striking streets in Manhattan. Sprinkled with more than its fair share of barbershops and hair salons, Doyers looks like an actual movie set.

———•+•———

Walk through Doyers to the end and turn left. Walk north on St. James Place, which will soon become Bowery. Cross Canal and walk north one more block. Turn left on Hester Street.

10. Hester Street. The Statue of Liberty declared, "Give me your tired, your poor," and they came—from all over and in large numbers from places in Europe to a land where they hoped to make better lives for themselves and their children. If they were lucky, they might even realize the American dream, which differs for every person who lands on these shores. From Eastern Europe, a huge number of Jewish people fled tyranny, poverty, and pogroms, and settled here in the New York City brought to life in *Hester Street*.

———•+•———

Continue west on Hester and turn right on Mulberry Street. Walk north to Grand Street.

11. Mulberry and Grand Streets. Northeast corner. They were late for their dinner reservation, but Gina (Jeanne Tripplehorn) stopped right here, because Michael (Hugh Grant) was running in such a silly way that he was making her laugh too hard. She begged him to run normally, but *Mickey Blue Eyes* told her, with his patented puppy-dog look of despair, that he had been running normally and that he was hurt by her comment. Not a good start to the evening.

———•+•———

Turn left and walk west on Grand Street. Turn right on Centre Street and stop at number 240, the beautiful, large building that runs the entire length of the block.

12. 240 Centre Street. This building is now the address of some pretty expensive condominiums, but years ago, in real life and in *Madigan*, it was the

central police headquarters and where the offices of Police Commissioner Anthony Russell (Henry Fonda) were located.

Continue north on Centre and turn right on Broome Street. Walk east on Broome, then turn left on Mulberry Street and walk north to Spring Street. There is a playground at Mulberry and Spring.

13. Playground at Mulberry and Spring. Charlie (Mickey Rourke) was *The Pope of Greenwich Village*, but he spent a good amount of time down here on the northern fringes of Little Italy. During one of many conversations held in this playground, Diane (Daryl Hannah) begged Charlie "not to go," without even knowing where he was planning to go.

Continue north on Mulberry and stop at the

door in the brick wall, on the east side of Mulberry Street, between Prince Street and Jersey Street.

14. Mulberry Street (between Prince and Jersey Streets). Door in Brick Wall. After Johnny (Robert De Niro) shot his gun from a rooftop, he and Charlie (Harvey Keitel) hid out in

the cemetery behind this door, taking refuge from New York's *Mean Streets*.

Years later, Frankie (Nick Scotti) and his friend Joey (Domenick Lombardozzi) watched in horror as two guys kissed in front of this door. A common occurrence in many parts of Manhattan, such a sight was rare for guys who worked in a Bronx pizzeria in *Kiss Me, Guido*.

Return to Prince Street, turn right, and walk west to Lafayette Street. Turn right on Lafayette and walk north until you reach the Jersey Street alleyway.

15. Jersey Street Alleyway. Off Lafayette. It's not the best spot for commerce, to be sure, but this is where falafel vendor Mustafa (Omar Townsend) stood, day after day, trying his best. He had very few customers, but one of them, Mary (Parker Posey), was sexy, persistent, and a *Party Girl*.

Continue north on Lafayette the short distance to the front of the Puck Building.

16. The Puck Building. 295 Lafayette Street. Having finally figured out the serial killer's modus operandi, fireman-turned-sleuth Nick (Kevin Kline) set out to snare the killer before he struck again inside this building. With the help of Bernadette (Mary Elizabeth Mastrantonio), the mayor's daughter, Nick set out to rid the city of *The January Man*.

This beautiful building houses the office of Grace Adler (Debra Messing) in the Emmy-winning television show *Will and Grace*.

Turn back and walk south on Lafayette Street. Turn right on Prince Street and walk west to Crosby Street.

17. Crosby Street, just south of Savoy (at 70 Prince Street). Gwen (Sandra Bullock) had made it through *28 Days* of rehab and was hoping to get her life back on track. But to keep her alcoholism in check, Gwen knew she would have to put behind her not only her drinking days, but certain friends and lovers as well. As she turned the corner in front of the Savoy, right where you are now standing, Gwen saw her boyfriend Jasper

(Dominic West) sitting on the stoop of her building a short distance down Crosby Street. Jasper was ready to resume where they had left off, but Gwen knew that she had to make a clean break.

Continue west on Prince Street and stop at Broadway. Dean & Deluca is on the corner.

18. Dean & Deluca. 560 Broadway (at Prince Street).

While Sam (Matthew Broderick) divided his nights between his two apartments (one he shared with sloppy roommates and one

he had by himself for two nights a week), he spent his days working behind the cheese counter here in *The Night We Never Met*. Little did he know that the woman buying caviar at this counter rented Sam's apartment on two other nights and had special plans for the caviar.

Resume your westward trek on Prince and stop at Fanelli's, on the southwest corner of Prince and Mercer Streets.

19. Fanelli's. 94 Prince Street (at Mercer).

While his gang watched from a nearby vantage point, Frankie (Ed Harris) had a sit-down here with Borelli (Joe Viterelli). The meeting put Frankie in a state of panic because the topic of

discussion was how best to deal with Frankie's brother Jackie (a typically out-of-control Gary Oldman). In *State of Grace*, Borelli told Frankie to "solve" the problem, or else it would be solved for him.

———•◦•———

Continue west on Prince and turn right on Greene Street. Walk north on Greene until you reach Kelley & Ping, at 127 Greene, on the west side of the street.

20. Kelley & Ping. 127 Greene Street. Finn (Ethan Hawke) left a formal cocktail party that was largely in his honor and raced through the streets of Manhattan in the pouring rain. When he got to this restaurant, he stormed inside and interrupted Estella (Gwyneth Paltrow), who was having dinner with her fiancé, Walter (Hank Azaria), and some others, and asked her to dance. Forsaking the others, Estella danced with him and then left the restaurant with him. At long last, Finn realized his *Great Expectations* as they consummated the passion that had been simmering between them, unspoken, for years.

———•◦•———

Turn back and walk south on Greene Street. Turn left on Prince, walk east, and turn right on the east side of Mercer Street. Stop when you reach number 112. It will be on your left.

21. 112 Mercer Street. A few floors up in this loft building, Sam Wheat (Patrick Swayze) and Molly Jensen (Demi Moore) lived together in *Ghost*. Unlike many New York locations, where only the exteriors of the buildings are used, the scenes that took place in their home were actually filmed inside this building.

Continue south on Mercer until you reach the intersection with Spring Street.

22. Spring Street and Mercer Street. Intersection. After a lunch that could only be described as awkward, Max (Wesley Snipes), Mimi (Ming-Na Wen), Karen (Nastassja Kinski), and

Vernon (Kyle MacLachlan) stood at this intersection. Much had happened to these two couples, and they learned that a *One Night Stand* was not always just a one-night stand.

Turn right and walk west on Spring Street. Stop at number 139, after Greene Street, but before Wooster Street. It is on the north side of Spring Street.

23. 139 Spring Street (at Wooster). Several years after figuring out how to deal with his brother Jackie in *State of Grace*, Ed Harris was figuring out how best to deal with another Jackie—

in this case, his ex-wife. In *Stepmom*, Luke (Ed Harris) had divorced Jackie (Susan Sarandon), the mother of his children, and was planning to marry Isabel (Julia Roberts), a much younger woman, which made Jackie feel anything but warm and fuzzy. Having left his house in the suburbs, Luke was ready for a change and lived with Isabel in a loft in this building.

Continue west on Spring Street and turn right on West Broadway. Look for OTP (Otto Tootsi Plohound) at 413 West Broadway, on the east side of West Broadway.

24. OTP. 413 West Broadway (north of Spring Street). With time running out on his mission, Nicky (Adam Sandler) began approaching people in the street, trying to lure them into the special flask he had been given. Apparently, that is how one catches evil spirits: they turn into smoke and get pulled into a small bottle. Go figure. Nicky even pulled a man off a passing bicycle in front of this store. *Little Nicky* may have been Satan's son, but his fighting skills left a lot to be desired. The man beat him mercilessly before continuing on his way.

Walk north on West Broadway and turn left on Prince Street. Walk west and stop at 172 Prince Street, on the south side of Prince.

25. 172 Prince Street. This seemingly obscure doorway leads to the apartment where Savannah Wingo (Melinda Dillon) lived. Savannah was the sister of Tom Wingo (Nick Nolte) in *The Prince of Tides*, and after Savannah attempted suicide, Tom came to New York and stayed here, hoping to find out what led his sister to such a desperate act. He did.

Continue west on Prince, the short distance to Raoul's, at 180 Prince Street, on the left.

26. Raoul's. 180 Prince Street. A SoHo favorite, this was the location of the restaurant owned by Anton (Tcheky Karyo), the man who stole the heart of Linda (Kelly Preston), the girlfriend of Sam the Milky Way Man (Matthew Broderick) in *Addicted to Love*. Sam got himself a job as a dishwasher in the restaurant, working for his nemesis, and exacted his revenge with the help of Maggie (Meg Ryan), the woman spurned by Anton.

—————

Walk west on Prince and turn right on Mac-Dougal Street. Stop at Provence, on the east side of the street.

27. Restaurant Provence. 38 MacDougal Street. Billed as one of the most romantic restaurants in a city filled with romantic restaurants, Provence is often the place where "guys" pop the

question to their "dolls." In *Crossing Delancey*, however, it is where author Anton Maes (Jeroen Krabbe) took Isabel (Amy Irving), who had a crush on him, for lunch on a first date. Anton had a proposition for Isabel, but it wasn't the one that she had expected.

Turn back and head south on MacDougal. Turn left on Prince Street and walk east. Make a right on Thompson Street and stop in front of SoHo Laundry, at 101 Thompson.

28. 101 Thompson Street, near Spring Street. He was about to be married, and for a professional football player with a pretty large following, that was a pretty big deal. While his friends looked on, ready to rib him mercilessly, Lance (Morris Chestnut) signed autographs, flirted with and charmed a small group of female admirers. After he shared a few moments with his fans in front of this store, Lance and his friends, in *The Best Man*, walked north.

Continue south on Thompson. Stop at the handball courts on the right, north of Spring.

29. Thompson Street. North of Spring. Handball Court. Frankie (Nick Scotti) caught his girlfriend having sex with his brother and decided it was time to make a change. He answered an ad for an apartment and moved in with a "guy with money." At least, that's what he thought "GWM" stood for in the ad, in *Kiss Me, Guido*. He ultimately learned that it meant "gay white male," but by that time he had nowhere else to live. One afternoon Frankie and his friend from the Bronx, Joey Chips (Domenick Lombardozzi), played handball on these courts.

Threatened by the rapid rise of young newcomer Josh Baskin (Tom Hanks), toy company executive Paul (John Heard) challenged Josh to a game of paddleball on these courts. Josh soon learned that in paddleball, as in life, not everyone plays by the rules and that being *Big* came with bad things, as well as good.

Continue south on Thompson. Cross Spring

Street and stop at 75 Thompson, on the west side of the street.

30. 75 Thompson Street. After Eliza (Hope Davis) found a love poem among her husband's belongings, she and her entire family packed into their station wagon and drove to New York to find out what secret her husband, Louis (Stanley

Tucci), may have been keeping from her. In *The Daytrippers*, Eliza's family staked out this building and, sure enough, watched Louis emerge from behind the blue door with a woman. But his secret was yet to be learned.

Continue south on Thompson and turn right on Broome Street. Walk west on Broome and turn left on Avenue of the Americas. Walk south to Watts Street. Lupe's East LA Kitchen is at 110 Avenue of the Americas, at Watts Street.

31. Lupe's East LA Kitchen. 110 Avenue of the Americas (at Watts Street). Northeast Corner. Poor Charlie Driggs (Jeff Daniels). Seemingly content with his none-too-exciting existence, he came here for a peaceful lunch. After lunch, he met Lulu (Melanie Griffith), who offered to drive him back to his office. But Lulu kidnapped Charlie instead and, proving to be *Something Wild*, took Charlie for the ride of his life.

Continue south on Avenue of the Americas to Grand Street.

32. Moondance Diner. Avenue of the Americas and Grand Street. Although Monica Geller (Courtney Cox), one of television's *Friends,* wanted nothing more than to be a chef, for a short while she had to settle for working here as a waitress. To make matters worse, she was forced to wear a padded bra and tacky blond wig while serving her customers.

Turn left on Grand Street and walk east to Thompson. Café Noir is on the northwest corner of Thompson and Grand.

33. Café Noir. 32 Grand Street (at Thompson). People write letters to erotic magazines about such encounters, but Constance Sumner (Diane Lane) was going to keep this one to herself. After unexpectedly running into some friends while on her way to meet her clandestine lover, rare-book dealer Paul Martel (Olivier Martinez), Constance found herself stuck with "the girls" at a table inside this popular gathering place. Constance was thrilled to see Paul show up and head for the bathrooms in the back of the restaurant. Excusing herself, Constance followed him, and moments later she and Paul had a wild sexual encounter while her friends waited for her. Afterward, slightly disheveled from her tryst but happy, nonetheless, Constance sat with her friends, and they engaged in a discussion of the pitfalls of being *Unfaithful*.

You have now reached the end of **Walking Tour 13: TriBeCa to SoHo**.

Walking Tour 14
THE SOUTHERN TIP

Walking Tour 14
THE SOUTHERN TIP

In the beginning, Lower Manhattan was New York. Bordered by water on three sides and Wall Street on the north, most New Yorkers at the time lived within this small area. Little by little, people pushed north and tamed what is now the Village, Murray Hill, Midtown, Sutton Place, and the Upper East Side, to name but a few of the neighborhoods of this great metropolis. However, Lower Manhattan continues to be both the reminder of what New York was and the evidence of what it continues to be.

Contained within **Walking Tour 14: The Southern Tip** are hints of New York old and new. And though its landscape was forever changed by terrorist acts on September 11, 2001, when the twin towers of the World Trade Center were destroyed along with the lives of thousands of innocent people, New York has endured and will continue to thrive. For the alternative is unthinkable.

In light of the terrorist attacks that changed the world on September 11, 2001, **Walking Tour 14: The Southern Tip** begins, fittingly enough, at the Criminal Courthouse in Lower Manhattan, at 100 Centre Street, just north of Hogan Place.

1. Manhattan Criminal Courthouse. 100 Centre Street. This building is where the trial of Mr. Hoover (Anthony Hopkins) took place. Mr. Hoover believed that his daughter, *Audrey Rose*, killed in a car crash, had been reincarnated into the body of a twelve-year-old girl named Ivy Templeton (Susan Swift), and when Ivy's parents didn't go along with him, he took custody of the girl and was subsequently charged with kidnapping.

This is also where Assistant District Attorney Adam Bonner (Spencer Tracy) prosecuted Doris Attinger (Judy Holliday), who was accused of the attempted murder of her husband. What made this case such a thorn in Bonner's side was that the defendant's counsel was Amanda Bonner (Katherine Hepburn), who just happened to be Bonner's wife, in *Adam's Rib*.

Two out-of-town businessmen were found shot to death in a car, and two young men were arrested for the crime. While crowds of reporters waited outside this building for the men to emerge, Robin (Amelia Campbell) struggled to get a good photo in *The Paper*.

Following up on his *Conspiracy Theory*, Jerry (Mel Gibson) followed a familiar-looking man into this building. He noticed DEPT OF COMMERCE in the lobby directory, confirming his belief that "spooks" (in other words, the CIA) operated from somewhere within the building.

————•◦•————

Head south on Centre Street and stop when you reach the New York Supreme Court Building, at 60 Centre Street.

2. New York Supreme Court Building. 60 Centre Street. The year was 1947, and Santa Claus was on trial. Only a miracle could save him, and that miracle was delivered, thanks to the love and faith of Susan (a very young Natalie Wood), the belief of Doris (Maureen O'Hara), the legal skills of Fred (John Payne), and some misdirected mail, courtesy of the United States Postal Service. The verdict: the man on trial, Kris Kringle (Edmund Gwenn), must be Santa Claus. The movie was *Miracle on 34th Street,* and the courtroom scenes took place inside.

When *The Godfather*, Michael Corleone (Al Pacino), exacted revenge, he went all out. In a classic scene, while his godson was being baptized, Michael's order to rub out the heads of the other crime families took place. One of those men was killed by a hit man dressed as a police officer as he walked down the steps of this building.

Luckily, Pacino did not meet a similar fate years later when he descended these same steps. Carlito (Al Pacino), whose conviction had just been overturned after he had spent five years in prison, exulted in his freedom as he walked down the steps with his attorney, Dave Kleinfeld (Sean Penn), in *Carlito's Way*.

After his arrest for insider trading, Bud Fox (Charlie Sheen) was dropped off in front of the courthouse and walked up the long steps to the front door to face the music. His short, but interesting and profitable run on *Wall Street* had come to a sudden end.

Recently teamed *Legal Eagles* Tom Logan (Robert Redford) and Laura J. Kelly (Debra Winger) defended Chelsea Dierdon (Daryl Hannah) in her trial for murder in this building.

At 60 Centre Street, dedicated jurors, played by the likes of Henry Fonda, Ed Begley, E. G. Marshall, Jack Klugman, and Martin Balsam, spent agonizing hours trying to decide the fate of a young man accused of murder in *12 Angry Men.*

After being cleared of all charges against him, former fugitive Mark Sheridan (Wesley Snipes) left a press conference held on the steps of this courthouse, bid farewell to Deputy Marshal Sam Gerard (Tommy Lee Jones), who had led his team of *U.S. Marshals* in Mark's pursuit, and descended these steps to freedom.

———————

Turn from the courthouse and look west across Centre Street. There is a small park called Thomas Paine Park, and there are numerous benches in the park.

3. Bench just west of 60 Centre Street. Rocky Graziano (Paul Newman) wasn't sure that marriage was for him, but Norma (Pier Angeli) loved him, and that was a wonderful thing. While trying to decide whether to go across the street to get a marriage license, the two of them sat on this bench. In *Somebody Up There Likes Me*, Rocky realized that somebody down here liked him, too. And he decided to do something about it.

———————

Beyond the benches is a tall, modern-looking building directly across from the Supreme Court Building, on Federal Plaza, at the intersection of Lafayette and Worth Streets.

4. 26 Federal Plaza. Their marriage was a sham, just a way for Georges (Gerard Depardieu) to get a *Green Card* so he could stay in the United States. But the Immigration Service caught up with Georges and Bronte (Andie MacDowell) and made them take a test to see if they were really married. After the test, they walked out of this building to ponder their fate.

Turn left and walk south on Centre Street. Stop at the plaza just south of the Federal Courthouse, at 40 Centre Street.

5. Municipal Building Plaza. In *The Devil's Advocate*, senior partner of all senior partners John Milton (Al Pacino) walked alongside young protégé Kevin Lomax (Keanu Reeves) in this plaza.

As they crossed the street, Milton offered to take Kevin off the big murder case he had been working on so he could tend to his ailing wife, but Kevin declined.

This plaza must remind filmmakers of the devil, because it was used in another "devil" movie. In *The Devil's Own*, after escaping from the back of a police car and shooting Officer Eddie

Diaz (Ruben Blades), Rory (Brad Pitt) ran through here with Officer Tom O'Meara (Harrison Ford), his former mentor, in hot pursuit.

———•—•———

Turn into the plaza and walk along (the Federal Courthouse should be on your left, and the enormous Municipal Building should be on your right). Continue until you reach One Police Plaza. The red sculpture will be on your left.

6. One Police Plaza. The movie was *Cop Land*, and mild-mannered but righteous cop Freddy Heflin (Sylvester Stallone), having stood up to the rogue cops for the first time in his career, delivered cop-in-hiding Murray (Michael Rapaport) into the waiting hands of Internal Affairs Detective Moe Tilden (Robert De Niro), right in front of police headquarters, here.

———•—•———

Continue along the plaza (but don't head toward One Police Plaza) until you reach the staircase leading to the subway stairs under the archways of the Municipal Building.

7. Staircase to Subway at Municipal Building. 1 Centre Street. Would-be muggers at this location pulled a knife on *"Crocodile" Dundee* (Paul Hogan) and his girlfriend Sue (Linda Kozlowski). Not impressed by the puny knife sported by the muggers, Dundee declared in his

inimitable Australian accent, "That's not a knife," and thereupon pulled out his own much larger weapon and displayed it for all to see, saying, "That's a knife."

If you stand at the top of the stairs long enough, you may see undercover transit cops Charlie (Woody Harrelson) and John (Wesley Snipes) pass you as they descend these stairs. They did just that in *Money Train* after being chewed out by Chief Patterson (Robert Blake).

Continue your walk around the Municipal Building (keeping the building on your right). Walk through another archway (the traffic on Centre Street will roar by on your left). Watch for a bench under the archway and see if you recognize the men sitting on it.

8. Municipal Building. 1 Centre Street. Bench under Archway. He lost a case his office considered a sure win, but he did it on purpose.

Soon-to-be-former Assistant District Attorney Michael (Brad Pitt) sat on this bench with life-long friend Shakes (Jason Patric), contemplating his next move, in *Sleepers*.

Continue in the same direction until you reach the front of the massive Municipal Building.

9. The Municipal Building. 1 Centre Street.
In a pivotal scene, after the *Ghostbusters* convinced the mayor that the demons must be stopped, the army was seen mobilizing from beneath the arch of this building.

After his source, Manny Feldstein (Joe Grifasi),

backed away from his corruption story, Jack Taylor (George Clooney) spotted him outside this building, followed him inside, and chased him to the roof. There Manny added to Jack's troubles on Jack's *One Fine Day*.

Deputy Mayor Kevin Calhoun (John Cusack) and Abe (David Paymer) worked at *City Hall*, but paid a visit to Larry Schwartz (Richard Schiff) of the Department of Probation here.

They had only known each other for a day, but they knew it was right. Also, *The Clock* was ticking, and Joe (Robert Walker) didn't have much time left on his leave in New York City. So Joe and Alice (Judy Garland) came here to get married.

Police Officer Mike Brennan (Nick Nolte) had shot a man, and Assistant District Attorney Al Reilly (Timothy Hutton) was assigned to the case. Reilly had lots of questions, but very few answers, and he did not yet know that he might be in over his head. In *Q & A*, a number of conversations took place in front of this building.

Cross Centre Street on the north side of Chambers Street, which begins (and ends) at the

Municipal Building. Walk west on Chambers and stop at the first building on the right.

10. Surrogates Court. 31 Chambers Street. Dora (Mena Suvari) was no *Loser*, but she was in a tough spot. Her family income prevented her from qualifying for financial aid to attend college, which she did here in the city. But her job didn't enable her to cover tuition. So Dora came here to her school's financial aid office to see about getting a second job. In actuality, this building houses the New York State Surrogates Court. If the building is open and you have time, go in and look around. You will see why they do so much filming in the first-floor lobby and on the staircase leading to the second floor.

In *Great Expectations*, Finn (Ethan Hawke) showed up fashionably late to a fancy party held here. Finn was the guest of honor, but he had more on his mind than idle cocktail-party chatter and art, even if the art was his. With thoughts only of Estella (Gwyneth Paltrow), Finn quickly left the party and ran through the rain-soaked Manhattan streets, hoping to find her. He did (see **Walking Tour 13: TriBeCa to SoHo,** Location 20).

Return to the corner of Chambers and Centre Streets. Turn right and cross Chambers. Head south on Centre until you reach the stairs to the subway. You'll see the Brooklyn Bridge to your left.

11. Centre Street Subway Stairs, across from Brooklyn Bridge. Actor Nick Lang (Michael J. Fox) came to town to find out what the life of a real New York City cop was like. And New York City cop John Moss (James Woods) drew the short straw and had to let Nick tag along as he went about his day. But Nick soon learned, *The Hard Way,* that portraying a cop in the movies is much safer than being a cop in real life. He was pinned down by gunfire on the subway platform, and Moss came to the rescue after racing down this staircase.

Now turn to your left and get a good look at the legendary Brooklyn Bridge.

12. Brooklyn Bridge. Built more than a hundred years ago and still going strong, the Brooklyn Bridge is one of the most recognizable structures in all of Manhattan. Because of its beauty and longevity, it is not surprising that the bridge has served as a backdrop in so many films over the years. Even Tarzan has scaled its cables and beams. In *Tarzan's New York Adventure*, Tarzan (Johnny Weissmuller) was a long way from home and forced to fit his muscular physique uncomfortably into a suit. But that didn't stop him from climbing the cables of the bridge to the top, while the police gave chase. But Tarzan was a breed apart, and as the cops inched closer and capture seemed imminent, he dove into the East River below.

Nebraska attorney Jerry Ryan (Robert Mitchum) chose a much more civilized method of crossing the bridge. Moving to New York after his divorce, he bypassed the cables and beams and strolled along the center of the bridge into Manhattan at the start of his new life and the beginning of *Two for the Seesaw*.

Sophie (Meryl Streep) also walked along the bridge, but her past was a lot more terrifying than Jerry Ryan's. She had survived the Holocaust, and New York represented not only freedom, but an opportunity to try to forget the horrors she had endured. One night she, Nathan (Kevin Kline), and their friend Stingo (Peter MacNicol) walked across the bridge, opening a bottle of champagne to celebrate along the way. They toasted Stingo as the next great American writer, but at the end of *Sophie's Choice*, Stingo crossed the legendary span alone.

Literary success may have eluded Stingo, but not Ivan Travalian (Al Pacino). His play was being mounted on Broadway. But Ivan's love life wasn't in great shape. After his wife left him, Ivan figured he'd be going it alone, but then Alice Detroit (Dyan Cannon) came into his life like a hurricane, and the two of them strolled along the bridge in *Author! Author!*

John/Judas (David Haskell) headed across the bridge, wheeling his multicolored cart into Manhattan to gather the other free spirits at the start of the rock opera *Godspell*.

And back in the days when the Brooklyn Bridge was under construction—1876 to be exact—Leopold Alexis, Duke of Albany (Hugh Jackman), followed Stuart (Liev Schreiber) onto the bridge and through a time machine of sorts into modern-day New York. There a creature like none the duke had ever before encountered awaited him: the modern New York woman, packaged nicely in the form of Kate McKay (Meg Ryan), in *Kate and Leopold*.

During *The Siege*, New York had already seen terrorists blow up a bus, a theater, and a government office building. After the president gave the order, the army was mobilized and, led by General Bill Devereaux (Bruce Willis), lumbered over the Brooklyn Bridge to set up camp.

It's probably no longer there, but many years ago a shack under the Brooklyn Bridge on the Manhattan side offered live bait and shelter from the rain.

13. Shack under the Brooklyn Bridge. Skip McCoy (Richard Widmark) lived in just such a shack in *Pickup on South Street*. The shack advertised LIVE BAIT and FISHING TACKLE FOR RENT, and Skip received more than his fair share of visitors. But the traffic increased dramatically after Skip lifted a wallet containing microfilm from the purse of Candy (Jean Peter) on the subway, and Skip realized he may have chosen the wrong wallet to steal.

From his shack, Skip may have gotten a great view of a boat passing under the bridge.

14. Boat on the East River, under the Brooklyn Bridge. Supposedly dying of a mysterious ailment, Hazel Flagg (Carole Lombard) was given a whirlwind "last gasp" around the city. Crack reporter Wallace Cook (Fredric March) took Hazel out on a boat on the East River, but in *Nothing Sacred*, nothing was sacred, and Hazel knew something nobody else did.

Also on the water, but moving somewhat more slowly on a tugboat, were Aaron (William Fichtner) and Martha (Demi Moore). They cruised the

East River and passed under the Brooklyn Bridge, prompting Aaron to declare the bridge his favorite, in *Passion of Mind.*

<hr/>

Turn right and leave the bridge behind. Walk along Centre Street (which becomes Park Row) until you reach the gate leading to City Hall, on your right. Keep walking until you get a good view of the building.

15. City Hall. Park Row. Office of the real mayor of New York, as well as various fictional mayors in the movies.

This is where Mayor John Pappas (Al Pacino) worked in *City Hall*. And where Jack Taylor (George Clooney) confronted the mayor known as Sidney (Sid Armus) about corruption in the sanitation industry in *One Fine Day*. And where the *Ghostbusters* convinced the mayor known as Lenny (David Margulies) that the days of fire and brimstone had fallen on the city. And where Mayor Flynn (Rod Steiger) struggled to protect both his daughter, Bernadette (Mary Elizabeth Mastrantonio), and his city from a serial killer terrorizing all in *The January Man*. And also where Police Officer Charlie (Nicolas Cage) received a citation for bravery on the steps of City Hall in *It Could Happen to You.*

<hr/>

Cross Park Row (away from City Hall) at your earliest, and safest, opportunity and turn right. Head south and turn left on Beekman Street. Walk east until you reach Nassau Street. Turn right on Nassau and walk south. Stop at the south side of Liberty Street and turn to the left. The Federal Reserve Building, with its castle-like turrets, is now north and east of you.

16. Federal Reserve Building. William and Liberty Streets. A madman, Simon (Jeremy Irons), was loose in Manhattan and had planted enough bombs all over the place to occupy the time of John McClane (Bruce Willis), his colleague Zeus (Samuel L. Jackson), and the New York City police force in *Die Hard With a Vengeance*. While the cops searched for a bomb in every school, Simon led his team into the Federal Reserve Building, intent on removing the gold supply. Some went in through the front entrance. Others drove trucks along the side of the building and through a hole created by a bomb detonated on a subway train.

Although stuck in bed with a nasty cold, he was still in charge. Willing to meet the demands of the hijackers who had taken over a subway train, the mayor (Lee Wallace), in order to save the lives of the hostages onboard, authorized the payment of $1 million to the perpetrators in *The Taking of Pelham One, Two, Three*. With only minutes to go before the deadline, the police gathered the money in this building, placed it into a police car, and sped off to get to the subway car in time and make the payoff.

———————

Turn and continue south on Nassau Street. When you reach Wall Street, take a good look at the pillars of the New York Stock Exchange across Wall Street and slightly to the right.

17. New York Stock Exchange. 20 Broad Street. Although Eugene (Ron Silver) seemed like a normal guy by day, working on "the Exchange" as a trader, he was leading a double life that was becoming more of a headache for New York. As his nighttime activities increasingly turned to murder, the police stepped up their efforts to nab him, and police officer Megan Turner (Jamie Lee Curtis) made his capture her number one priority in *Blue Steel*. Megan had a special interest in finding the killer, since Eugene had obtained the gun he used for his crime spree during a supermarket robbery attempt in which Megan had interceded.

Cross to the south side of Wall Street and turn around. On the corner diagonally across from where you are standing should be 14 Wall Street.

18. 14 Wall Street. On an otherwise deserted Wall Street in the early hours of a new day, Murray Burns (Jason Robards) and Sandra (Barbara Harris) walked along and stopped in front of 14 Wall Street, realizing that the two of them were all alone, surrounded by all the money that these buildings  represented, in a city that contained many more than *A Thousand Clowns*.

Look across Wall Street to your right. The statue of George Washington confirms that you are gazing upon the Federal Building.

19. The Federal Building. Wall Street and Broad Street. Try to remember the scene in *Ghost* where a reluctant Oda Mae Brown (Whoopi Goldberg), at the insistence of Sam

Wheat (Patrick Swayze), gave a $4 million check to the shocked nuns from the Saint Joseph's Shelter for the Homeless while they solicited donations at the base of George Washington's statue.

Mayor Ebert (Michael Lerner) was giving a speech in front of this building. The speech ended abruptly when *Godzilla* stepped ashore in Lower Manhattan.

———◦•◦———

In the intersection of Wall and Broad there is a sewer plate.

20. Sewer Plate on Wall Street, in Front of the Federal Building. Another serial killer was at large in the city. The best hope to track him down was a quadriplegic, Link (Denzel Washington), confined to bed and unable to do anything for himself. But Link was intent on catching the killer known as *The Bone Collector*, and he enlisted the help of an initially uncooperative young cop, Amelia (Angelina Jolie), to be his eyes and ears. With time running out, Amelia and other cops entered the sewer system through the sewer plate right in front of you to try to find a kidnapping victim before she became a murder victim.

———◦•◦———

Turn around and head south on Broad Street. The New York Stock Exchange should be on your right. Stop when you are across from 30 Broad Street.

21. 30 Broad Street. The headquarters of Linus Larrabee (Humphrey Bogart) and his family were located in this building in the original *Sabrina*.

Another rich and powerful man spent some time in this building, but his fortunes quickly changed. Avery Bullard (an unbilled Raoul Freeman), the head of the Treadway Furniture Corporation, collapsed to the ground as he exited this building, and his death set off a ruthless scramble for power high atop the company's offices in the *Executive Suite*.

Walk a bit further and you will reach 40 Broad Street.

22. 40 Broad Street. This building, which sits just south and west of the subway station entrance with its distinctive red-and-white globes on the light poles, is where Lawrence Garfield (Danny DeVito) worked as a takeover king, ruthlessly coveting *Other Peoples' Money*.

Continue to the corner and turn left on Exchange Place. Walk east to William Street. Note the building on the southeast corner of William and Exchange Place.

23. William Street and Exchange Place. Southeast Corner. After setting out on her own, Laurel Ayres (Whoopi Goldberg) had to have an office, which she found here, along with her loyal assistant, Sally (Dianne Wiest), in *The Associate*.

Turn right on William and walk to Beaver Street. Delmonico's is on the corner.

24. In front of Delmonico's. 56 Beaver Street. Her illness grew worse with each passing day, but her senses were more heightened than ever. As they passed this corner in their car, Charlotte (Winona Ryder) put her hand over the heart of Will (Richard Gere) and could tell that he was lying. Realizing that he had been unfaithful and that he would never change his wild ways, Charlotte got out of the car at this spot. Their summer had become *Autumn in New York*.

Continue on William until you reach the downtown Manhattan fixture Harry's of Hanover Square.

25. Harry's of Hanover Square. 1 Hanover Square (the downstairs entrance). Jack Prescott (Jeff Bridges) and Dwan (Jessica Lange) sought some shelter and a drink here in *King Kong*. With the gargantuan ape at large in New York, the town was crazed with fear, and people were either fleeing from the beast's path or heading into battle with it. The place was empty, but Jack and Dwan helped themselves to drinks and enjoyed the few minutes of solitude it afforded them. Then while sitting at a table, Jack figured out where Kong would be heading, and the two of them rushed to that spot, hoping to get there before it was too late.

Turn back the other way on William and walk north until again reaching Exchange Place. Turn right on Exchange Place and walk until you reach the front of number 20.

26. 20 Exchange Place. This building is where the offices of the North Coast Fidelity and Casualty Company were located. It was 1940, and the insurance company, run by Mr. Magruder (Dan Aykroyd), employed such people as George Bond (Wallace Shawn), Betty Ann Fitzgerald (Helen

Hunt), and C. W. Briggs (Woody Allen). All seemed rosy until Betty Ann and Briggsy came under *The Curse of the Jade Scorpion*.

━━━◆━━━

Return to William Street, turn right, and walk north to Wall Street. Stop in front of the staircase leading down to the subway.

27. Wall Street and William Street. Subway Entrance. It was a festive night, and Charlie (Woody Harrelson) had had too much to drink. Or had he? He stumbled down Wall Street and gingerly made his way down this staircase. As it turned out, Charlie was an undercover cop, and his behavior was part of his disguise, in *Money Train*.

━━━◆━━━

Turn right and head east on Wall Street, stopping at 48 Wall.

28. 48 Wall Street. Things didn't go according to plan, and Steven Taylor (Michael Douglas) had to give $400,000 to David Shaw (Viggo Mortensen) to keep him from telling the authorities that the two had planned *A Perfect Murder*. Steven came to a bank at this location to withdraw the money from his account.

━━━◆━━━

Walk east on Wall Street until you reach the east side of Water Street. Walk north on Water until you reach Wall Street Plaza, between Maiden Lane and Pine Street. Stop at the tree closest to the main entrance.

29. Wall Street Plaza (between Maiden Lane and Pine Street). Tree. Imagine you are Bud Fox (Charlie Sheen) and had just learned that your idol, Gordon Gecko (Michael Douglas), had pulled a fast one on you and was planning to dismantle your father's company, Blue Star Airlines, once he had taken it over, thanks to your help.

Shocked, dismayed, numb, you left the meeting of lawyers and finance people, walked along Water Street, and stopped at this tree, leaning up against it for support. That's what Bud Fox did. Right here, in *Wall Street*.

Turn back south on Water Street, then turn left on the north side of Wall Street. Walk east until you are in front of 120 Wall, just west of South Street.

30. 120 Wall Street. He was a multimillionaire, but he wasn't going to tell that to Shotzy (Lauren Bacall), who was co-authoring the book on *How to Marry a Millionaire*. But Tom Brookman (Cameron Mitchell) was smitten, nonetheless, so he decided to chance it. Although Tom looked just like the guy next door, he owned the company located here in the building named for him.

No need to cross South Street, but try to get a view of the enclosed tennis courts on the other side of the elevated FDR Drive.

31. Wall Street Tennis Courts. Wall Street and East River. Having just met as part of a blind date to play tennis with some friends, Alvie Singer (Woody Allen) and *Annie Hall* (Diane Keaton) emerged from these courts. Annie offered Alvie a wild ride home in her car.

Turn right and head south on South Street. Walk until you reach the sign EXIT 1, BATTERY PARK, STATEN ISLAND at the southern terminus of the FDR Drive. You should be in the shadows of

55 Water Street, and the Vietnam Veterans Memorial Plaza should be on your right.

32. South Street at Vietnam Memorial Plaza. There was something rotten among "New York's Finest," and Officer Frank Serpico (Al Pacino) thought he should do something about it. In *Serpico*, he decided to tell what he knew and got into a car parked right around here. By talking to the higher-ups, Serpico knew he was taking his life in his hands, but he felt he was doing the right thing, and that was what mattered in the end.

If you can climb up to the Vietnam Memorial Plaza, or walk around the block and enter from Water Street, you may see some thirteen-year-old boys with a dilemma on their hands.

33. Vietnam Memorial. Water Street and Coenties Slip. Having learned that it could take six weeks to find the Zoltar machine that had granted his wish to be *Big*, Josh Baskin (Tom Hanks) and friend Billy Kopecki (Jared Rushton) spent a few minutes hanging out in this plaza.

Look across the FDR Drive to the Downtown-Manhattan Heliport.

34. Downtown–Manhattan Heliport. At the beginning of *They All Laughed*, John (Ben Gaz-

zara) stood near where you are standing and watched as Angela (Audrey Hepburn) emerged from a helicopter at the heliport. He was a private detective, and he was hired to perform a service, but the lovely Angela was someone he was glad to keep an eye on.

Continue along South Street until you see the Staten Island Ferry Terminal across the way.

35. Staten Island Ferry Terminal. Hoping to improve her lot in life, Tess McGill (Melanie Grif-

fith), an honest *Working Girl*, took the ferry each day to and from her home in Staten Island. This terminal is where she disembarked in Manhattan.

Cross to the terminal, then keeping it on your left, enter Battery Park. Walk along the path, all the while keeping an eye on the water. With any luck, the ferry may appear.

36. Staten Island Ferry. They had each other, they had their drug addiction, and they had their friends, but for Helen (Kitty Winn) and Bobby (Al Pacino), that wasn't enough. So they boarded the ferry and headed to Staten Island to get a puppy. On the return trip, Bobby put their new puppy down while he and Helen went into the bathroom to shoot up heroin. When they finished, they looked for the dog, but all Helen could do was scream as she saw the defenseless puppy fall into the churning waters behind the ferry, another victim of drugs in *The Panic in Needle Park*.

———•—•———

Follow the path until you come to the Soldier's War Monument. There are concrete walls on both sides of the plaza. If you can't find it, ask a New Yorker. We're a friendly lot.

37. Battery Park. Soldier's War Monument. Movies about terrorism now seem both timely and inappropriate, but like terrorism itself, they are a painful part of life. Two madmen came to New York and embarked upon a crime spree. They killed innocent people and filmed the torture and subsequent murder of Detective Eddie Flemming (Robert De Niro). With the help of a tabloid news show, their film footage even aired on television. But arson investigator Jordy Warsaw (Ed Burns) decided that their *15 Minutes* of fame had gone on fifteen minutes too long. After a trial ended in a verdict of not guilty by reason of insanity, attorney Bruce Cutler (playing himself) led one of the killers, Emil (Karel Roden), through the crowd that had gathered here. But Jordy was in the crowd and knew which buttons to push. In response to Jordy's baiting, the killer revealed the truth. His fifteen minutes, and his freedom, were indeed up.

———•—•———

Walk through the plaza and exit down the steps and turn right. Walk north on the Admiral Dewey Promenade.

38. Battery Park. Admiral Dewey Promenade. Bored with her life as a housewife, Roberta (Rosanna Arquette) sought excitement, and found it in the life of Susan (Madonna). In one scene, while she was *Desperately Seeking Susan*,

Roberta had an encounter along this promenade with someone who was also searching for Susan.

College freshman Clark Kellogg (Matthew Broderick) had gotten himself into a hell of a mess, involving agents of the federal government, a rare but apparently tasty komodo dragon, and a mysterious man who bore more than a striking resemblance to Don Corleone from a certain film about the mafia. It was no coincidence, of course, that the man was played by Marlon Brando in full Corleone regalia. This movie is *The Freshman*, and in it Clark stood at the railing in front of you, staring out at the Statue of Liberty and contemplating his next move.

Adrift and alone in New York, Kevin McAllister (Macaulay Culkin) rose to the occasion and took himself on a whirlwind tour of Manhattan in *Home Alone 2: Lost in New York*. In one scene, Kevin stood along the same railing as Clark Kellogg and admired the Statue of Liberty through one of the viewing machines just above the promenade

Now follow the lead of Clark and Kevin and admire the Statue of Liberty, rising majestically from her pedestal, floating in the harbor above the Hudson River.

39. Statue of Liberty. She stands proudly, torch in hand, casting her light on the entryway to the United States and the American way of life. Severely challenged by the terrorist attacks of September 11, 2001, attacks for which Miss Liberty had an unenviable front-row seat, she continues to represent everything that is right about freedom. Imagine how a young Vito Corleone (Oreste Baldini) might have felt when he, though quarantined upon his arrival at Ellis Island, was able to gaze upon the Statue of Liberty through the windows of his tiny room in *The Godfather Part II.*

Miss Liberty has made it into other films, but she hasn't always been treated with such reverence. In *Up the Sandbox*, a bored housewife, Margaret (Barbra Streisand), used to imagine her life being more exciting than it was. In one such fantasy sequence, Margaret and her cohorts sailed to the statue and pulled a caper inside, causing it to fall into New York Harbor.

Running from the cops, Mr. Fry (Norman Lloyd) climbed to the top, crawled outside, and clung to the torch, and then his nemesis, Barry Kane (Robert Cummings), arrived. Despite the enmity between them, Barry did his best to save Fry, grabbing on to his sleeve and holding on for dear life. But then, in classic Hitchcockian fashion, the sleeve ripped away from the jacket, thread by thread, and Fry plunged to his death, with Barry holding only a sleeve, in *Saboteur*.

On a sunny day, a mermaid (Daryl Hannah) emerged from the surrounding waters, clambered up onto Liberty Island, and approached the statue, much to the shock and delight of onlookers, in *Splash*.

And then the world came to an end. At least the world as we knew it. When astronaut Taylor (Charlton Heston) rode along the shoreline on horseback, he came upon one of the most frightening scenes ever to darken the silver screen: Miss Liberty, or what was left of her, lying on the sand. For the *Planet of the Apes* was not somewhere out there, at the far reaches of the galaxy, but it was here, on Earth. And not just on Earth, or in the United States, but really here, in New York. Armageddon had come somewhere along the line. Liberty was gone, too, with only a grisly reminder in the sand of what had once been and perhaps would someday be again.

It's a chilling reminder of what Miss Liberty had to witness on September 11, 2001, when Armageddon struck for real, and the towers of the World Trade Center crumbled by the design of the devil's henchmen, who continue to walk the Earth.

Take a breath and look out in the Hudson River. Maybe a tugboat will pass by.

40. Tugboat in New York Harbor. Of course, if you're really lucky, you might be able to see, and hopefully hear, Fanny Brice (Barbra Streisand) standing on the deck of the tugboat and belting out *Don't Rain on My Parade* in *Funny Girl*.

Something about tugboats must make people want to sing. In *Godspell*, from a tugboat, the happy-go-lucky group also belted out a song, this one about living in the light of the Lord.

Continue north on the promenade. As you approach Castle Clinton, look for a bench.

---

41. Bench on Promenade. Near Castle Clinton. Veteran operative Kay (Tommy Lee Jones) and potential newcomer Jay (Will Smith) sat on one of these benches while Kay laid out for Jay just what his job in the alien-monitoring organization would entail. Required to sever all human ties, Jay spent the rest of the day and night sitting on this bench, considering whether to join the *Men in Black*.

Circle around Castle Clinton and follow the path out of Battery Park. Walk east on the street just north of Battery Park (Battery Place) until you are across from the windowless building just west of Greenwich Street.

42. Battery Place (between Greenwich and Washington Streets). Administration Building. Beneath this seemingly innocuous building, the highly secretive organization that tracked and fought alien invaders was located, in *Men in Black*.

Continue east until you reach the large museum (identified as U.S. Custom House near the top) at the southern tip of Broadway. Cross Broadway and walk to the front of the museum.

43. 1 Bowling Green. Museum. It had been quite a year for cop-turned-lawyer Sean Casey (Andy Garcia). After his father was shot in a drug bust, Sean was selected as the assistant district attorney who would prosecute the defendant. And before long, his boss the district attorney, Morgie (Ron Liebman), was felled by a stroke, and Sean was elected to succeed him. During a restless evening, Sean, knowing that police corruption had hit particularly close to home, wandered the streets of Lower Manhattan, finally ending up at this building trying to decide what to do in *Night Falls on Manhattan*.

Convinced he was the target of a giant conspiracy, cabdriver Jerry Fletcher (Mel Gibson) made a habit of barging in on Justice Department employee Alice Sutton (Julia Roberts) in *Conspiracy Theory*. In the movie, the Justice Department offices were located in this building.

This building is now a museum, as it was in *Ghostbusters II*, when the spirit of evil emerged from a painting of Vigor, "the Scourge of Carpathia, the Sorrow of Moldavia," and declared, "Now is the season of evil." Vigor commanded meek art restorer Janosz Poha (Peter MacNicol) to find him a child so that he might live again. And Janosz almost gave him the child of Dana (Sigourney Weaver), on whom he had a crush, but luckily for Dana and the rest of New York, the Ghostbusters again saved the day.

Walk a few yards north to a spot on the curb to the right of the small plaza in front of the Customs House.

44. Whitehall Street across from Beaver Street. Northeast of Customs House. They were doing their best to get along, despite the fact that one lived in the jungle of Manhattan and the other in an actual jungle on the other side of the world. After a heated argument, Michael Cromwell (Tim Allen) chased his son, Mimi Siku

(Sam Huntington), through the streets of Lower Manhattan. He caught up to him here, and in *Jungle 2 Jungle*, Michael taught his son how to hail a cab: a first step toward getting by in the jungle that is New York.

Continue north on Whitehall and stop in front of the bull that adorns the plaza between Whitehall and Broadway. Look at 26 Broadway, to the east.

45. 26 Broadway. Against his better judgment, Bud Fox (Charlie Sheen) agreed to do some dirty work for Gordon Gecko (Michael Douglas) in *Wall Street*. Bud had to trail British financier Larry

Wildman (Terrence Stamp) to find out what he was doing in town. Bud hopped his motorcycle, tracked Larry's Rolls-Royce downtown, and followed him into 26 Broadway. Bud even managed to force his way onto the same elevator as Larry and his entourage.

Monty Brewster (Richard Pryor) had just seen the $30 million he had inherited in *Brewster's Millions*. It was piled high in a vault at the First Bank of Manhattan, which was also located in this building.

———•—•———

Cross to the west side of Broadway and continue north until you reach number 71.

46. 71 Broadway. Editor Henry Hackett (Michael Keaton) had it pretty rough. His wife Martha (Marisa Tomei) was pregnant, scared, and vulnerable, and Henry had a deadline to put his paper to bed. The offices of *The Paper*, "The New York Sun," were located here.

———•—•———

Continue north on Broadway until you reach Liberty Street. Turn left, but there is nowhere to go. Just stop and look.

47. The World Trade Center. Twin Towers. They are gone, but they will never be forgotten. And one scene from one movie seems to capture the enormity of the fall. Jack Prescott (Jeff Bridges) knew that *King Kong* would eventually find the towers, because they reminded him of a structure near his home, as they reminded all New Yorkers of home. The great ape climbed the towers, with the lovely and lithesome Dwan (Jessica Lange) in his grasp. As the army mobilized below and whirlybirds circled above, Kong put Dwan down and nudged her to safety, choosing to face the machine guns himself. After such a display of gallantry, no one could blame Dwan for

shedding tears when Kong fell to his death on the plaza below.

You have now reached the end of **Walking Tour 14: The Southern Tip** and the end of *Manhattan on Film: The Deluxe Edition*. Please tell at least two friends and one cousin about this book. But make sure they go and get their own copies: potato chips are for sharing, not this book.

Movie Index

About the Author

Chuck Katz grew up on the South Shore of Long Island in a town that served as home to some of the original *Goodfellas*. He attended Union College in Upstate New York (the setting for the college scenes from *The Way We Were*) and Fordham Law School (in the neighborhood once fought over by the Jets and the Sharks in *West Side Story*).

Mr. Katz is a partner in the New York City office of Duane Morris LLP, specializing in public finance, the area of law that was the subject of such legal thrillers as *A Civil Action, And Justice for All, Erin Brockovich, Absence of Malice, 12 Angry Men,* and *QB VII.* Okay, maybe not. An amateur photographer (all photographs appearing in the book that are not movie stills have been taken by the author), Mr. Katz has been profiled in the *ABA Journal,* and his song parodies have appeared in industry publications. In addition to the *Manhattan on Film* books, Mr. Katz has written a novel, two screenplays, and ten television scripts.

Mr. Katz lives on Long Island with his wife, Ashley, and sons, Jaden and Austin, in a town where scenes from *Meet the Parents* were filmed.